The Blow-Ins

The Blow-Ins

Annie Roche

Contents

Dedication		viii
1	Susannah Hill, London, 1884	1
2	Eliza Barton, Devonshire, 1898	13
3	Donna Barnard, London, Ontario, Canada, 2012	31
4	Donna, Usbournes, Devon, April 2012	46
5	Susannah Usbourne, Devon, 1884	62
6	Eliza, Devon, 1889	70
7	Donna, May 2012 - Duvet Day	81
8	Clemency, Devon, 1896	94
9	Eliza, The Hiltons, Barnstaple, Devon, September 1889	104
10	Eliza, The North Devon Free Press, June 1890	116
11	Donna, May 2012 - Gran	120
12	Eliza, Exeter Gaol, November 1890 - Shoe stringing.	131

13	Eliza at Usbournes, December 1890 - The Blow-In	141
14	Eliza, December 1890 - The Night Terrors	160
15	Donna, May 2012 - The Records Office	164
16	Donna, May 2012 - Donna and Jude	178
17	Eliza, Christmas 1890	188
18	Eliza, December 1890 - Christmas Day	199
19	Donna, June 2012 - The Rottweiler	210
20	Algie and Donna, July 2012 - Billy No-Mates	224
21	Eliza, Wednesday 29th July 1891 - Salvation	228
22	Eliza, July 1891 - The North Devon Free Press - Vile Wretch	240
23	Eliza, August 1891 - The Inquest, Day One	243
24	Eliza, August 1891 - The Inquest, Day Two	256
25	Usbourne, August 1891 - The North Devon Free Press - Horse Whipping	268
26	Donna and Algie, June 2012	272
27	Eliza, Berry Hill, March 1892	279
28	Three Doors Close	287
29	Donna and Eliza. Eliza, London, September 1899	294
30	The Captain and Eliza, September 1899	302

31	Donna's Research Notes	310
32	The Wake, November 2012	312
33	Charlie, November 2012	317

About the Author   324

For HERA

*You know who you are,
with much love,
AMS xxx*

...with thanks and much love,

to my editor Adrian Smith @Things Other Publishing, Rosie Florence Artwork, Nicola Hedges and Lorna Howarth for all their support and encouragement and The Friday Freaks, who have listened to the prospect of me writing a novel for the last twelve years...it's here at last! XXX.

Copyright © 2024 by Annie Roche

All rights reserved. No part of this book may be reproduced in any manner whatsoever without written permission except in the case of brief quotations embodied in critical articles and reviews.

First Printing, 2024

1

Susannah Hill, London, 1884

James Henry Hill lay dying. He knew he wasn't long for this world - every fibre in his body told him so. His limbs burned and ached. His chest felt so constricted it constantly rebelled against every new in-take of breath. Molten tears burned deep into the crevices of his face as the battle for breath entered its final throes.

He failed to notice the ticking of the wall clock carefully metering out the rhythm of his remaining time. Yet now it seemed to burst into life ticking loudly. How could he have missed it?

Tick, tock...breathe in...breathe out.
Tick, tock...breathe in...breathe out.
Tick, tock...breathe in...breathe out.

It lifted his spirits to see that Hetty had entered the room. She stood over him reassuringly and held his hand. Susannah, their daughter, was already holding it tightly, but Hetty managed to slip her ghostly hand in and loosened her daughter's grip.

She bent over and whispered into his ear: -

"Let go…"

Only his eyes could express his apprehension.

She said it again.

His wife's whispered words filled his senses with a warmth and contentment he'd been denied for many years.

His body started to feel free from the shackles of pain and liberated from the burden of worry. It generated a lightness of being that confused him.

Overwhelmed by these new metaphysical sensations, he realised that he was drifting away from consciousness… The war of attrition was finally over, and he succumbed to the inevitable.

Tick, tock…breathe in…breathe out…

breathe in…breathe in…BREATHE IN!…

His final view was of the white ceiling as he looked towards heaven.

The final sounds of that infernal clock continued without him.

No breath… no pain…no life… gone.

Philip was the first to notice there were only two of them left in the room. "At last," he thought. "The old bastard has finally had the decency to give up."

He carefully rolled his father's eyelids closed. He didn't want his sister to see the bloodshot eyes staring vacantly.

He had little comprehension of how dramatically their lives

would change without his careful guardianship. A new life without the old boundaries would open new possibilities.

He placed his shaking hands upon Susannah's shoulders in a bid to calm her heaving frame. He understood her capacity for grief. He had experienced it some years before, with the unexpected passing of their mother. Only the numbing effects of laudanum, surreptitiously laced into her milk had soothed Susannah's restless spirit last time. He needed new supplies: the little brown bottles of tincture were surprisingly empty.

Susannah realised that her father had passed. She had been holding his hand when finally all life had drained away. It had not been within her power to stop him from slipping away – no matter how hard she had gripped his hand.

Not yet cold and yet everything had changed. She liked to believe they were alone in the world - just her and her beloved Philip. The thought that she would soon be usurped in her brother's affections, no longer the mistress of the house filled her with dread. She was struggling with her grief and sense of abandonment, but she knew she was expected to conduct herself with dignity. Philip's firm touch soothed her inner maelstrom. She battened down her emotional hatches. Calm was temporarily restored.

They eventually left the bedroom together, holding each other's hands as if trying to reclaim their childhood.

Downstairs in the hallway they passed the three long-cased clocks standing in a row, a few feet apart. The first had been purchased for their great-grandfather Henry Gordon Hill and was considered a very fine specimen. A family tradition founded on grief; the clocks were dutifully replaced upon the demise of the patriarch.

The James Henry clock was a beautiful mahogany Brockbanks of London. It stood proudly at ninety-three inches tall and was considered to reflect both the stature and character of the man – proud and dependable.

The clock graveyard unnerved. Their ghostly forms were constant reminders of the dead. Disembodied chimes would echo and startle as the hour struck.

They witnessed everything.

They scorned.

They judged.

They dominated even in death.

The mistresses of the house were almost forgotten. They had the occasional portrait or faded photograph, but nothing as imposing as a chiming mahogany monolith.

What traces of her existence would Susannah leave? The prospect of dying or leaving the security of her home made her shudder.

She had barely left the confines of the house since she was fifteen – a consequence of her mother's fatal accident. Witnessing her absent-minded mother step out in front of a speeding horse and carriage permanently altered her perspective on the safety of the outside world.

These deep-seated feelings of anxiety were consolidated when her beloved father had been beaten and robbed in the street. He never recovered from the brutal shock of a savage attack ...all for the price of his dented timepiece. The police had failed to apprehend the assailant. With no witnesses they offered little hope of an arrest.

Outside there was danger, a place where only violence and poverty flourished. Susannah had no desire to leave the safe perimeters of her home. No desire to engage with the outside world or society in general. No desire to walk in the park or visit friends. She had no friends. She wore her loneliness with a sense of pride.

The mere thought of leaving the house filled her with a deep, sickening sensation. Her frantic heart would beat so loudly that she could no longer understand her own thoughts. Her world would spin, her hands would perspire.

Philip led her to James Henry. He placed his sister in front of him facing the clock. He remained unnaturally close behind pressing his body firmly against hers. He placed his hands on top of Susannah's and like a carefully rehearsed dance of intimacy they stopped the hands of the clock at two twenty-five p.m.

Susannah reached down with both hands to the shaft of the pendulum stopping it swinging decisively to and fro. She could feel the resistance as she held it firmly in her hands. She applied more pressure to stop the mechanism from swaying again. The clock continued to resist.

Philip's body pressed further into her back and buttocks. She grew increasingly uncomfortable. Were the ancestors watching?

"I can't, I feel like I'm smothering him." She withdrew herself to a safer distance.

Philip brushed her rejection aside and held the pendulum firmly until it finally stopped.

"It's only a clock for heaven's sake!" Philip always knew how to belittle.

Susannah moved away and observed the brown paper wrapped article in the corner of the hallway.

"Is that what I think it is?" she asked suspiciously.

Philip walked over to the item and started to pull off the wrapping.

"This is our new master of ceremonies!" he announced proudly.

She stared at the new timepiece.

It left her cold.

"You can't replace him that easily..."

"Don't be so melodramatic! It's a wedding present from Cecily's father - it arrived this morning."

"Well I don't want to see it. You should send it back!"

Philip had no intention of continuing such a disagreeable discourse and reached for his hat and coat.

"That's it, turn your back on me...you always do!"

"Necessity, not pleasure! I need to notify the authorities of father's death. I shall pay the Pryors a visit out of courtesy. They should hear the news from me rather than from hearsay."

He had managed to untangle himself from a potential conflict of interest between his ever-demanding younger sister and his future in-laws, just by ignoring the offending request. He gave Susannah a brotherly kiss on her forehead and left her side before she could use any other forms of emotional blackmail to prevent him from going about his business.

Another abandonment, the second of the day. Guilt was setting in. Susannah knew her emotions should be centred on her father's passing and yet the thorny subject of Philip's betrothed needled her. He was delusional if he thought that she would ever accept Cecily as her 'sister' or her newly bestowed authority at Grove House.

She seethed. The unwanted addition to the ancestral

collection unnerved her. The thought of ever losing her brother was unbearable - a world without Philip inconceivable, unnatural. She wanted him to reconsider his engagement. She favoured the siblings sharing their dotage, untouched by the outside world and free to conduct themselves how they pleased.

She had conveniently forgotten her own betrothal to Captain Usbourne. A contract born out of financial convenience, without love or her consent. Both parties seemed reticent about fulfilling their engagement and both were secretly relieved when another shipping commission turned up to prevent the marriage. They corresponded regularly, but Susannah never believed there was any real prospect of marriage owing to their mutual lack of commitment.

Hit by exhaustion and the urgent need to lie down, she ventured back upstairs. Her father's bedroom door was left ajar. A childlike need to speed pass without looking was supressed. She was wary of her ancestors' disapproval.

She stood transfixed at the object that was once her father. All life had been sucked out as if through a straw – only a pale and fragile husk remained.

Plagued by a spiteful, nagging pain in her head, she needed the sanctuary of her mother. Hetty's room had changed little since her untimely death. No overnight guests were permitted. Nothing was removed but the dust and the occasional dead moth. This was no shrine to the dead, no temple to the matriarch.

Part sanctuary, part camera obscura, this room was Susannah's window to the world. She would spy on the coalman as he delivered his dirty trade. She would watch the race between the gardeners as they scooped up the black gold left by the horses.

The roses would be good this year.

Then there were the ladies of The Crescent, promenading in their finery, their air of sophistication undermined by a lack of care wading through the horse piss. They were oblivious to the staining of their finest from Paris, although the servants took note.

It was obvious.

Filth and danger respected no boundaries.

This self-inflicted exile was comforting, protective…essential. A loneliness worn with a misplaced sense of pride. It was jarring.

The deep red velvet curtains were drawn close. Now womb-like, the room seemed smaller, darker, safer. She unfastened her dress and loosened her stays. She collapsed without grace onto her mother's soft bed and started to drift into a deep and much needed sleep. Untouched by emotion, Susannah lay unconscious for many hours…

***

Full of Pryor's brandy, Philip returned to find the house devoid of company. He placed a small wooden box of tinctures on the table and prepared a sample to take to his sister.

He found Susannah's bedroom door was open – the room empty.

He called out to her, but there was no response. He continued his search with increasing urgency.

Of course she was with mother, laying on Hetty's bed, deep in slumber.

His own self-awareness recognised that he needed her too much.

He placed the oil lamp on the side table and let it cast its soft, wavering light invitingly over her body. Susannah's peaceful slumber exposed her vulnerability. She unknowingly needed protection.

Boots were quietly kicked off. His waistcoat removed. He slid down beside her and drifted into an uneasy, alcohol-fuelled oblivion.

Susannah was the first to stir. Surprised to find her brother next to her, breathing heavily, but not quite snoring.

Philip woke, turned to face her, and smiled. He gently pushed her hair away from her face and curved it around her ear. He studied her brown eyes pained with sorrow. He bathed in their weakness. It was mesmerising. Philip drew her close to him and gently placed his hands either side of her face.

He kissed her. First in a gentle, brotherly way and then with more purpose. Fraternal or something deeper? Something darker, something dangerous?

He gently traced the edges of her closed eyes with his wet tongue. He kissed her eyelids tenderly one, by one. His tongue prised open her lips.

Moved or confused? Both. He took her lower lip and teased. She recoiled as he started to bite.

He pressed close into her as she stiffened with horror.

Susannah started to push away in fear of immediate violation.

Why was he doing this? She didn't understand, maybe the blame was hers?

Her body prickled with terror as he kissed the contour of her neck. He brushed the straps of her camisole from her shoulders and continued to kiss her with urgency. His bliss was intense and sublime - his need was overwhelming.

No matter the consequence. Power was always in his possession, a compelling aphrodisiac. Her fear fuelled his desire, her objection an invitation.

His loss of control, his reasoning was overpowering. He suddenly stared into the dark pit of eternal self-hatred. He was diving into murky waters forever trapped by the unbreakable stranglehold of guilt.

He stopped. In urgent need of an exit-strategy he slapped her hard across the face. "Whore!" he screamed, "You fucking whore!"

He scrambled off the bed in an obvious state of arousal. He didn't dare look at her. He didn't want her to see the look of self-disgust written upon his face.

He left her confused, ashamed and so alone.

Her ears rang from the intensity of the slap. A sense of utter betrayal that would sting for decades.

***

Four days of avoidance and excruciating self-reproach.

Four days to ruminate and reformulate, then a summons to his study.

Susannah had been draping squares of black silk over the clock faces of her ancestors. She could no longer bear their judgement. Her shame too deep. Determined to remain contrite and composed, she entered the room in silence.

"That can never happen again! You cannot stay near me…There is something deeply wrong with you…" he stated, delegating all responsibility.

The severity of his contempt struck her harder than when he slapped her. She bit her lip and started to fiddle with her bracelet.

He then moderated his voice in a more practical, measured tone: -

"Our father will be buried the day after tomorrow. On Sunday the banns will be read for both our marriages. Both parties shall be married at the earliest convenience. You will then join your husband to live in Devonshire on his family estate. You will no longer have any connection with Grove House. Any communication will be through my wife and, you will not return here under any pretext."

"And what if I refuse?" Her phobic considerations outweighed her fear of violation, filling her with a false sense of option.

Philip grabbed her by the back of her neck and pulled her close.

"If you refuse, I shall have you placed in an institution." He was determined to expel this she-devil from his life.

"Marriage or Bedlam, it's your choice." His tone of menace was hard to ignore. He gave her hair a final tug and then released her.

His spite twisted and filled her with rage. She was shocked by her capacity to loathe. All her life was spent loving him. He was the saviour of the family; he had saved them all from ruin – her mother often told her so. He was brave, clever, and handsome - a pedestal so tall, it was dizzying.

"I hope your shame dies with you!" she hexed.

Simple words that cut deep. Her look of betrayal would forever haunt him. He would never be able to look at Cecily without seeing Susannah. Their future intimacy forever ruined by his shame. His feelings permanently altered. Their marriage empty.

Susannah had no intention of providing Philip with any more ammunition. She calmly left him to wallow in his own self-loathing. Her head was filled with his vile rhetoric. The ancestor's disapproval echoed with increasing intensity.

"Unnatural whore!"

"She-devil!"

Their judgmental utterances screamed to a heady crescendo.

She retreated hastily to Hetty's room. The door was safely slammed. The cacophony of profanities instantly ceased.

She placed a chair against the door to stop the outside world from seeping through. She could trust no one. Memories of her beloved parents were contaminated by her brother's betrayal. She buried herself under the bedding.

If only she could return to Hetty's womb.

2

Eliza Barton, Devonshire, 1898

Eliza had avoided the village for years. She was unwelcomed -permanently uninvited. Her ailing father had begged her to run an errand for him – to pick up a parcel from Marshalls. Not long for this life, she could hardly refuse. He was her one true ally, her protector and salvation.

Out of his six surviving children, Eliza was the one Tom Barton worried about the most. He spent his final days fretting how she would cope without his protective guardianship. He could depend on Becky and Percy to stand by her, but he wasn't so sure about the others. Weak willed sons with money grabbing wives were his main concern.

Village memory was harsh and unforgiving. Judgement was final and without clemency. This sister of Berry Down had betrayed the laws of humanity and deserved to be cast out. Eliza's apprehension was completely justified.

She left the protection of the farm and stood at the top of the hill. This had always been her favourite view. The chequered oblongs of moss green and jade marked the boundaries of the strawberry fields on this south-facing hill. These precious strips of land were rich and bountiful. A welcome financial lifesaver that helped those who struggled through the leaner months.

Today the strips were shrouded in mizzle that hung depressingly in great clumps of opaque dampness. Normally you could see from Top Town down to Seaside and on a good day you could see over to the Welsh coast. But for now, the village's beauty lay secretly hidden and would wait for the return of spring before revealing its treasures again. Eliza passed the church and graveyard which was full of her departed kindred including her beloved mother. One day she hoped she would join her and the way she was feeling today she hoped it would be soon. The fine damp mist was beginning to seep through her clothes making her feel slightly shivery and her fair, curly hair was starting to frizz at the edges. She pulled her shawl across her chest firmly in a bid to conserve heat, but it didn't work. She still felt chilled, damp, and miserable and was keen to get the trip to the village over as quickly as possible.

There were plenty of villagers in the High Street going about their business. Harassed mothers shopping for groceries with their little ones and workmen that were coming out of the Pack after a crafty mid-morning pint.

As Eliza progressed down the cobbled road carefully tiptoeing past various deposits of excrement, she became aware of how quiet everyone was. The villagers had stopped greeting each other and she became more aware that she had been noticed. A mother with her daughters past by hurriedly and Eliza heard her forcefully instruct her girls not to look and to hurry by.

At first Eliza thought she was imagining it, but as she carried on through the High Street, she realised that she was being avoided. People started to cross to the other side of the road or would turn their backs on her. As she stopped to look at the window of the toy shop someone tapped her on the shoulder. A pregnant woman with a battered pram with two infants top-to-toe looked her straight in the eye and spat in her face viciously.

"Bitch!" she screamed and then sped away with her precious cargo.

Eliza was used to public humiliation and had become accustomed to such an outburst. The attack merely hardened her resolve to pick up her father's parcel and to quickly retreat home never to return. She wiped away the clotted green slime from her face and proceeded directly to Marshall's.

As she entered the shop she noticed two women deep in conversation, one of them was her Aunt Wynn. Both women stopped in mid-sentence as Eliza approached the shop counter, Wynn had no intention of communicating directly with her niece in public. Sarah Marshall, a short, stout, charmless woman breezed in, surveyed the ensemble, looked Eliza in a disapproving manner and shouted for her husband. Jack Marshall made an instant appearance not wishing to risk the wrath of his wife by loitering unnecessarily.

"Take her out back, I don't want her in the shop," she said

with no discretion, "I thought you said the order was for Becky Barton."

"It is. She came in a couple of weeks ago, she didn't mention anything about this one coming to pick it up." replied the down – trodden tailor. He walked over to the shop floor and politely escorted Eliza into a back room. As she was leaving, Eliza overheard Wynn say to Sarah and the other woman,

"She maybe kin, but she shouldn't have got away with it. They should have let her swing at Heavytree and left to rot."

The image of Eliza's rotting corpse swinging from the gallows gave the women a short-lived snap of satisfaction.

Eliza wanted to protest her innocence and let the gossips know how wrong they were, but instead she contained the strength of her feelings in a bid to escape as quickly as possible. Eliza didn't want to make a scene, she never did - and it was part of her problem.

The tailor hurried to retrieve the order from the adjacent stockroom. It was a plain mid-brown wool jacket with discreet leg-o-mutton sleeves, a matching skirt, and a plain, undecorated, white cotton blouse. The ready outfit was obviously the result of a collaboration between her sister and father.

Eliza had always felt uneasy in the presence of Jack Marshall, he was too sycophantic and leering. She asked him to wrap the goods up so that she could hurry home. Jack insisted that she tried the clothes on for good measure. Eliza reluctantly agreed and disappeared into the only changing room. She could feel his lechery beyond the safety of the heavy curtains as he eagerly waited for her to dress. She brushed by him as she made her way to the mirror. Despite the be-frizzled state of her hair she looked quite presentable. The jacket sleeves were a little long.

A detail that did not escape Mr. Marshall, who hurried over with pins in mouth to fix back the offending surplus. She felt a distinct broach of her personal space and felt her back straighten in response to the proximity of his person. She could smell the kippers he had for breakfast and the acrid odour of Woodbines on his breath. The nauseating combination made her lean backwards. As he leaned forwards, they both lost their balance and crashed into a pile of newly delivered boxes together. Eliza's instant reaction was to kick out at the assailant in panic. Sarah's prompt return to the back room resulted in an instant resolution of Marshall's position and left Eliza looking stupid and undignified.

"Get her out through the yard when she's finished. She's not coming back through here," she demanded.

Eliza scrambled to her feet and returned to the changing room and quickly put her old clothes back on. She presented him with a pile of fabric that he proceeded to fold and to parcel up into a neat package held together by string. They exchanged embarrassed apologies and niceties in equal measure, and she left unceremoniously via a dark passageway at the back of the shop parallel to the High Street.

Eliza stopped a moment to take a deep breath and recover from her ordeal. Tears were involuntarily running down her face. She mopped them up with the same handkerchief that she cleaned the clotted green slime and returned it to her pocket. Eliza made a vow to herself that she would never go back to the village again and trudged her way back to the safety of the farm.

***

Eliza continued to replay the awkward events of the morning. She became increasingly irritated by her lack of retaliation.

Why was she always so polite when people were so unkind?

Frustrated by all her would-be witty retorts, her tormentors remained unchallenged. Her replayed mumblings were clearly audible, and she started to sound like the village mad woman who lived in the caves.

Eliza resolved to regain her composure. She didn't want her father to know that she was publicly bullied by his own sister – it would only cause him unwanted distress and would cause further trouble in the family.

As she walked up Lime Kiln Hill, she noticed a small gathering surrounding something on the ground. Her instinct told her that something was wrong, and she started to run faster towards the dilapidated dry-stone wall that marked the entrance to the farm. Eliza realised it was her brothers standing over her father who was lying on the ground in some distress. She dropped the brown paper parcel on the ground and hurried to her father's side.

"What's the matter? He shouldn't be out in this weather."

She loosened his collar so that he felt less restricted. But she soon realised that her actions were pointless, he was already dead. His eyes stared vacantly into the ether and his lips turned an eerie shade of corpse blue.

"You shouldn't have touched him Eliza, questions will be asked," mumbled Tom who had instantly assumed the role of head of the family. Will immediately stepped backwards in retreat.

"Perce, go down village and get the doctor," Eliza instructed.

"What's the point he's gone. Better off getting a bobby now that you've touched him. A bloody doctor's not going to bring him back!" Tom said as he started to make his way back to the farmhouse. "Stupid cow!" he muttered under his breath.

Tom and Will were secretly relieved that Eliza could shoulder the blame. They knew they should never have asked their father to come out to help with the walling.

Percy's instincts were to place his trust in Eliza and to ignore his brothers. He grabbed a horse and rode bareback to fetch the doctor.

"Don't leave him in the rain. Gives us a hand," she cried.

"A bit of mizzle isn't going to make any difference now he's dead. Better wait for the police to give us the all-clear," Tom said coldly. "I don't want to end up before a judge like you, I might not be so lucky."

Her elder brothers ignored her pleas and continued to walk to the farmhouse. They were determined that they would not touch their father's body until they had received reassurances from the authorities that they had no case to answer. They left their sister totally bereft and in disbelief that they could be so callous as to leave her poor father's body out in the seeping misery.

***

Thomas Barton's body was dressed and open to viewing in the front room. It was a rarely used room, reserved for 'best' and for lying-in-wait bodies that were soon to be interned. Eliza had made a special effort to make the room look presentable and had managed to salvage some late autumn flowers to add some colour to an otherwise depressing diorama. The family had yet to decide whether she would be allowed to attend the funeral. Tom, Will and Wynn had made their objections known. Becky and Percy were trying to fight the injustice on her behalf. If only Alf weren't serving in the navy, he'd tip the balance. Eliza knew her protestations were falling on deafened ears and was waiting for Aunt Esther and Uncle Walter to arrive to cast their deciding vote.

Eliza was not expecting miracles – Eliza had fallen from her aunt's grace many years before Eliza's troubles had begun and found it hard to believe that she would suddenly see her in a benevolent light. Eliza busied herself in the kitchen, making sure that there were enough plates and cups to go round and that she had made plenty of bread. Becky was the first to arrive and planted a solid sisterly kiss on Eliza's cheek and gave her a big, generous hug that instantly made Eliza feel human. Becky came with two boiled crabs from Esther's tearoom and placed them on the side.

"Esther and Walter are out front talking with the boys. They've brought Little Eliza with them." Becky knew the unexpected arrival of Eliza Warren would cheer her sister.

The thought of seeing Little Eliza after all these years lifted her spirits and she ran to the window to look. She instantly forgot the gravity of the conversation that was taking place between the boys and their aunt and looked for the ten-year-old. There she was, beautifully dressed for church waiting politely behind Esther. She had grown to be a pretty girl with long, golden hair that was braided up by her temples with a ribbon. She seemed disinterested in the grown-up conversation and was looking around to see if there were any other children. Leaving the bored child outside, the deciding party entered the farmhouse. Esther and Walter barely acknowledged Eliza's presence and walked directly into the front room to pay their last respects to their brother-in-law. Eliza observed her aunt walking round the coffin whilst muttering to her husband. They stayed with Tom Barton for over twenty minutes pondering the dilemma and gesticulating to each other. At last, they left the room. Esther carefully closed the door behind them to prevent her words from offending the deceased. Eliza braced herself for the verdict.

"The Family don't want you at the funeral. However, he was your father, you have a right to be there. You won't speak or sit with them, and you must stay at the back. You will not be welcomed at the graveside, so you better say your last goodbyes now before the coffin is closed," Esther pronounced judiciously.

Eliza bowed her head gratefully and entered the front room to say her tearful goodbyes. Becky allowed her a few precious moments with their father alone and then she decided to go and console her sister. Eliza knew it would be the only time she would be allowed to share her grief with a member of her family, and this added to her pain. After a few short minutes Tom, Will, Percy and Walter solemnly entered the room and secured the lid of the coffin. Thomas Barton was then carried off outside to the hand-drawn cart. Esther and Walter took their places at the front of the family procession, followed by Becky, Wynn, Tom and Will and their newly acquired wives Bronwyn and Nell. The steep incline of the hill meant that the pall bearers had to steady the coffin which was precariously balanced on the cart. Eliza waited until she could see the procession arrive safely at the church before she left. She noticed that Eliza Warren was missing from the family gathering, but she was nowhere to be seen.

The church was full of relatives and fellow villagers who

held Tom Barton in high esteem. Eliza sat at the very back of the church and would be able to make a quick exit at the end of the service. The last thing she wanted was for another enraged local to cause a disturbance.

Eliza was painfully aware that she was being watched and judged. She ignored the spiteful whispers and kept her head down throughout the service.

The sermon dragged on. The vicar made the most of his newly extended audience and didn't want to miss the opportunity to recruit.

The church was hot and airless.

A big bass drum started to beat violently in her chest.

Her head felt unpleasantly woozy and light.

Faint with hunger and emotional fatigue, she hurried from the service in search of fresh air and clarity. The clean, cool sea air soon stimulated her senses back to reality. She started to review her precarious future.

Eliza knew that the cuckoo sisters Bronwyn and Nell were poised to move into the farmhouse with their husbands. She knew she would be pushed out of the nest, left to perish.

She pinned her fragile hopes on building a shack on mum's strawberry strip on the hill. Maybe she could eke out the money made on strawberries throughout the year and grow enough food to sustain herself.

Eliza warmed to the idea of a solitary life, No lecherous men, no vile gossips, and no beatings from those who thought they knew better.

Becky and Percy could visit and bring her news of Little Eliza.

Maybe one day, she may even visit.

Eliza might even allow herself the luxury of a little happiness with her simple life on the hill.

She spied Little Eliza skipping in the churchyard.

What an opportunity. Would she be remembered? Would she still love her? The child approached.

"Why aren't you in church?" the little girl asked.

"I wasn't feeling too well ... I needed some fresh air."

"I don't like churches they're creepy, they make me think of dead people like Uncle Tom and Jesus," said the little girl. A wry smile came over Eliza as she realised that the two had a lot in common.

"I don't like them either, they're full of people who don't believe in what they say! So, what do you like?" Eliza asked, desperate to keep the conversation going.

"I don't know...playing...cake and Becky... oh and Christmas." the little girl said gaily.

"I like those too, especially Becky." Eliza was always ready to sing her sister's praises.

"Are you Cousin Eliza?"

Big Eliza paused before she answered. The term cousin still cut to the bone.

"Yes, I'm Becky's big sister... you remind me a little of Becky when she was a girl."

"Becky told me that you used to look after her when she was little, when her mama was working."

"That's right, I used to look after all the little ones, including you." Eliza instantly knew that she had said too much.

"What do you mean?"

"I used to look after you when your mama was working – before she got the teashop. Do you remember?"

"No. It must have been a long time ago; I only remember the teashop."

The conversation was interrupted by some of the mourners emptying from the service. Eliza was desperate to keep these precious exchanges going,

"Do you know that back at the farmhouse that I have made loads of cake?"

"Really. I love cake!"

"But you live in a teashop, you must have cake all the time...you lucky girl."

"No. That's for other people. I only get cake if Becky sneaks me some when mama isn't looking."

Excited by the prospect of unrestricted cake, Little Eliza gave her cousin a big, squeezy hug.

Unfortunately, the Warrens came out of church to witness the exchange of affection between the two Elizas. Esther starred venomously at her niece.

The girls quickly parted.

The little one raced back to her mother's side, only to be chastised for not staying in church.

Eliza senior decided to hang back from the crowd spilling out from the church. She didn't want to risk the wrath of the local outraged and wanted to keep away from her family.

A respectful distance was kept. She felt her fragile heart rip as she witnessed her father's body hastily lowered into the ground.

Unwelcomed and unmissed, Eliza decided to ditch the wake in favour of a long walk. She new Esther would ensure that Little Eliza was kept away from her.

Becky could cope with the demand for tea and crab sandwiches, she would understand…she always did.

Father would forgive her absence. He had been the most forgiving and accepting man. He always looked after his eldest daughter no matter what.

Eliza walked for a couple of hours before she realised that the light was fading fast. She found herself a vantage point on top of North Hill to survey the gradual exodus from the wake and the twinkling of lights in the village.

Eliza decided to return to the farm when she was confident that most of the non-family mourners had left. She made her way to the kitchen to help with the clearing up. Becky looked tired and worn, and Little Eliza was asleep in her uncle's old chair. The boys had already made their way down to the Pack to drink their sorrows away and their wives had gone back to their lodgings. Walter sat silently in the corner supping at a bottle of brown ale and chewing on the remains of a crab claw.

"Becky, it's time for you to take Eliza back to our rooms. We've an early start in the morning," instructed Esther who had just finished washing the crockery.

"Right maid, I need to talk to you, sit down." She beckoned Eliza. They waited for Becky and Little Eliza to say their goodbyes and made their exits. Becky wanted to spend longer with her sister to make sure that she would be alright, but Little Eliza had eaten too much cake and needed some fresh air and her bed. Esther practically pushed them out and bolted the door to ensure that they would not be interrupted.

Eliza had been dreading this moment for a long time. Her father was aware that once he was gone that the others would push Eliza away from her family home and they had spoken about it openly. In many respects Eliza knew that the farm was to be split between the eldest boys and she would be expected to leave the homestead even before the family rift.

"Right, let's get this over and done with. I don't know why this has been left to me, I am not the head of the family, but the boys felt that it would come better coming from me. As expected, your father has left the farm to Tom and Will equally. He didn't want to divide the farm up so it's unworkable and has left Alf and Percy a small sum of money each. You and Becky have got your mother's strawberry strips." Esther paused dramatically... "However, you have stained this family with an evil that won't wash away. Their wives don't want you near their children ...and the boys hate you. They fear you, and they want you out of here for good. We have clubbed together to buy your strip from you so that you can move on," said Esther with a thinly disguised air of pleasure. Eliza found this all hard to take in. She knew she couldn't stay at the farm anymore, but she never considered that they would try to rob their mother of her dying wish that she should get one of the strips.

Before Eliza could respond Esther pushed a small dirty bag of coins her way. The arrogance of the gesture made her defiant and she pushed the offending bag away.

"I don't want your bloody money. You can keep it! You have no right to take away my strip. Ma worked extra hours for years to buy it from you so that Becky and I had something to fall back on. How could you deny my mother's wishes so easily?"

"Don't you bring your poor mother into this; God rest her soul. You helped to her to grave in the first place!" Esther snapped back. Esther's accusation hit Eliza hard as if she had been punched in the stomach and winded. She paused to gain strength and shouted back, "How can you blame me for ma's death. She was too old to have that baby."

"It wasn't the baby that killed her, but the worry you caused her being stuck in the assizes again. She made herself sick with worry and when her time came, she had little strength to cope with it all. Your father has kept the truth from you. I told him it was a bad idea, and that truth will out and now you know," Esther said spitefully.

"I don't believe it you spiteful old witch!"

Esther's only response was to hit her niece hard about the face with an almighty slap. Eliza wanted to strike back, but she noticed Walter from the corner of her eye get up from his chair and start to take his belt off. Eliza only hoped that neither Becky nor Little Eliza had ever felt the weight of his belt.

Eliza backed down, the last time she was ganged up on she had three broken ribs - the pain from which troubled her still. She didn't want to risk it. Despite the pain and the ringing in her ears, Eliza sat down on her chair. She paused for a while whilst she reassessed her position. Life would be very difficult if she insisted on staying. She would find it impossible to find anyone to do business with her in the village and she would struggle. If she took the money and disappeared, she would confirm everybody's worst thoughts about her. She couldn't bear the thought that Becky or Little Eliza would think badly of her. She had two summer's worth of earnings saved up. She could manage without out their bloody money. Eliza realised that she was beaten.

"The strip is not for sale. I shall give it to Little Eliza so that she has something to call her own when she's older. Becky will show her how to look after it for her until she's old enough.

One day I hope that you will have the decency to tell her why I have given it to her," Eliza said calmly.

"I'll leave the money on the table. Jed Hooper is going into Barnstaple tomorrow at eight. You can catch a lift with him. If the money is still there by then, the offer will be withdrawn," Esther said triumphantly.

"I hope you're pleased with yourself. You have managed to rob me of everything that was precious to me."

A defeated Eliza left the room to pack her few worldly possessions and to write letters to Becky, Alf, and Percy. She decided to write a letter to Little Eliza that Becky would keep safe until the time was right. She would have to find work, somewhere where she wasn't known. As she was writing her farewells, she spied the brown paper parcel that had been forgotten about since her father's death. It was then she realised why her father insisted buying her those clothes.

After a sleepless night, Eliza gathered her bags together and put her new clothes on – she wanted to leave in style. Eliza took a yellowing crumpled piece of paper from her drawer and studied the words of His Lordship, Mr. Justice Littleton that were burned upon her memory: -

"There is little doubt that Eliza Barton gave birth alone and I submit to you that the injuries described by Mr. Mitchell, the surgeon were caused by a very problematic self-delivery, and they were not the consequence of a deliberate murderous act by the prisoner. There can only be one conclusion and I urge you to find the defendant NOT GUILTY..."

The declaration was printed in the smallest font and placed in the bottom right-hand corner on the back page of the newspaper, where only the truly dedicated readers would delve. She took a deep intake of breath at the irony of the situation. Her innocence was greeted with both suspicion and scepticism and her liberty had left her confined and rejected. At least she had seen her Little Maid one more time and that gave her hope. She shook herself from her reverie and neatly folded the newspaper clipping and placed it in her front pocket. Eliza took herself into the kitchen to scout around one last time to make sure she didn't leave anything of sentimental value. She grabbed her father's old clay pipe from the mantelpiece and retrieved her mother's large, chipped, china willow pattern cup and carefully wrapped them in brown paper and put them securely in her carpet bag. She paused for a moment or two as she looked at the bag of coins on the table. A part of her wanted to check how much the family were prepared to pay for her absence. Even though she knew the house was empty, she decided against it in case she was discovered by someone lurking in the background sneakily watching her every move. She didn't want to give anybody the satisfaction of her curiosity. She gathered her belongings and exited the farmhouse.

It wasn't long before Jed pulled up with his old nag and cart. Jed didn't even look at her, nor did he help her with her bags. After all, he had only been paid by the Barton's to drop her off at the station, he certainly wasn't going to put himself out for the likes of her. She hiked her bags onto the cart and took one final look at the family homestead. She looked up at her old bedroom window and she could see a shadowy figure pointing down at the ground. It looked like her father, but it couldn't be. She looked again and the figure had gone. She decided to look at the ground where the figure had been pointing and realised there was her father's lucky rabbit foot lying on the turf. Her father had always said that if he could come back that he would. She picked up the gift from the beyond and saw it as proof that she was being watched over and protected. It gave her the faith that she needed to carry on knowing that she would never return to the farm or her family.

3

Donna Barnard, London, Ontario, Canada, 2012

"Oh, for fuck's sake!"

Donna was struggling with her groceries. She tried to prise the various front door keys from her teeth to her hand to get into fortress Barnard. She practically fell in through the door and plonked the shopping down on a chair. As she entered the family abode a large, pushy ginger tom cat brushed past by her guiltily.

"Who let that bloody cat in again?"

No one replied.

It's not that Donna disliked cats, she just objected to other people's cats coming and taking the piss. Her feet were pulsating with pain, and she vowed never again to squeeze her extra wide feet into a pair of stilettoes. She peeled off the offending shoes and suddenly realised that she was a great deal shorter and less elegant than she was thirty seconds ago. Her weekly vow never to wear fashion shoes again occurred almost as regularly as her vow never to have a third glass of wine or a second chocolate biscuit. A pointless, yet compulsive private ritual that she performed to save herself from her own self-indulgence... it never worked.

"Tammy, mum, anyone want tea?" she yelled, but there was no reply.

Donna made her way to the kitchen and her foot squelched into something cold, slightly furry, and unpleasant. She peered down to find that she had trodden in a pile of cat vomit which was now squeezing through her toes and making her feel slightly queasy. She hopped precariously into the downstairs bathroom and shoved her vomity foot into the rarely used bidet and turned the tap on.

Her foot felt surprisingly soothed by the application of cool cat sick, a notion that bothered her for a moment or two until she was further distracted by the telephone. She quickly dried her foot and ran back into the hallway to find that the phone had stopped ringing. Just another petty annoyance to round off a day of irritation and shittiness. Once she cleaned up the offending cat leavings and thoroughly scrubbed the carpet, she continued her original mission to make everyone a cup of tea.

Donna found them on the balcony already with half-drunk cups of coffee, admiring the panoramic views of the surrounding hillside across the valley. The patio heater radiated its warmth keeping the old lady and her carer from freezing. Donna gave her mother a kiss on her cheek which was barely acknowledge or reciprocated. Joanie Barnard was not a cold or uncaring woman - she had loved her only daughter dearly, but her Alzheimer's had drained her memory of all but a few fleeting remembrances and today she had barely a flicker of recognition.

"How's she been?" Donna asked Tammy.

"Oh, you know a little hazy, but she's had her moments," answered the juvenile carer.

"What do you mean?" Tammy escorted her back inside into the lounge.

"Well look...". The whiny youth pointed to a glass coffee table with two half-filled glasses, one with bourbon and the other with gin and tonic. The ashtray had two stubbed out half-smoked cigarettes delicately poised at angles in the grooves of the glass. One had a ring of red lipstick on the tip of the filter.

"Is this a joke?"

"No honestly, I needed the bathroom and when I returned a few minutes later I found this. I didn't even know she smoked," Tammy insisted, "but the really creepy thing is that she said that a man had been here with her."

"What man?"

"She said his name was Eric...do you know who that is?"

"My Dad was Eric. She hasn't really spoken about him for years. Are you sure she said Eric?" Donna needed to get the facts straight.

"Definitely Eric, it's not a name I would make up."

Donna felt more than a little alarmed. Either Tammy was playing some form of sick trick, or her helpless mother had managed to procure a packet of cigarettes (she hadn't smoked since the onset of her illness) and played a prank on the unsuspecting care-worker. It briefly occurred to her that an intruder may have wormed their way in, but why would they help themselves to a fag and a drink and not their possessions? Donna was aware that even though she thought she knew her mother's limitations Joanie would surprise them every so often and she did used to have a wicked sense of humour. Donna decided to dismiss the incident as one of those mysterious things that happens when you live with someone with dementia.

"Any chance you can stay on for an extra half-an-hour whilst I take a shower and change?"

"I'm sorry, I've got to go - I'm on a promise!"

Donna understood that the prospect of looking after an incontinent, demented, geriatric for another thirty minutes was not high on the list of priorities of a beautiful and libidinous nineteen-year-old girl.

Donna wanted to put her foot down and insist that she stayed and worked the extra time that Tammy owed her, but she didn't want to seem sour.

"Don't do anything I wouldn't do!" she shouted.

"You really don't do very much".

"Well piss off then and have some fun!"

"I'll see you Wednesday, its Keira's turn tomorrow... bye." Tammy rushed off in case Donna changed her mind, after all she did owe her an extra hour after she slept in last week and she didn't want to disappoint her boyfriend waiting outside.

Donna decided she needed to take a shower anyway. She lovingly escorted Joanie indoors and ensured the balcony window was locked. She placed her mother in front of the TV and placed the key in her bedroom draw.

She wouldn't be long. She just needed to freshen up before the next round of semi-masticated food and any other shit that the day could throw at her came her way. Donna normally liked to luxuriate in the ceremony of having a shower, but today she powered her way through her daily ablutions with clinical expertise in a bid to ensure her mother was not up to any more shenanigans. Cleansed and refreshed Donna returned for dinner duty. She popped her head around the lounge door and noted that her mother was intently starring at the TV and gently nodding her head every so often. It was criminal how such a disease could reduce an intelligent and vibrant person into a confused and vulnerable creature, almost devoid of any semblance of the original person. Before her brain had turned to mush Joanie had been a leading research scientist – a specialist in female contraception and its effects on the body. She had travelled worldwide to share her research with universities, conventions, and pharmaceutical companies on her groundbreaking theories. She was held in high esteem by her colleagues and leading feminist writers of the time. It was rumoured that a Nobel nomination might becoming her way, but it came to nothing and now they only way she was going to win a major prize would be posthumously.

Joanie's condition first started to show itself with the usual forgetting of names of people, objects and then events. Whole passages of time would disappear, and she would replicate tasks repeatedly. Her colleagues started to question whether her work was becoming too stressful...she was starting to make serious errors.

At first, petit mal epilepsy was diagnosed which part-explained her increasing vagueness. Donna started to notice the dramatic change in her mother, but by the time it was finally diagnosed the disease had a firm hold on her and no one was surprised with the new label. Joanie's form of Alzheimer's was particularly aggressive, and her sad decline was almost complete.

Deep down Donna knew that her mother was coming to the end of life, but it caused her great pain to even think about losing her. Donna realised that she was upsetting herself again and tried to change the direction of her internal monologue. To stimulate some form of food memory for her mother she decided to 'do English' and have veggie bangers and mash. She knew she would have to be careful to cut the food up in non-chokeable bite-size pieces, but she thought it was worth a try.

Joanie was oblivious to the canned laughter on the box. Instead, she was more interested in the return of Eric. She hadn't seen him for so many years and yet out of the blue here he was. He was still attractive despite being short, fat, and middle-aged. She had really missed him and was so pleased to see him.

At first, he didn't speak, merely gesticulated, and nodded his head. He turned the TV off. He always found it irritating and felt that Donna spent way too much of her time in front of it. He poured a couple of drinks, a G&T for Joanie, and a bourbon for himself. They walked together to the balcony. He opened the door with the key and led them out to the outstanding view of the valley. It was this view that sold the place to them back in the seventies and it became a daily ritual to come out to the balcony and have a drink and smoke together at the end of the day.

Eric took a cigarette in his mouth, lit it and in a gentlemanly fashion offered it to Joanie. She gratefully accepted, she hadn't been allowed to smoke for a while, but couldn't remember why. He offered her the drink which she sipped cautiously. Her hand started to shake a little and he placed his hand on top of the shaking one and calmed it still again. He kissed her lovingly on the lips and gently brushed her cheek. She could hear his gentle encouragement to drink up. The alcohol felt warm and comforting. Its effect was immediate.

Joanie inhaled deeply on the cigarette. She enjoyed the nicotine rush and started to feel extremely mellow. There was a strange fluttering in her head. Butterflies were dancing around in her grey matter.

The perimeter of her vision was narrowing...

Eric's smiling face was beginning to fade into the ether and she wanted to follow him. Her surroundings were changing from light to dark...and then nothing.

Donna was just starting the mash the potatoes when she noticed the smell of burning. Not trusting her culinary skills, she double checked the oven and the hob, but she had already switched the electric off. The smell was getting stronger. It was the smell of sulphur from a freshly struck match with a hint of cigarette smoke.

It was coming from upstairs. She knew instantly that Joanie was up to her old tricks again and rushed upstairs to make sure she wasn't burning herself or the bloody house down.

Joanie was no longer planted in front of the TV.

A rush of ice blasted past her cheek. Donna spied the open balcony window,

"How the fuck did that happen?" she asked herself. Donna was convinced she had locked the balcony and put the key in her room. She could see Joanie sitting outside looking towards the wooded hills.

"Mum, you know you're not allowed out here. How did you get out by yourself?" She leant over her mother to put out the cigarettes and then realised as she brushed past her that something was very wrong.

Donna checked for a pulse but there was nothing. She propped Joanie up and somehow managed to drag her onto the sofa. Donna tried desperately to resuscitate her, but it was hopeless. She was gone. She starred at her mother in disbelief.

How could this happen?

She couldn't understand how life could evaporate so quickly.

Donna took a few intakes of breath and took stock for a moment or two. She was still puzzled by the bizarre nature of the situation. She knew that phoning for an ambulance should be her priority, but she had to satisfy her mounting curiosity. Instead of reaching for the phone she went back to her bedroom. She opened her drawer and there placed neatly on an old diary was the balcony key. No matter how Donna tried to figure it out she could not understand how her incapacitated mother could pour and consume two glasses of alcohol, light two cigarettes and magically open the balcony window.

A whiff of Floris No. 89 and stale cigarettes wafted by. She sensed her father's presence and felt comforted.

***

The funeral of Joan Clemency Ruskin-Barnard was a quiet and dignified affair. It was a Humanist ceremony, mercifully brief and lacking in sentimentality, just how Joanie would have wanted.

Donna managed to hold it together as she had cried herself stupid in the proceeding ten days enabling her to cope on the day. She was pleasantly surprised how many people made the effort to pay their respects and was particularly impressed with a couple of Joanie's ex-colleagues who had travelled over from the States. Joanie's carers were there, including Tammy who was visibly upset by the loss of her first client and was still affected by the novelty of death.

The reception was held back at the house and the mourners gathered in the balcony lounge to give their condolences and admire the vista. Donna had hired a local catering company to provide canapés and drinks. She felt that given her reputation for being able to burn water she ought to provide her guests with edible offerings and give her mother a proper send off.

Donna was surprised to hear the doorbell above the general hubbub of mutterings and despite the day's open-door policy she found that she had to go to answer it. Donna took a sharp intake of breath as she discovered her ex-husband Colm on the doorstep.

"I'm so sorry that I missed the service – my plane was late," he said as he kissed her on the cheek and breezed in uninvited. "What happened to the old girl in the end?"

"A massive stroke – a bit of blessing really, she was going down-hill fast," came the well-rehearsed response.

"Why the fuck are you here Colm, I don't remember inviting you?" Donna said with sudden realisation that her ex had turned up, waltzed in, and was already making her feel defensive.

"I'm just here to pay my respects and do the right thing," he said earnestly. She could feel him weighing up the situation.

He was already registering how sophisticated she looked in mourning – the LBD she was wearing suited her. Donna's hair was swirled up and smoothed over into a chignon and her mother's pearl necklace and earrings added another level of finesse. She somehow looked taller and more elegant than he remembered.

"I'm sorry Colm, I just don't buy it. I haven't seen your arse for dust in these last three years. You haven't so much as called or text to see how we were coping and now she's gone you want to do the right thing."

Colm looked crest fallen. He genuinely thought he was doing the right thing. Yes, he'd been a bit of an insensitive bastard over the last few years, but he could always depend upon Donna to forgive him and move on.

Donna saw the look on his face and felt slightly ashamed that she was feuding with her ex on the day of her mother's funeral. She really didn't want to make a fuss in front of everyone.

"Seeing as you are here you can make yourself useful. Go and mingle, pass drinks round, introduce yourself as the long-lost son-in-law if you like."

The problem with Donna was that she could never stay cross with Colm for long – no matter what he did. He always seemed to retain some likeable charm.

Donna realised that her feet were throbbing with pain and decided to take her heels off, get a third glass of wine and eat a second chocolate biscuit. He noticed that she was suddenly shorter and was no longer as elegant.

After a couple of hours of Donna watching Colm mingle and Colm watching Donna play host, many of the guests took their leave. Donna had been observing his every move and the sudden realization dawned upon her that she still found him incredibly attractive. Tammy, who had obviously worked through her grief was propped up against the wall sucking her boyfriend's face off. The sudden exposure of an empty room made the amorous couple self-conscious and they took their cue to leave.

Donna was surveying the mess that had been left behind... lip-stained glasses, golden flakes of pastry and wine stains on the carpet. The mess surprised her as she thought mourners might be a little more considerate. Much to Donna's further surprise she noticed that Colm had got a black bin bag and was emptying plates of leftovers and picking up litter.

This was not the inconsiderate bastard of old. She had brought up his children from another marriage, kept a beautiful home and juggled with her own journalistic career. Donna felt she had sacrificed her best years so he could screw around and make a laughingstock out of her. Maybe he had finally matured.

There's no way she would put up with that kind of shit now. She had done all her caring for others, and it was now time for her to do what she wanted. And... she was going to start tomorrow...

"I wouldn't worry about that too much. I've got cleaners coming in to give the place a deep clean tomorrow. There's no need for you to stay if you want to go."

"There's no rush. I thought it might be good to catch up if you got time."

"Fancy a glass?" She gently shook a half empty bottle of Shiraz as an incentive.

"Why not, I can always get a cab if I need to."

"Not worried about pissing Jenna off then?"

"Are you fishing for something?" They sat down together

on the sofa. "Jenna left some time ago. Called me a commitment-phobe."

"She's right, you've been married twice, and you still can't commit."

"A bit harsh Dons. I did try."

"Well done you! Look Colm it is was it is. You're rubbish at fidelity. Monogamy really doesn't suit you. You are a serial adulterer and are much better off single." There was obvious sexual tension.

She had him at a disadvantage. He knew that he had behaved badly, and he had paid the price ever since. He bitterly regretted screwing around, believing that accepting Donna would always have him back. In all fairness to Donna, she offered him the branch of reconciliation time and time again. He hadn't considered that once the kids had gone off to uni that she would cut her losses. The stupid thing was that once she left him the only thing, he could think about was her.

He went through the same old routine of going out with much younger girls that would eventually want some form of commitment whether it was living together or babies and then he would want out. But he always come back to thoughts of picking up with Donna again.

He was puzzling her. What was his game? What the fuck did he want? Donna was not prepared to go back in time and play the doting wife and gamble on him screwing things up again. She was not prepared to take the risk.

However, the house freaked her out since the Floris No. 89 affair, and she didn't want to sleep alone on her last night. The thought of familiar sex was comforting, and she would be happy to let him stay.

Colm wondered which strategy to employ. Should he turn on the charm and beg her for forgiveness and hope that one thing would lead to another? Or should he start talking about Joanie in a caring and sensitive way, hoping that one thing would lead to another? Of course there was always the 'let's get back together' ploy, but that would firmly place him in the position of having to alter his relationship status on Facebook. He wasn't sure he was up for that kind of commitment.

"Do you want to stay the night?" Donna asked bluntly.

Before he could reply they were already making up for lost time. It wasn't long before they made their way to the comfort of Donna's king-size. They were in the process of stripping each other's clothes off when Donna insisted on stopping. Colm watched her scurry over to the other side of the room worried that she maybe having second thoughts. Donna's unexpected departure had little to do with him, but was an urgent need to close her bedroom door. In the throes of passion she had the irrational thought that Floris No. 89 was still watching over his daughter, and it was putting her off ... and she had no intention of sleeping alone that night.

***

A part of Donna felt like a bit of a slapper. She wasn't in the habit of sleeping around or having one-night stands. In fact since leaving Colm she had become a born-again virgin and hadn't slept with anyone else. They were both free agents, but bringing a lover back home still felt like a bit of a taboo, despite both her parents being dead.

Anyway, no matter she had a flight to catch, she just hadn't told Colm. She had forgotten what a heavy sleeper he was. He managed to sleep through the irritating sound of her radio alarm going off, her taking a shower in the adjacent ensuite and then blow-drying her hair. Time was passing by and he left her with no alternative but to wake him up forcibly with a mug of black coffee and to tell him to sling his hook.

"Colm, Colm. You've got to wake up, I've got to go." He started to make vague mumbling sounds, but nothing that resembled coherent speech.

"Come on lazy, you can't stay." He finally started to come round as she shook his arm.

"What's up? Where are you going?"

"England."

"What?"

"I said ENGLAND!" she shouted into his ear.

"This is a joke, right?"

Then he noticed Donna's packed cases near the door and realised that she was serious.

"I've decided to take a sabbatical. I've inherited my gran's old farmhouse in Devon. I've nothing to keep me here. I'm renting this place out and the paper are happy for me to a write a column about what it is life is like back in the old country. I'm going to split my time between renovating the place and travelling."

"Yeh, but you're coming back, aren't you?" He was unused to having this kind of conversation with anyone, let alone with Donna.

"I haven't decided yet. I'll see how I get on. If I decide to stay, I'll sell this place. I was never particularly fond of it – I always resented being dragged away from England in the first place."

"If you are so fond of England, how come you've left it 'till now?" Colm was desperately trying to make sense of the situation.

"Too many other people pleasing commitments I suppose. First Dad died and I felt I couldn't leave Joanie. I went to uni. Met you and inherited your children, then mum fell ill and now for the first time in my adult life I have no responsibilities."

"What about us?"

"What about us? You made your lifestyle choices many years ago. Just think of this as just another one of your many conquests. I'm sure your ego can take it if you reframe it."

"That's so unfair. I really was hoping for us to get back together." He felt forced to play the reunion card after all.

"Do you really think that we could make this work? Because I don't. You can't help yourself. As I said last night, you are a serial adulterer and should stay single."

Donna could hear a car waiting outside.

"Anyway, I've got to go. The cleaning team will be in at eleven. Just put the key in the post box on your way out."

Donna leaned over him and kissed him goodbye.

"I'm sorry Colm this is what it feels like."

"What do you mean?"

"You know," she said enigmatically.

"I'll call you!" he said as a feeble attempt to re-engage her in conversation. But it was too late. She was already in the cab on her way to the airport.

4

Donna, Usbournes, Devon, April 2012

Donna's first night at Gran's cottage didn't bode well for the future. She arrived in the early evening to find what used to be a well-kept rose garden had been reclaimed by nature. The abundance of spiky brambles and twisted bind weed had fortified the entrance to her new home rendering it impenetrable. The back yard was equally impassable due to antiquated, abandoned farm equipment blocking the way.

Donna had forgotten how remote the cottage was and found that the few neighbours in the hamlet seemed to be out. She also had underestimated how few ATMs there would be in North Devon and realised that she had no access to cash. She had no alternative but to spend another night in Gertie the camper van and sort out the mess in the morning.

Gertie had been Donna's one indulgence since Joanie died.

She wasn't in the habit of spending money on herself as a rule. Normally any spare cash had been spent on the kids. But they had grown up and abandoned their devoted stepmother in favour of less complicated lives for themselves away from any feelings of guilt or divided loyalty between her and their father.

Donna had always loved the romance and freedom of the old VW Samba and made it her priority to get one as soon as she arrived in England. She wanted to tour the country first, as she knew that once she took over the cottage there would be no time for travel and soon her year would be up, and she would have to return to work.

The lack of ready cash meant that Donna had to dine on fridge surprise again. A speciality chez Gertie was any old crap left in the camper van's dilapidated 1960's box fridge. Last night's Russian roulette of a meal consisted of a hardboiled egg and some semi-fizzy tinned spaghetti that had been opened the best part of a week, followed by some flat Chateaux Fanta vintage circa 2012. It was a rancid combination that left Donna particularly nauseated and with chronic indigestion. After she had recovered from her gourmet meal, she tried in vain to access the internet, but realised that there was no bloody signal. She wondered how the locals coped without easy access to the net and realised that she might find it more difficult to adapt to life in rural England than she first anticipated.

Donna bedded down for the night on the couch as she couldn't be bothered to pull the bed down and run the risk of pinching her fingers in the springs again. She snuggled down in her ancient nylon sleeping bag that still had a faint odour of teenage promiscuity, dope, and stale beer from her years at university. It took her back to the days when her life was so full of potential and the notion that everything was possible.

But what had she achieved? She was forty-five, divorced, childless, orphaned and potentially stateless. Her career was on the skids, she had been living in a camper van for the last two months. She smelt like an old bag lady, and felt like she was going to throw up… Still there was nothing like a good old rant to yourself about how shit your life is to put everything into perspective.

She was exhausted, but she couldn't settle. First, she couldn't get comfortable as she tried to balance herself on the Gertie's narrow couch. Then she tried to free herself from a particularly uncomfortable wedgie as she hadn't bothered to change into her nightclothes. As the night progressed the temperature dropped, and Donna was faced with the eternal dilemma of should she get out of bed to get a blanket or should she stay put and stay balanced. After much prevarication, she decided that the blanket was a good idea, but had problems re-balancing on her return. She just drifted off when she heard some drunken giggling. She looked out of the window to see an older couple and a female friend stagger home after a good night out.

"Inconsiderate bastards!" she thought to herself and tried in vain to return to sleep. After a few hours of light sleep she needed the toilet. She returned to the old dilemma of whether to stay in the warmth of her bed or to negotiate balancing on the barely disguised bucket in the cupboard. Her bladder won that debate as her body needed to rid itself of the flat Fanta. As she balanced precariously on the chemical toilet, she noticed to her annoyance that the early dawn chorus was already starting. The opportunity for more sleep was rapidly vanishing. Donna decided to give up and make herself a cup of tea. She consoled herself with the thought that she should be able to get into the cottage and catch up on her sleep at her leisure.

Donna dozed off sitting up. Her steaming mug of tea tilted precariously as she slipped back into the land of nod. Someone started to bang loudly on the cottage door.

"Eliza! Open up. It's past seven o'clock. I'll be late to feed the pigs," shouted a young sounding man.

There was no reply. Donna prised open the curtains a little to see why somebody should be banging on Gran's cottage door. No one was there. Donna assumed that she had been dreaming, placed her mug down on the table and closed her eyes again. She was just on the verge of drifting off again when she heard the banging even louder.

"For goodness' sake Eliza, open up." shouted the man.

Donna looked out again and still couldn't see anyone. She assumed that the sound was carrying over from one of her neighbours and was starting to realise that life in the country is not always so peaceful. Donna could clearly hear the latch of a door being lifted and some mumbling between the young man and a woman. The weak cry of a very young infant could be heard.

"My God Eliza! What have you done?... I'll better get help."

At this point Donna leapt out of the camper van in fear that a neighbour's baby might be in peril. She squinted to see properly in the shock of daylight, but she couldn't see anybody. She tried listening again, but the couple had stopped talking. She followed the road round to her nearest cottage, but all seemed peaceful and calm. The only thing she could hear was the bleating of lambs on the hillside and the end of the early morning chorus.

The fridge surprise started to curdle violently in her stomach and with no warning she found herself throwing up a pile of fluorescent orange stringiness in a nearby hedgerow.

Donna acknowledged to herself that if the food was fizzier than the soda then it shouldn't be trusted. She made another pointless vow to herself that she was going to adopt a much healthier lifestyle now that she was living in the country.

After a stomach churning few minutes, the potential for vomit subsided and with no more noisy neighbour activity, Donna returned to the van. She wrapped the old crochet blanket around her shoulders and tried to doze off again. She had just drifted off into a dream where she was being chatted up by a rather handsome young under-graduate, when someone banged loudly on the van. She opened the back door.

"What the fu…" Donna stopped herself mid-obscenity as she realised it was one of the old ladies who had returned worse for wear last night.

"You can't park here love; this is private property," said the lady with purpose.

"What?" Donna responded like a truculent teenager.

"I said you can't park your van here. It's private property. I saw you here last night, but it was a bit late."

"I know, you woke me up!"

"I know your type. If you want to camp out there are plenty of sites up the road. If you don't move your van, I'll get the police to move you along."

"This is bloody ridiculous. I am entitled to park here, I…"

"Look young lady I am aware that your generation have an

all-embracing sense of entitlement, but this property belongs to someone, and you DO NOT have the right to park where you want."

Donna's patience was rapidly running out. "Look here, I have every right to park my bloody van outside my own property."

"Don't you pull the wall over my eyes young lady. I've lived here for over twenty years, and I know the old woman who used to own it."

"Yes, MY grandmother, Mrs. Ruskin."

The woman paused to process this new information. She immediately adjusted her tone.

"You must be Joanie's girl! Why didn't you say? I'm Judith Walters, your neighbour from across the way. You can call me Jude." She held out her hand.

"Yes, I am. I'm Donna... hi!"

"I'm awfully sorry about that. Just a misunderstanding. I'm always having to move surfers and doggers on from parking here. I am always clearing up used condoms and stuff. You 'll never believe what people get up to now days."

Donna was taken by surprise by Jude's jolly attitude to other people's sexual deviances.

"You look dreadful. Why don't you come in for a cup of tea and a chat?" Jude enquired... "and a shower?"

"That would be most welcome!" Donna grabbed a towel, some clean clothes, and followed her new neighbour to her abode.

Jude lived just about a two-minute walk from Usbourne cottage.

Much to Donna's surprise Jude's place was a modern 1970's

lodge style creation, not unlike her place back in Ontario. Jude explained that the original house was bought by her grandparents on their retirement. The old cobb walls caved in when they tried to extend and had to start from scratch.

It wasn't the most attractive house, but it offered unparalleled views of the breath-taking surrounding countryside and a silvery sliver of the Atlantic in the distance. Once Donna had showered and changed, Jude served the pot of tea and rounds of toast on the balcony, and they started to chat. Donna soon forgot about her night from hell in the camper van and the strange behaviour of their neighbours and started to relax in Jude's easy company.

Jude was saddened to hear Donna's news about Joanie. They had never met but she had heard so much about her from Lottie that she felt she knew the family intimately.

Jude had been a good neighbour to Lottie. She used to get her pension and shopping every Thursday and would drive her to the doctor's surgery when needed. Over the years they had got to know each other well and became firm friends. She greatly admired Lottie's determination to stay at home and remain independent.

Lottie was a game old bird in Jude's estimation and any grandchild of Lottie's would always be welcome.

Donna explained her set of family circumstances and of her plans for the renovations to the cottage.

"You do realise that it's going to take more than a year to get that place straight," Jude said with an air of disbelief.

"It shouldn't take long to fix up the old place. Why do think it will take time?"

"It's been neglected for decades. It's been empty for over

ten years and poor old Lottie didn't do anything to it since the fifties. The roof is going home, and the electrics will need replacing. Then to top it all there's the size of it."

"But it's just a tiny cottage!"

"Let me show you," said Jude and she took Donna by the hand.

They walked round to the front of the cottage.

"Look, the property is 'L' shaped. This is just the entrance to the small part," Jude continued as she escorted Donna round the corner. There was another, much larger garden that had also returned to the wild. It belonged to a much more substantial property and was in a dreadful state of neglect.

The front of the property was obscured by wisteria and ivy. It was hard to identify the white rendered exterior underneath the flourishing vegetation.

It looked as if the two properties were individual freeholds, but they were attached to form an 'L' shape.

"Then there are the outbuildings and those cottages over there, as well as the land," continued Jude.

Donna surveyed her inheritance with a mixture of awe and dread. The land was obviously farmed by someone, and the cottages looked occupied.

"I don't understand. I just remember Gran living in a cottage, no one ever mentioned any of this." Donna was still reeling from the enormity of the task.

"As Lottie grew older, she found the property too much. She had it partitioned and rented the rest out."

"When was this last leased?"

"This part hasn't had tenants for some years, but the cottages and the land are still rented out."

"So, who's getting the money from all this?"

"I assume you or your mother."

"I've got all of mum's paperwork and she has never received any income from this estate. In fact, it has been a financial millstone. Mum has been paying an agent to maintain the property since Gran died, which is a bloody joke because nobody has done anything." Donna paused. "Right, I'm not having this I am going to sort this out today," Donna said with an air of determination. "Fancy coming? I might need a witness." She beckoned to Jude as she started to walk back to Gertie, the tangerine dream.

"Let me get my keys, I won't be a minute." Jude was beginning to see a great deal of Lottie in her granddaughter.

Donna and Jude had a productive morning at Austyn and Simms property agents. It was clearly a shock to Leighton Collins that any one from the Usbourne estate would ever walk in unannounced. He knew that Mrs. Barnard lived in Canada and had been trying to persuade her to sell the estate for years.

Donna pointed out that her late mother had paid maintenance of more than £26,000 over the eleven years since Mrs. Ruskin had died and it was obvious by the sorry state of repair that nothing had been done. She demanded that a clearance team be hired immediately, so that the frontage could be cleared to gain access to the property by the afternoon. She also pointed out to the obsequious manager that her husband - 'a leading Canadian commercial lawyer', would be in contact concerning the missing rent from the estate.

The bemused manager ignored Donna's last reference to the missing rents but assured her that a specialist team would be over by mid-morning and profusely apologised for the over-sight and any inconvenience caused. He issued Donna with an impressive bunch of ancient looking keys and wished her luck.

Jude was impressed with how Donna had managed the whole situation and imagined that Lottie would be proud of how her granddaughter stood her ground and showed the Uriah Heap clone in the office how to do business.

Donna was just relieved that she got what she wanted without swearing at the little prick.

It was past six in the evening before Donna was able to get to the cottage. The yard had been cleared by a couple of local farm lads who managed to drive most of the tractor artefacts out of the yard and towed the rest of the rusting rubbish away. The space was transformed from a dumping ground to a large courtyard hemmed in by various dilapidated farm outbuildings and a large barn that was screaming out for conversion. It exposed the back of the larger part of the 'L' shaped building, and it was the first time that Donna could gain any real scale of her new abode.

The clearance team at the cottage battled for a couple of hours to chop the foliage back but decided that it would be quicker to flame it. The scorched Earth policy worked and after the front garden had been dampened down Donna was able to gain access. She was a little pissed off that some of the white rendering had scorch marks, but soon realised that in the great scheme of things a little lick of paint was the least of her worries. Donna soon abandoned any prospect of exploring the buildings that evening, as she couldn't find the electric box and re-scheduled the mission until the morning.

Donna spent a much more comfortable night in Jude's

spare room. Jude enjoyed entertaining and was pleased to have the company. She offered to cook her speciality Thai green curry, but Donna was still suffering from the after effects of her self-inflicted food poisoning and felt that she was safer with tea and dry toast. They were both excited by the prospect of exploring what Usbournes had to offer and were happy to sacrifice a lie-in and to make the most of the day.

***

Donna managed to open Gran's cottage with ease and Jude found the Bakelite electric box under the stairs and switched on the electrics. Donna surveyed the dimly lit cottage enveloped by a cosy mist of nostalgic reverie.

Very little had changed since she last saw it before being unwillingly dragged away to a foreign land. The front door opened into a narrow hallway with a room either side and a small twisting staircase to the first floor.

The kitchen was very basic comprising of a Belling electric hob, an old, chipped Belfast sink, and a few door-less wooden cupboards. There was a cheap transistor radio with the dial eagerly hovering over radio four on the kitchen shelf. Next to it was a curious mustard coloured ceramic fish with its open mouth full of crochet hooks.

Donna had to fight her way past a luridly coloured plastic streamer fly screen that hung precariously above the back door, before she could make her way into the courtyard.

The view across the paddock was obscured by the large barn that was loosely connected to the cottage by a piece of corrugated steel roofing. The yard offered little of any interest and Donna retreated into the dimly lit kitchen. Jude was standing outside the sitting room in the claustrophobically small hallway waiting for Donna to return. Jude seemed a little reticent to go in by herself.

"Are you alright?" asked Donna.

"I found her in there. Your Gran, I mean. I returned from getting her shopping one day and there she was cold in her old chair with the Archers on, completely lifeless."

"I had no idea you were the one that found her, it must have been horrible for you."

"I half expected to find her dead every time I came to see her, but it was still a shock when I finally did. It's not as bad as what happened afterwards though."

"Why, what happened?"

"Oh, another story and at some point I'll fill you in with all the boring details. Come on, let's look," she said, quickly changing the subject.

A smell of dusty old books hit them as they entered Gran's sitting room. The ancient, shredded net curtains had yellowed with age and had a tentative grip on the wooden curtain pole. The tiny windows seemed to suck the light out of the room and spectacularly failed the amazing view of the hills.

The main focal point of the room was not a television, but a rather stylish wooden Ecko radiogram with a pile of well-thumbed Radio Times stacked on top. A couple of dilapidated armchairs with multi-coloured crochet anti-macassars draped over the arms were plonked in the centre of the room. The slippery wooden floor was masked by a large faded blue Persian rug. Its treachery remained.

Three-quarters of the room was entombed by wall-to-wall bookshelves with an eclectic collection of literature from Archer to Voltaire. A confusing mix of rare first editions and

Reader's Digest abridged classics. A dangerous looking paraffin heater was placed where you would expect a fireplace and there were no radiators to be seen. A slight whiff of fuel hung in the air.

Finding Gran's sitting room a little depressing they decided to venture upstairs. This comprised of Gran's and little Joanie's bedrooms and a tiny bathroom and toilet. Donna decided that she was going to have Gran's larger bedroom which had the best views to the front of the cottage. It had a large brass knobbed bed covered with a patchwork quilt that had been crafted from any old random remnants of material. There was a plain dark wooden blanket box at the end of the bed which contained some holey crochet blankets and a few dead over-fed moths. A curious smell of moth balls and blood emanated from the box, making Donna feel queasy again. She clearly hadn't fully recovered from her bacteria filled feast from the other night.

"So, what do you think?" asked Jude.

"I'd forgotten how basic this place is. I don't know how Gran managed without a telephone or central heating." Donna realised she had remembered the cottage through a rose-tinted haze.

"I'm not sure I can manage a project like this, and we haven't even been next door yet," she added, suddenly feeling overwhelmed by it all.

"Let's take a look, it might not be as bad as you think," encouraged Jude with an added sense of adventure.

Jude's misplaced sense of optimism rallied Donna's flagging confidence and persuaded her to look at the main house.

Initially, Donna struggled to find the right key from the array of ancient keys that Uriah Heap had given her. It was poorly lit, and they struggled to find the electrics in the boot room adjacent to the back door. The first main room they entered was a large farmhouse kitchen which came equipped with a spidery black range cooker cocooned by a thick stone hearth and an ancient bread oven snuggled into the corner.

A substantial iron hook was suspended from the beamed ceiling where meat used to be cured. There was a large oak table underneath, undulated by generations of servants heavy scrubbing.

The grey slate floor generated an eerie echo as Donna and Jude's boots chinked and clunked with every step. It had a cold, unloved feel to it which made Donna feel uneasy. The kitchen was centrally situated to the left was a small bathroom and toilet and another crooked staircase leading to the upper floor. Right at the very end of the corridor was an empty room with another deep-set hearth and a door leading to the front garden.

Donna and Jude decided to explore the south side from the kitchen. On the left-hand side was a wooden panelled dining room complete with a large dining table, chairs and various sideboards with fine cut-glass decanters and glasses that were laced with the silk of spiders and glittered with dust.

The whole of the corridor was carpeted in dark grey which revealed a dark green hue underneath once the thick film of fluff was disturbed. The room to the right of the kitchen was a large, panelled reception room which housed the most impressive stone hearth in the house. There were a few armchairs that were covered with dust sheets randomly scattered around and a rather fine walnut drinks table in the centre. Jude and Donna walked around in silence as they struggled to understand why

Lottie Ruskin had decided to live in the grotty part of the house.

They mounted the second, grander staircase of the house to the upper level to discover a long corridor with exposed grey stonework walls and various bedrooms sprouting from the main stem.

Along the outside wall stood a horologist's dream... a collection of four grandfather clocks, their faces obscured by squares of black silk that had been draped over each one.

Jude lost her nerve. "I've got to get out of here, this is too much!" She made her way down the stairs.

Jude's sudden change of attitude took Donna by surprise and not wanting to stay near the clock graveyard on her own she decided to follow her neighbour.

Jude insisted on going back to her place to make a pot of tea.

"What was that all about?" asked Donna.

"Nothing I'm just being silly, I spooked myself that's all."

"I know we've only just met, but I know that something creeped you out about those clocks, what was it?"

Jude poured two strong cups of milky tea and unusually she put a couple of teaspoons of sugar in hers.

"Well, it goes back to the day I discovered Lottie dead. I saw her in the morning and got her a cup of tea before going into town. She seemed very chatty, and I left her listening to The Archers. I was gone a few hours as I had to go into Barnstaple. When I returned, I found your Gran dead in the chair where I had left her, her tea remained untouched, and the radio was still on. I checked for a pulse, but she was already starting to stiffen a little... so I knew she had been dead a while. I popped outside to get a signal and phoned an ambulance. When I returned to switch the radio off when I noticed something that frightened me.

Someone had placed a square of black silk over her face like a veil. I double-checked the back door which was locked and decided to look upstairs in case some weirdo had come in behind me. But there was nobody there, the house was completely empty. Knowing that Lottie was dead when I discovered her, I couldn't understand how she could be sitting there with a shroud on her face. It made my skin crawl and I had to get out of the place. Seeing those grandfather clocks with the same cloths over their faces brought it all back to me... had to get out."

The hairs on Jude's arms started to prickle.

Donna couldn't come up with any rational answers. She had only known Jude for a couple of days, and she seemed a very rational, practical person who wouldn't normally be prone to inventing wild stories about the recently departed. Her own experience with Floris No. 89 had made Donna more receptive to other unusual occurrences.

Donna decided not to dwell on Jude's strange tale for too long. She was going to have to sleep in the cottage by herself and didn't want to be kept awake by the strange noises and shadows of the house. Another sleepless night in Gertie was not an option...it was killing her back.

She determined to sleep in Gran's old room and comforted herself with the thought that Gran would have been delighted that she had returned. She rationalised that Lottie always loved and looked after her in life and would do so in death - just like Floris. She had no need to worry.

5

Susannah Usbourne, Devon, 1884

The carriage that transported the newly wedded Captain and Mrs. Usbourne was an old bone shaker, and the suspension needed an overhaul as a matter of urgency. The journey had been particularly uncomfortable since they deviated from the main road and were negotiating the lumpy track leading up to the village of St. Nectan's. They were making their final detour up to the estate.

The Captain observed that his new wife looked particularly anxious. Her arms taught and her knuckles whitened as she gripped tightly to her seat. She was in considerable distress.

His failed words of reassurance were greeted by an unnerving silence.

Despite their nuptials the day before, she was still dressed in mourning, shrouded by a black veil. It was only when she moved her head to one side that he caught a glimpse of her large, sorrowful eyes and a hint of her fine bone structure - a promise of beauty that lay beneath.

It had been the strangest twenty-four hours of his life.

A day of celebration, yet the Hill siblings were quite clearly in mourning. Theirs was not the only family wedding being celebrated that day and that he was merely a minor player in a rather bizarre double ceremony involving his new brother-in-law and a Miss Pryor.

There were a few wedding guests mainly from Miss Pryor's family, a trio of irritating sisters with their mother all in their finery and a loud bulldog of a man who would rather be down at the races.

Susannah had no friends or ladies in attendance. She failed to speak to anybody or raise a smile not even to her brother, whom he knew she was particularly fond of. A day drained of all joy and excitement with an economy of emotion and all conversation carefully measured. A fine balance was maintained between politeness and austerity, a joyless and bizarre spectacle that lacked any hint of the feminine romantic ideal.

He knew that something was wrong but, was unable to pinpoint the source of discontent other than the obvious. It puzzled him that the unnaturally devoted siblings could barely look at each other and they parted with such emotional efficiency that they seemed like strangers.

He looked at his terrified wife and started to question the merit of the marriage and why Phillip insisted on the wedding so close to the loss of Mr. Hill.

What had he married into? What burden of responsibility had he undertaken?

The pragmatic Captain failed to dwell on the dilemma for too long and focussed on the sizable dowry and annual income that Philip had generously offered. This commercial venture bore no romantic attachments and it was advantageous to have a member of the family on the estate, freeing him to conduct himself as he pleased in London.

What was done, was done and if this partnership failed to provide fulfilment, then there was always the welcome sanctuary of The Millen Club and the welcoming bosom of his London housekeeper.

Susannah sat bolt upright as if struck by premature rigour mortis. Her breath was fast and shallow, her beating heart louder than the metallic din of the hoof and the clattering of the carriage. Like a blinkered horse, she avoided all exposure to the world outside apart from her narrow frame of reference. She could only gaze straight ahead.

He could not compare to her beloved, but he was not an unhandsome man. Distinguished looking, clean, and freshly manicured, his greying hair was fastidiously combed, and his unassuming attire had been chosen with care.

He had remained silent since she first rebuffed his gently spoken re-assurances, but her priority had been to concentrate on containing her body's potential to rid itself of the bitter bile and acid that was rising in her throat and to save herself from an unbearable disgrace.

"We are nearly there, if you look out of the window you will see the approach to Usbournes," said the Captain, in a vain attempt to encourage his wife to look at his estate.

At first Susannah hesitated, her irrational fear of the unfamiliar made her reluctant to engage with the view. She realised that this may be the only opportunity to survey her new environment without the need for her physical involvement.

The uneven, stony road passed through a hamlet of six or so labourers' cottages, neatly thatched with greying straw and sharply rendered in white, with crisp straight walls like tiny sugar cubes nestling in the green.

She had never seen such large swathes of countryside and the sheer size of the hills, and the vividness of the colours was overwhelming.

Susannah was used to viewing her world through the comfort of a frame. Limited by her mother's window, she had failed to experience anything on this scale before. London maybe the world's largest city, but everything seemed small and confined by comparison to the vastness of the Devonshire countryside.

The view failed to excite. It was a sizeable property but lacked the gravitas and grandeur of the sweeping gravelled drive and the carefully tended gardens that she had imagined. She had expected exotica like roaming peacocks and carefully handcrafted shrubs and perhaps even a small lake or fountain.

Instead, there was a muddied road, aggressive geese running round a small weed filled pond and a few forlorn looking rose bushes that were clearly struggling to survive outside a modest entry porch to the house.

The carriage pulled up suddenly. Susannah heard the driver jump down, indicating that she would soon have to leave the relative safety of the carriage. She was engulfed by a new wave of anxiety as she started to hyperventilate.

The door was opened, and the Captain exited the carriage immediately holding out his hand to his new bride. His gallant gesture was ignored... there was an awkward pause. Susannah seemed rooted, unable, or unwilling to make her way from the carriage. Invisible hands gripped her feet rendering her unable to move. Another pair of hands seemed to grip at her throat, squeezing tightly.

The Captain patiently coaxed his new wife from the vehicle and finally succeeded in his mission as she took a deep breath and clumsily fell into his arms.

After an apologetic recovery, they were greeted by a severe looking servant dressed in navy with a spotless apron.

"Welcome to Great Usbourne House," she greeted in a soft, feminine voice that conflicted with her austere exterior.

"I am Mrs. Waits, the current housekeeper," continued the servant in a warm and welcoming tone. Her thin, pinched face and pallid complexion was a reflection on the hard life she had led rather than her character. Whilst she had a reputation for being an excellent and efficient housekeeper, she was also known for being a kindly, nurturing soul and was held in high regard by most in the village.

The newly-weds were escorted into the morning room at the end of the house. It was a small, functional room offering panoramic views of sheep laden hills and bracken filled moors.

Susannah took an immediate dislike of the room and its open vistas.

"I shall bring tea in presently," said the servant, but before she could leave the room an overanxious and exhausted Susannah stood up.

"Please forgive me if I seem rude, but I am feeling rather unwell, and I would rather be shown to my room," she informed her surprised husband.

"Of course. Mrs. Waits would you kindly show Mrs.

Usbourne to her new room?" The Captain's patience and understanding were beginning to wane.

"Certainly. Please come this way."

When they reached the room Susannah hurried the servant away and bolted the door. She made her way to the washbasin and was violently sick. She splashed a little cold water on her face and carefully placed a nearby towel over the offending bowl.

Susannah stared at her face in the oval, silver filigreed mirror. Her deep brown eyes stared back at her with barely a flicker of self-recognition. Just for a second, she saw the face of a stranger. A plain looking woman with short curly hair and the look of utter surprise. Within a blink, she had gone and was instantly forgotten.

The mirror's crazed right-hand corner caught her eye. She studied how it reflected and refracted the shafts of sunlight, acting like a prism dividing the light into delicate shards of metallic colours, steely and harsh. She looked away, but the image had imprinted onto the corner of her right eye. The shaft of light cracked into a myriad of kaleidoscopic patterns and colours, followed by a sharp pain which split across her eye like a pick to ice. She closed her eye, but the images transferred seamlessly over to the left side, leaving her dazed and disoriented.

Susannah collapsed on top of her new bed without taking off her boots and clothes. A violent battle started to rage through her head, spiteful and twisting. Lights of electrical intensity flashed across her eyes. Comfort was beyond her. Hours dragged past, desperately seeking refuge from pain. Traumatic events of the last few weeks replayed over and over. At some point she drifted off into a deep, coma-like state.

***

Susannah was woken by the bleating of sheep and the aggressive spat of territorial sparrows fighting on the window-ledge. These unfamiliar sounds jarred and irritated, they were not London noises. She was alarmed to find that she was in a strange room... how she longed for the sanctuary of Hetty.

The drapes had been drawn and she had been dressed in her nightgown and placed in the warmth of the covers. Order had been created out of the chaos of her arrival. Bonnet and veil carefully placed on the table. The bowl of disgrace emptied and scrubbed clean.

Susannah got up from her bed slowly and with care. Weakened from the migraine assault and lack of nourishment, she drank slowly to ease her sore, dry throat. The water was sweet and unlike anything she had tasted before. She washed and dressed and made her way to the dining room.

It was a unique experience for her to explore a new abode. She had been born in Grove House and was rather hoping she would die there. New things did not suit her, nor did new people, it was all so crushing.

She regretted the unpromising start to her new life and marriage, but this was an opportunity to create a new and more fulfilling existence. She was freed from parental expectations and her cloying, suffocating brother.

This was a relationship where she could set the boundaries and not have them forced upon her by parents eager to ensure that Phillip was adored and idolised at her expense. Her lack of self-worth and her limited experience ensured that all perspective had been lost. Their love had developed a depth and intensity that defied the normal boundaries. A love that would never truly diminish. A love so engrained that she would never be truly free. No real space for her to love another.

6

Eliza, Devon, 1889

Eliza was lying on a grassy patch, allowing herself a few rare moments of tranquillity before gathering up the little ones after a long day picking strawberries. The freshly picked scarlet jewels had been packed up and loaded and already on the way to London. The fruits of their labours would soon be devoured by society's elite for tomorrow's afternoon tea and would soon be forgotten within the day.

Her eyes were firmly closed observing the mottled impressions left on her eyes of the trees and cottages after she had been looking at the sun.

It was too quiet...

Suddenly, she felt the warm sensation of over-ripe stickiness being joyfully squashed onto the back of her shoulder. A peel of uncontrollable giggling signalled to Eliza that her unnaturally quiet siblings had been enticing little Eliza to squash strawberries onto her back.

"You little horrors!" She gently pulled the little one on to the ground and started to tickle her. Little Eliza's chubby little legs started to kick around playfully in the air. The excitement of being tickled and the force of her rotating legs swinging perilously close to big Eliza's face meant that not only did she accidentally kick her in the nose, but she passed a noisy little puff of smelliness in the process. Becky picked little Eliza up when she noticed that her big sister's nose was starting to bleed. The little ruby beads dripped onto her strawberry stained pinafore.

"Right then you horrible lot. We better make our way home," Eliza said as she picked up a punnet of squashies to take home for tea.

"The sea, the sea!" Alf and Percy shouted joyfully as they ran off over the hill-top in the direction of the shore.

Becky and Eliza took it turns to carry the little one until they reached the beach. The tide was in, and the sea was glassy, gently lapping against the sides of the fishing boats that were tethered to the harbour wall.

The Barton children waded in and washed their sticky fruited hands in the shock of the cool water. Eliza knelt and cupped some of the sea into her hand to wash her face. She watched as the crimson mixed with the crystal-clear water in large swirls twisting and spiralling until they melted away. She wiped her face with a large kerchief and took her pinafore off to wash in the water. It looked like she'd been butchering. Even the salted water wasn't enough to bleach out the incriminating evidence of strawberry indulgence and accidental violence. Eliza knew her mother would fret over the ruin of yet another pinafore, but pride prevented her from sending her eldest daughter into the village with badly tarnished clothes. She would insist on making Eliza another one.

Eliza sat down on a washed-up tree trunk and watched the boys chasing the little one around the beach. Becky was searching for fresh lava to take home for tea.

Eliza soaked in this moment of pleasure. Her face gently tingled with the warmth of the day and the salt air. She closed her eyes again to see what kind of impressions would be left on her eyes. She sensed an unwanted presence sitting beside her on the trunk. She squinted one eye open to find Billy Evans had rudely invaded her perfect moment in the early evening sun,

"What do you want?" Eliza said grumpily.

"Nothing. I thought you looked lonely, and I thought I'd come and see if I could cheer you up."

"Well, you thought wrong, now bugger off!"

"That's not a friendly thing to say to someone who is only trying to cheer you up," Billy responded with an air of misplaced charm and sexual expectation.

"I don't need cheering up thank you, I'm perfectly happy as I am."

"Maids like you always need cheering up."

"What do you mean, maids like me?"

"You know…maids that have been around a bit!"

"I don't know what you mean." Eliza could feel her hackles beginning to rise in fury.

"Well THAT over there," Billy said as he pointed to little Eliza. The children looked up as they could sense that something was wrong. Eliza refrained from responding as she didn't want to frighten the little one.

"You didn't get that on your own, did you?" Billy slipped his hand down Eliza's unbuttoned top.

"Take your filthy hands off me, you bastard... she's, my cousin. I look after her when her mam's working." Yet another maternal betrayal, she felt more like Judas with every denial. Eliza needed to be careful, one day she might just spirit away the truth and she would be left with nothing.

"You want to watch what you say round here, 'cos if it gets back to my brothers, they'll shut you up for good. Now piss off and don't come near me again!"

Billy noticed that a couple of fishermen were returning to their boat and were watching their spat with interest. He didn't like being shown up by that scabby bitch, but he wasn't going to run the risk of being sorted out by the two burly blokes in the harbour.

"I wouldn't touch the likes of you with a barge pole any way, everyone in the village knows that kid's yours... the only problem is trying to work out which one of your inbred brothers is the father!" Billy scrambled away up the mound of shingle.

Eliza was tempted to kick him hard in the balls as he fell during his retreat but decided against it in favour of picking up and protecting the one referred to as THAT.

Becky rushed to her sister's side and called the boys back up the beach.

"What was that all about?" asked Becky.

"Nothing to worry about. Just Billy Evans being an idiot and trying to throw his weight around. He won't be so cocky if bumps into Tom and Will after a skinful at the Pack. Promise me Becky, that when you're older, you'll keep away from the likes of him. He's nasty. Boys like him don't know how to treat a nice girl like you. You make sure that when you start courting that you choose a nice boy that will look after you. Not a badden like him."

"Like Sam?" asked Becky who was beginning to blush with embarrassment with the talk of courting a boy. No one had mentioned Sam Goodenough's name for a long time, and it took Eliza by surprise.

"Yes, like Sam or Dad. Just make sure you marry a gooden." Tears started to blur across her pale blue eyes. She cocooned little Eliza with her shawl and held her close to her chest and showered the infant with kisses. She didn't want to think about poor Sam and decided to focus her attention onto something happier. It was such an idyllic day in the sun, surrounded by her charges, and she didn't see why a little fucker like Billy Evans should spoil the moment.

It took an exhausting forty-five minutes to get the little ones to tramp up Lime Kiln Hill back to Berry Hill Farm. The boys were fractious and had started to fight and little Eliza had fallen asleep under the protective fold of the shawl. Mrs. Barton was sat at the table chatting to her youngest sister Esther who had come with news.

"I'm not sure Est, what about him? I don't want history to repeat itself," Mrs. Barton said with some concern.

"I promise you; she'll be safe. They soon packed him off abroad and no one has heard from him since. He might be dead for all I know," replied Esther in a convincing manner. The sisters stopped chatting as soon as they realised they had company.

"Where's my favourite niece then?" said Esther abstractly.

The girls kissed their aunt dutifully on the cheek. Esther uncovered the red cheeked cherub from beneath the shawl.

"Look at the state of her, the colour of her face!" Esther exclaimed loudly as she prised the infant away.

Little Eliza woke with a start and feeling exposed she started to cry loudly.

"What a terrible noise! You can tell she's been sparing the rod!" Esther always had something to say about how the child was being dragged up.

Eliza dreaded her visits.

"She wouldn't have started if you hadn't snatched her away," Eliza retorted haughtily.

"Elizabeth, are you going to let your daughter back-chat me?" Esther appealed to her sister.

"Eliza, go and get washed and get some bread and dripping for the boys, they look as if they are going to drop at any minute!" Mrs. Barton intervened.

Eliza was happy with the distraction. She loathed how Esther would fawn over little Eliza. She hated her aunt's acidic tongue and bitching tone.

The little one sensed the tension and reached out for Eliza,

"That's it! Time for bed!"

"Is it that time already? Can't she stay a little longer?" asked Esther.

"No, she's been on the go all day. She needs to know that its bedtime, after all I can't spare the rod, can I?" Eliza bristled.

Little Eliza did the rounds of kisses before being whisked upstairs to bed with the boys and it wasn't long before all three had fallen asleep.

Becky and Eliza returned to the table to hear Esther's news.

"Walter and I are going to wed next month. His mother kicked the bucket a few weeks ago and left him a small amount of money and the lease on a teashop in Lynmouth. I'm giving my job up, and we shall start getting the place up to scratch to open for next year."

"It means that my position at the Hiltons will be going, and it will be ideal for Eliza. I can put in a good word in for her," continued the aunt.

"I'm not looking for a job. Who will look after the baby?"

"I will," said Esther curtly. "I shall be able to have her in the shop whilst I work."

"She's not yours to take, she's perfectly happy here." Eliza had an increasing fear that her whole world was about to collapse.

"What can you offer her? What kind of future will she have with you? Walter and I can offer her a good home with a steady income. Your mum and dad can't keep you forever. They need you to start earning...the sooner the better from what I hear. You need to get out into the world and find yourself a husband. You won't find a fella with a baby hanging round your neck!"

"You can't have her. Mum, tell her she's wrong we can manage, can't we? I don't want a sodding husband; I'd rather keep my baby!" An increasingly distraught Eliza looked towards her mother for support.

They both knew that the farm was having a bad year. They couldn't get a good price for their mutton, and they had lost a lot of new-borns to the cold during lambing. Mum was working down the laundry whilst Eliza looked after the little ones, but Alf started school this year and Percy would shortly follow - little Eliza was keeping her from earning.

"I'm sorry love, but we've had a terrible year. If we have another bad lambing season, we might have to sell up and move on. You knew that this day would come, Esther always said that when she was settled, she would help us out," Mrs. Barton said sorrowfully.

"She said she'd help us out, she didn't say she'd take my baby… I knew she wanted her for herself…she's always bitching at me… saying that I'm a bad mother. She's happy to tell me that I've brought shame on this family by having a bastard…and what about love? Who do you think will love her more…me or that evil witch over there?"

"Hang on, missy. Just you show some respect! I'm happy to take that little bastard off your hands and bring her up as our own. It will give you a chance of making a half-way descent life for yourself. In a few years' time when you're married, you'll look back on this as a blessing. If you are anything like your mother, you will have many more babies and you will forget this one… You're just being a selfish little bitch." Esther knew she had a battle on her hands.

"Why don't you go and have one of your own instead of trying to steal what's mine!" Eliza knew this would cut deep.

"You know I can't have one of my own."

Eliza remembered the day when her aunt was dramatically lifted from the cart by her father, ghostly pale and bleeding. She was delirious, close to death.

A bodged-up, back-street job that nearly killed her. The bastard responsible was happy to pay, to sort it out before she started to show. He was more than willing to risk her life to save the precious family name.

Esther was left butchered like a filleted fish and with an

infection which rendered her baby-making days over. Her misplaced feelings of loyalty and the thin promise of job security ensured that she remained in their employment.

"Let's stop before this goes too far. Esther, you go and pay Wynn a visit until this all blows over. Becky it's time for you to go to bed, you've heard too much already... I need to chat with your sister," Mrs. Barton intervened.

Becky was already in floods of tears at the prospect of little Eliza living with Esther. Becky was wise beyond her thirteen years, and she knew that ripping the baby away from her mother would be devastating. Eliza had already suffered so much. Becky felt a strong need to stay with her sister but knew that her absence was required more than her presence and reluctantly left for her bed.

Esther and Wynn were kindred spirits. Esther knew she would receive sympathy and gin in equal measures, and she would return knowing that she had a new ally in the war of little Eliza's future. She left the Barton's trusting that her sister would talk some sense into her stupid niece and that little Eliza would soon be coming to live with her and her new husband in Lynmouth.

"Bitch!" shouted Eliza, as Esther slammed the door.

"Now just you stop! Do you really think that you're helping yourself by calling your aunt names? You've been brought up better. I know this is difficult for you but swearing at Esther isn't going to help you or little Eliza," said Mrs. Barton.

"But mum, how can you be on her side, she wants to take our baby away?" Eliza sniffled as she was reduced to the role of being a small child again. Her mother beckoned her to sit close by and gave her a hug and tried to kiss her furrowed brow smooth.

"I'm not on her side, you foolish child. I just want what is best. It will break my heart to see Eliza move away, but I know that she will be loved and cared for. You may not like Esther, but she can offer so much more than we can."

"I can't give her away she's all I have left of Sam," said Eliza as the dam of tears finally over-flowed into a major flood of anguish and loss.

The truth was that the Barton family were struggling with money. Last winter they had to appeal to the parish for outside relief. The shame still burned on the memory and hung over them like a persistent damp cloud of Devonshire misery. One step away from destitution, the threat of the workhouse was only one more bad season away.

There wasn't much more they could do. Tom and Will were needed by their dad on the farm, even though they weren't earning a crust. Becky was already helping with the strawberry strips and was soon going to join her mum at the laundry. The hot, hard work was poorly paid, and Mrs. Barton was keen to get Becky out of there as soon as she could.

Eliza could go into service if the little maid was reared in Lynmouth with Esther. It would help to tip the balance. They could keep the farm going and escape the workhouse.

Her sister was right. Eliza would stand a better chance of getting a husband if she didn't have the little one to look after. It was rare to find a man who was willing to take on another man's babe.

"Listen child," said Mrs. Barton said in a soft, soothing manner, "Why don't you take the Hilton job and save your earnings up for a while. Esther and Walter can't take the maid on for a bit, as they will be busy getting the teashop ready. You never know, the farm might be doing a bit better by then and we might be able to manage." She knew though there was little real hope that the farm could make such a quick turn-a-round.

It wasn't an easy decision. Not yet sixteen, Eliza was still a child herself. Blinded by her misplaced optimism, she couldn't make a rational judgement.

It would be down to Mrs. Barton and her old man to sort it out. He'd keep out of it, and it would be left, as always down to her to sort the bloody mess out.

Elisabeth Barton knew that she would, with heavy-heart, hand the little one over to her grasping sister. It would be easier to make the break if Eliza was out of the way.

She would instantly regret her part in the betrayal.

A desperate decision made in haste.

A decision that would haunt for generations...

7

Donna, May 2012 - Duvet Day

"Morning Eliza, the door's locked, can you open up?" asked the unseen man.

He waited patiently for a couple of minutes whilst intermittently rattling the rusting latch.

"Eliza, open up, it's past seven o'clock, I'll be late to feed the pigs."

Donna could then hear the young sounding man trundle off through the courtyard. She looked out of the back window. No one was there.

She was pissed off. The last few mornings she had to be up early anyway. She needed to let the telephone company in to install the phone line and the electrician who had finally finished snagging after eight traumatic days of having the floorboards up to re-wire.

But today was going to be her lazy day. Her duvet-day. She had it all mapped out: -

1. Rise sometime before midday.
2. Chocolate biscuit breakfast.
3. Dexter box set back-to-back.
4. Down to The Anchor with Jude for a spot of roast and a drink.
5. Girly film extravaganza.
6. Slop back to bed around three in the morning.

Perfect!

Donna decided she wasn't going to abandon her original plan just yet and so returned to bed to grab another few hours shut eye. She was just starting to drift off again when she was disturbed by another round of rural domestics at the front of the house.

"For Goodness' sake Eliza, open up," shouted the man, pounding on the front door of the cottage. Donna's patience had expired. She had been putting up with a repetition of the same conversation for the last few days and had had enough.

"My God Eliza, what have you done?" said the man desperately, as Donna mouthed the words in perfect synchronicity. This couple really needed to get themselves together and get another key and stop being so bloody melodramatic.

"For fuck's sake, can't you two give it a bloody rest. Us normal people like to lay-in on a Sunday morning," shouted Donna from the front window. Yet again the illusive couple were nowhere to be seen and much to Donna's embarrassment she had shouted at the 'we are Rogers', who were being walked by their Dalmatians. Donna had been introduced to Monty and Diana Rogers a couple of nights ago at a soiree at Jude's.

"I'm so sorry, I didn't mean you. I was having a go at the couple who keep the pigs!"

"What couple? No one keeps pigs here, only sheep," said a bemused Monty.

"I keep hearing this young couple go through the same drama over and over again. I think she's called Eliza." Rather than shout from her window, Donna made her way down and grabbed her dressing gown on the way.

"Just us old fogeys here, no one called Eliza."

"They have a baby," Donna continued.

"Definitely no babies here. The old professor lives down that driveway at Little Usbournes, Gautier and Victoire live next door to us and Paul and Miranda live round the corner. Just us retirees I'm afraid," explained Monty.

"What about the people at the farm?"

"No, the Tresgothick's children have grown and flown the nest ages ago," the Rogers said together.

"It's just so annoying! This man keeps shouting out for Eliza to let him in otherwise he will be late to feed the pigs, whilst a tiny baby cries pathetically in the background. It's like conversation that's on a bloody loop, day in – day out."

"Maybe it's from one of the holiday cottages across the valley. You'd be surprised how sound can carry." suggested Diana. One of the Dalmatians started to pull away impatiently... "Sorry, must dash..." she said as she struggled to keep up with the hounds.

She was warming to the Rogers. They seemed a little stand-offish at first, but after today's encounter she realised they were just a very eccentric couple that doted on their fur-babies. In a flash of visual transference, she imagined herself as a dotty old dear being led by over-sized dogs and talking in unison with an imaginary partner that was a male clone of herself... it made her shudder.

No, the Rogers seemed like a very nice couple, and she made another pointless vow to moderate her language in public.

Donna walked back into the kitchen and put the kettle on. It was so nice to be able to switch the electric on safe in the knowledge that the plug wasn't going to spark and send a few volts up her arm. She took her mug of hot chocolate and her newly delivered newspaper upstairs and decided she was going to get back into bed and read for a while.

Donna opened the curtains for maximum reading light and settled into her comfy duvet. She had just started to read when she heard a faint and intermittent knocking sound. Donna stopped to listen more carefully. The last thing she needed was a problem with death watch beetle... nothing.

The noise started again, but it sounded more like a soft scrambling noise coming from inside her Gran's wooden chest at the bottom of the bed.

Worried that there might be a trapped rodent, she rolled up one of the more pointless Sunday supplements in anticipation of splatting a rat.

She carefully lifted the lid. A freshly blooded sheet weakly writhed at the bottom of the box.

Donna looked again and a neighbour's ginger tom leapt out and began to curl itself appreciatively around Donna's legs.

She was hit by an overwhelming smell of fresh blood and instantly vomited on a very shocked feline. The vomit splattered cat failed to appreciate the poetic justice and comic timing of the whole event.

"Fuck you!"

Donna found the whole role reversal vaguely amusing. The cat sped out of the room flicking warm chocolaty liquid up the newly painted walls and made its escape from the open kitchen window.

She double-checked the contents of the blanket box. Just a few moth-eaten crochet blankets that her Gran had made and a faint whiff of cat piss. The poor cat must have been trapped over- night; she was lucky to have heard him.

Feeling weak stomached, she decided to leave clearing the puddles of puke up and decided to remove her sticky brown PJ's and have a relaxing soak in a perfumed scented bath surrounded by the soothing light of multiple candles. Donna was determined to claw back her day of indulgence and get back onto her duvet- day schedule and she had plenty of time for a bath before Jude would pop over for lunch.

***

Duvet Day Afternoon.

"The lying bastard!" Donna held a pregnancy test result up to light to double check.

"What does that mean – a yes or a no?" enquired Jude, who was getting used Donna's preferred method of expression.

"It means you're right." Donna seriously thought she was menopausal and didn't bargain at being a first-time mum at forty-five. She was shell-shocked.

"Colm said that he had finally got round to having the snip when we separated, but he obviously lied... Shit!" Donna sat down to take the news in.

"Did you never want children of your own?" Jude asked, not knowing whether Donna's news was welcomed or not.

"It was never really a choice. Colm made it perfectly clear that he didn't want any more children under any circumstances."

"That's a bit selfish," added Jude.

"Not really. He had a really bad experience with his first wife Kathy. She had extremely bad post-natal depression... it ended badly." The thought of her predecessor's suicide still haunted.

"What are you going to do...are you going to tell Colm?" asked Jude.

"I have absolutely no idea! I've had the last three months living on my own and I love it. I love being back in England...I love my newfound independence... I'm not sure if I want to turn the clock back and play happy families again."

"You will go through with it?" Jude wanted to gauge an appropriate response.

"I don't know. A part of me is excited... it's an unexpected gift. Another part of me just thinks that I'm too old to do the whole, nappy changing and sleepless nights thing. It is such a massive commitment – by the time this child is in its late teens, I will be..."

"My age! Be careful what you say! I reckon I could handle a stroppy teenager."

"I think I'm in shock! I've spent all my adult life trying to prevent conception and now I am toying with the idea of having my ex-husband's child, possibly as a single parent... I've really got to think this through."

It was all Jude's fault. If she hadn't brought Donna her 'little present', she would still be in complete ignorance of her expectant state and about to go down The Anchor for a bite to eat and a glass or three of wine. As an ex-midwife, Jude had her suspicions for a couple of weeks, but every time she discreetly tried to introduce the topic, Donna retreated under a cosy blanket of self-denial and moved swiftly on to a new subject. When Jude found out the explanation for the chocolate brown stain on the newly painted ceiling, she decided that the time was right to present her with the opportunity to get Donna to face the possibility of impending motherhood.

Donna's duvet day was way off schedule... she no longer had the resolve to continue with her pamper day.

She made her polite excuses to Jude and decided to stay at home and try to re-think her life. Donna was lucky, whilst not a multi-millionaire she could survive financially with either the rent or the sale from either the property in Canada or Usbournes. She could continue to write for the Ontario Echo or perhaps try to get some work locally.

One of her main problems was that she hadn't really decided on whether she was going to go back to Canada or make a new life for herself here in England. She had only been at Usbournes for a few short weeks, but she already felt at home and had started to make friends at St. Nectan's.

What about Colm? He did say that he wanted to try again.

She looked him up on Facebook, he had already changed his relationship status and was now with a twenty-five-year-old fitness instructor called Cherise. This would wipe the smile of his smug little face! Serve him right the lying, selfish bastard!

She had to speak to him in the week about the missing rent saga and she decided to hold back and see how his nascent relationship was shaping up.

Colm could wait she decided, it served him right. He really shouldn't boast to his ex-wife that he had permanently resolved his fertility problem in a pointless act of pseudo-macho bravery.

What about Donna? What did she want? Despite her time being a step-mum to two emotionally damaged children, she had enjoyed much of her experience and had found it very rewarding.

Deep down she had wanted her own child, but she had always understood Colm's fears of history repeating itself.

She knew the timing was far from ideal – the thought of her being the oldest mum in the playground didn't exactly thrill her. Another vision of an elderly Donna being licked to death by her substitute canine babies flashed through her mind. She found this potential future rather chilling.

Donna fortified herself with the notion that she had been a good stepparent finding a delicate balance between being emotionally available and not being worried that she was uncool when teenage manipulation set in. She had provided Colm's kids with a dependable foundation from which to grow and become independent adults, and if she could do that for someone else's kids, surely she could do that for one of her own?

All this intellectual soul-searching was making Donna crave for a return to superficiality and she decided to pop next door to see if she could find a decent mirror for her bathroom. She had been managing with an old cracked mirrored bath tile and she could only see her face in two separate halves if she bent her knees every so often. Her usually perfectly unblemished skin had started to erupt like a teenage volcano into small patches of sebum laden pimples on her cheeks. Donna had suspected the change in water, but with hindsight it was merely her body's way of rebelling against the unwanted wash of hormones that was infiltrating her middle-aged body. Donna was not particularly impressed by her return to an earlier incarnation of her pubescent spotty self but was thankful that after years of orthodontic persuasion to push her protruding tombstones back to an aesthetic acceptability, that she didn't have to put up with being called Goofy anymore.

Donna hadn't really explored the big house since the aborted expedition with Jude. She had been in briefly, to provide a constant supply of vital rocket fuel in the form sugary tea and coffee for her ever-thirsty electricians. The sacrifice of her prized packet of chocolate Hobnobs had been repaid with on-demand, safe electricity to lighten both the cottage and the big house and now offered her the freedom to fully explore her inheritance.

As she unlocked the back door and manipulated the rusty latch, she realised that it produced the same sound as the latch from the rural domestic drama loop – a cross between a rusting crunchiness and an irritating high-pitched squeakiness that could set any hardened black-board enthusiast's teeth on edge.

The new power supply switched on with ease and after few moments of dimness, the bulbs powered up and the transformation was complete. She bypassed the clinking harshness of the slate floor in favour of the soft- tread of the dust-laden carpet and mounted the main staircase. Donna's newly heightened sense of smell ensured that the damp odour did not go unnoticed. She revisited the collection of grand-father clocks and pondered why their faces had been shrouded with black silk.

No longer inhibited by Jude's over-reaction, Donna sequentially lifted the veils to reveal the individual character of each clock. She noticed that they had stopped at different times, each clock-face had a different expression. She assumed that the silk was placed to protect the faces from the scratching of dust particles and the bleaching powers of the sun. Donna carefully shook the dust from the silks away from the clocks and folded them up neatly and placed them on a dressing table as she entered the principal bedroom.

It was a large room with patches of mould trailing up the lime-washed walls in large swathes of musty, green-blackness. It was dominated by a large brass-knobbed, un-made bed with a dingy biscuit coloured mattress that could barely hide the embarrassment of the stains left behind by Donna's ancestors. It was a plain, functional room, that no doubt had been enriched by the addition of coloured drapes and colourful pictures at some point in the past.

In a corner, near one of the windows, a wooden vanity unit stood with a fine china bowl decorated with delicate hand-painted rosebuds and a companion water jug on top. Immediately above the washstand was a rather fine oval, silver-filigreed mirror that dazzled in the late afternoon sun. It was just what Donna needed to gain a full exposure to the damage that her galloping hormones were having on her complexion.

It was rather dusty and was dotted with black patches which added a certain character, but Donna was confident that with a bit of spit and polish it would be a welcome addition to her otherwise rather scabby bathroom. She took the mirror down with care and blew some of the dust and cobwebs away and decided to make her way back to the cottage.

As Donna looked up, she realised that someone had carefully replaced all the silk shrouds on the faces of the clocks. She transformed into feline mode as her hackles started to rise and the adrenalin started to pump round her body. She quickly re-entered the bedroom, only to discover that the silks had been taken from the dressing table. The thought that someone had crept in behind her to retrieve the veils was very unnerving and she wasn't sure what to do next. Semi-frozen in a state of bewilderment and not sure whether this was someone's sick idea of a joke or something darker, more malevolent, she decided to take her time, calm down and try to rationalise the situation. Regardless of the nature to this unwanted intrusion, she realised that she had to get from A to B and run the risk of bumping into whoever or whatever was spooking her and was going to have to brazen this situation out. She took a deep breath, picked up her treasured mirror and held it up to shield herself from any potential invading projectile and left the bedroom once again. She had often wondered why in creepy films that the protagonists would deliberately seek out the danger of the unseen and now she was in a similar position.

"Is anyone here?" Donna shouted nervously to her unknown assailant. She paused to listen in the unlikely event of a response. Her heart was thumping loudly, blocking out the signals from her inner coach which was instructing her to get the hell out of there and stop messing about. But there was a part of Donna that really resented being intimidated in her own property and her resentment was over-riding her need for self-preservation.

"So, you think you're funny, do you? Because I don't. I think you are a big coward, trying to frighten me without showing your face!"

The lack of response bolstered Donna's flagging confidence. She tiptoed nervously across the length of the hall crouching behind the ornate mirror. She cut quite a comical figure. Donna was struck by the absurdity of the situation as she passed a full-length mirror and caught a glimpse of herself cowering behind the reflective oval. She was nearly across the hall when her misplaced confidence encouraged her to shout out,

"See, I'm not afraid of you and your silly tricks. Now piss off and get out of my house!"

In an instant all the shrouds eerily slipped away from the clock faces and the hallway was filled with multiple versions of the Westminster chimes ringing out at different stages of the chime sequence. The air was full of ticking timepieces that echoed loudly, the sound reverberating off the exposed stone walls with increasing volume. It was at this point that Donna's flight or fight reflex finally kicked in and she sped down the stairs and out of the house without turning any of the lights off as she left. Donna could hear that the din of the clocks stopped as soon as she reached the courtyard. She was left shaken and grateful for the fact that she didn't lose control of either her bladder or bowels. She ensured that the door was double locked so the intruder could not escape,

"Take that you little fucker! Stay inside...you will need to come out some time, you creep."

Little did she realise that containment was exactly what

Donna's unwanted intruder required. Containment and solitude.

8

Clemency, Devon, 1896

Mrs. Clements was supping tea in the kitchen. It had been a busy morning and she was just waiting for the bread to bake before embarking on preparing lunch for the mistress. She had been with the Usbournes for over twenty years and was now on her fourth master.

Her first employer, old Mr. Lewis Usbourne was on his last legs when she arrived and duly expired within a matter of weeks. His successor Lewis the younger, was a hedonistic young man whose philosophy in life was to squeeze every drop of enjoyment out of any situation. In many ways he was a pleasure to work for - he was undemanding and often absent. He left a trail of broken hearts and illegitimate offspring all over the county and his newly born bastards were often abandoned on the doorstep for her to discover.

It was heart-breaking to hand over the little bundles to the priest, destined for the workhouse orphanage, knowing that they would probably meet their maker within a few short days. She learned to live with the guilt. She had her own children to care for and she saw no reason to take responsibility for her master's shoddy conduct.

It was the poor girls she felt sorry for. Broken promises and broken hearts left these young girls with tarnished reputations, unemployable and burdened with a baby they couldn't feed. They had no choice other than to abandon their children in the mistaken hope that they would have a better chance of survival without them.

Clements often wondered how many more little lives were surreptitiously snuffed out at birth or had ended up outside in the privy with all the other human waste, forever undiscovered.

Master Lewis had been on the verge of marrying and finally settling down, when he accepted a wager to race across the cliffs. In his drunken state, he misjudged the proximity of the edge and drove himself and his steed over the top to be violently impaled upon the jagged rocks below.

He was succeeded by his younger brother the Reverend Austin Usbourne who decided to leave the church upon his inheritance and enjoy the life of a gentleman farmer.

Clements had expected him to be a quiet, pious individual, but found to her surprise that he had obviously been heavily influenced by his elder brother and enjoyed a life of drinking, gambling and whoring.

Thankfully, she found no more little bundles of misery on the doorstep – he was a little more responsible than his brother. After a few years of rebelling against the confines of his earlier vocation, Austin settled down. The drinking and gambling ceased and the endless parade of loose women making their way to the hamlet suddenly stopped.

The Reverend's change of direction coincided with the arrival of the widow, Mrs. Waits who was employed as a live-in housekeeper. Mrs. Clements' suspicions that Waits had been the late Reverend's mistress were confirmed when he left her a healthy sum of money and the use of a small cottage in St. Nectan's.

After a respectable period of mourning and the new master and mistress had settled into the house, Mrs. Waits left the Usbourne's service to live in her little cottage in the village and looked after her young child and her elderly mother.

Life at Usbournes was more settled. The new mistress had surprised them all. Waits didn't think that a blow-in from the smoke would make it a month in the country and that she would end up packing her things and running back to London.

The new Mrs. Usbourne had breathed new life into the household. She was responsible for commissioning a new wing, which provided a proper washroom and walk-in pantry downstairs, a new recreation room for the master upstairs and a nursery for the baby which was due in a few weeks. She had the lower walls of the house panelled in oak, which stopped the damp from showing and made the house look a little grander.

The new mistress had also stepped into Wait's shoes on her departure and was able to run the house with equal efficiency and was happy to contribute and collaborate with the estate manager in her husband's absence. Her new mistress had proved that she could run the estate without her husband being constantly by her side and had proved to all her doubters that she could adapt to life in Devon.

Mrs. Clements was a little worried about the mistress of late. She seemed pre-occupied and not her happy self. There was a definite tension between the mistress and Verity the maid, and Clements had a notion that the new servant had ambitions to be of service to the master and this had been noticed. There had been a terrible row and the master had made a swift departure back to London. Verity had said nothing to her about the incident, but Clements had noticed that she would avoid the mistress at all costs.

Mrs. Clements looked out of the window to see if she could spy Jake Parkin, who had been asked to move some heavy furniture for the mistress. He promised he would return after checking if any more ewes had produced overnight and had obviously been delayed. It was at this point she heard the grating noise of heavy furniture being pushed across floor which was starting to reverberate throughout the kitchen and making the ceiling shake.

"Bloody hell Verity. Go and tell Parkin he's needed in here at once and I'll sort the Mrs. out!" Clements instructed.

Mrs. Clements hauled her heavy frame upstairs to discover Mrs. Usbourne and her ever-expanding bump trying to shove a large, heavy bureaux into the master's new room.

"For goodness' sake, you will cause yourself a mischief! What will the Captain think?" the cook cried out.

The truth was that Susannah didn't care what the Captain thought. She never had. He rarely troubled her thoughts, and she took no pains to hide her indifference.

"Come downstairs and I'll make you a cup of tea," coaxed Clements.

The worried cook escorted her bemused mistress down into

the dining room and poured her a cup of tea from the ever-ready pot in the kitchen.

Susannah rummaged around in her pocket and withdrew two crumpled envelopes and studied the messages written in Phillip's ornate script. The first one contained four simple words.

"Look in the mirror..."

The words of the second message were even more enigmatic.

"YOU KNOW WHY..."

She was puzzled, after two years in exile, her brother had started to scribe such cryptic messages.

It was unnerving. The last thing she wanted was for Phillip to come back into her life and spoil things. The worrying communications had arrived separately in the post yesterday and it had troubled her ever since.

Mrs. Clements brought her tea and reassured her that Parkin and a lad was about to move the furniture and that she was to put her feet up and rest.

Susannah went to get up to supervise the move, but the baby ground its elbow deep into the side of her ribs. It made her feel queasy. She flopped back down. She hadn't got used to the kicking and grinding of bone on bone. It physically revolted her.

Susannah had been greatly inconvenienced by her present condition and the thought of impending motherhood filled with her with dread. She was not maternal. The well-meaning failed to reassure her that she would feel differently once the child was born. This baby was not wanted. Susannah was being held to ransom by her pre-ordained biological destiny. She prayed for a boy and then she could move the Captain permanently into his new room in a bid to avoid further issue.

The Captain was elated. The impending birth of his son would ensure the bloodline for the estate. He could not comprehend his wife's lack of enthusiasm. It was great source of friction between them. He hoped for more.

Susannah was unequivocal. Once the little master had made his way into the world, the Captain would be consigned to the rooms in the new wing. The tension was unbearable, and his presence considered provocative. He retreated to the sanctuary of London.

A post-boy had called at the door. Susannah wondered if she would receive another of Philip's coded messages. She could hear Verity and Clements chatting in the kitchen. Something was amiss. There was concern in their voices. There was a timid knock at the door. Clements was holding a black edged envelope. Susannah sat staring at the letter. It was from Cecily. The thick band of black edging on the envelope could only mean one thing.

He was gone.

Susannah sat in disbelief. Dragged from the Thames. Drowned.

She knew Phillip had not lost his footing. His cryptic messages now seemed more sinister, more ominous.

Susannah understood that Philip had immersed himself in his work and spent most of his free time drinking at his club. She knew he was unhappy. She took comfort in the knowledge that all was not well in their marriage. His misery became her triumph.

She recalled their last words. They started to twist and

torment. They were intended to cut deep, to wound, but not to destroy. She was overwhelmed by the depth of her regret.

His shame was her shame. Their parting bitter and acrimonious. No room for reconciliation. No happy reunion.

The sunlight started to stream through the window. The refracted light cast complex patterns in rich oscillating colours onto the back of her hands. A deep throbbing pain pulsated behind her eyes. There he stood, captured within her shattered vision, the familiar cracking mirror splitting across her eyes. His presence suffocating and unavoidable.

She could not banish him, forever trapped. The eternal prisoner, trapped with her brother to marriage and motherhood. Sentenced to a life within the stonework of the walls.

***

God knew how to punish Eve. It took two and a half days before the doctor managed to pull the life-draining parasite from her exhausted body. The friction of the child being forcibly removed with forceps left her both violated and liberated.

It left a cold vacuum inside of her that she was determined would never be filled by another. The baby cried and was tightly swaddled in a soft white blanket and placed at her breast. She looked down disbelievingly at the tiny bundle of red, wrinkled flesh. It barely looked human, its bald head looked bruised and conical, and its disproportionate eyes bulged.

Susannah waited for the fairy-tale moment when she would be overwhelmed by a warm rush of maternal love for this child, but she realised that the longer she waited, the less likely it was to happen.

"You have a daughter," the doctor said in hushed tones.

She had risked her life and all she had to show for it was a girl. No matter. The Captain would be confined to his new quarters, he would have to be satisfied with a daughter.

Susannah found the child's failed attempts to suckle both repulsive and annoying. Each time it tugged away at her breast her body would respond with the renewal of abdominal contractions that would take her breath away.

Without warning, her body started to pump blood. Her heartbeat started to fade. The child was immediately ripped away from its dying mother and given to Clements.

Everything slowed down, action, speech – even the clock on the wall as it started to meter out her time at half the rate.

The Captain had been called into the room and he sat beside her holding her hand.

Displaced from time she noticed Philip had entered the room. She gasped for air. Her brother reached out for her hand and usurped the Captain's tight grip for his own. She looked into his deep brown, soulless eyes and she could see her own hollow image trapped within them.

"Let go!" he whispered into her ear. She tried to look away from her beloved captor, but wherever she looked his face would stare back.

"Let go!" he insisted.

He leaned over her and she could feel the coldness of his breath as he homed in on her dry chapped lips and kissed.

Susannah could see the Captain through Phillip's body and wondered why they had never shared such pleasure. Phillip caressed the curve of her neck and was hit by an intense bolt of pleasure.

He moved down her body, kissing each part tenderly. His legs wrapped possessively around her, and they continued to twist and writhe. She was becoming lighter and lighter and soon realised that she could see Samuel below her desperately holding onto her empty shell.

Who realised that dying could be so pleasurable? She was happy to abandon her husband and child, she wanted to leave with Philip.

Deep from somewhere she felt the sharpness of the slap. His screamed obscenities echoed through the room. Once more she felt his disgust and hatred.

She looked into Phillip's eyes and realised that with each new impassioned kiss he was sucking the warm breath from her body. He was sucking out her soul to replenish his own, leaving her brittle body ready to shatter into a thousand glassy shards.

Susannah realised that she did not want to be trapped for all eternity with his warped manipulations. The ancestors' condemnations, their revulsion demanded her attention. She looked down to witness the man she did not love weeping, desperately holding on to her cool, pale body. A tug of war between life and death… her survival instinct had started to kick in.

Gravity pulled her back from the brink, back to her death-bed away from Philip. His presence no longer commanded, he started to fade. She was liberated from his grip, his icy form melting away to reveal the Captain in full colour. A large intake of breath jolted her back to consciousness, a warm flush of oxygen banished death from her body.

"Thank God!" praised Captain as he kissed his wife.

She looked at him and smiled thinly. The doctor wiped her

brow with a cool, damp cloth. She was offered a sip of water, which she took slowly and refreshed her parched and painful throat.

"What shall we call her?" asked the Captain.

"Clemency...her name is Clemency." She waited in vain to be engulfed by an overwhelming wave of love and devotion.

Her return from the dead left her drained, empty and cold. Left behind was a pale imitation of the original, devoid of vitality and emotion, a paler shade of her former self. Philip had spirited away her intensity, her vibrancy. The Captain was left with a passionless, mediocrity and a contempt that he did not deserve.

9

Eliza, The Hiltons, Barnstaple, Devon, September 1889

Trafalgar Place had been the home of the Hilton's since 1806. Built with profits from war, this elegant three-storey, double-fronted town house was situated in the most fashionable part of Barnstaple.

The subsequent heirs to the elegant Georgian townhouse draped themselves in the comfort of material riches and cluttered their elegant abode brim-full of unnecessary treasures.

After a series of poor investments, William and Victoria Hilton were forced to economise on their household expenses. A household that once had a housekeeper, cook, scullery maid, two general maids and a full-time gardener, was humiliatingly reduced to a part-time plain cook, a part-time gardener, and a full-time maid-of-all work. The bulk of all the hard, dirty work fell to their newly appointed maid-of-all Eliza Barton.

After six excruciatingly long weeks, Eliza was still suffering from heartbreak and homesickness. She was expected to work in silent, obsequious servitude. Separated from all that she had ever loved, her isolation was complete.

The cook didn't have time for idle gossip either. She was always too busy trying to prepare her day's work in half the time. Eliza had been used to the constant chatter and the surreal hubbub of the family coming in and out of the house throughout the day. She yearned for her little maid; her days were meaningless without her. How she longed to be back at the farm.

Old Mrs. Lincoln, the elderly mother of Victoria Hilton was of a generation that forbade eye contact with her servants. Eyes averted and backs were turned. It avoided any possibility of communication with the lower orders. It gave her the power to dehumanise and humiliate.

Eliza was kept extremely busy. The farmer's daughter was used to hard graft. Rising at five in the morning and going to bed late came naturally, but her parsimonious mistress demanded that she account for every minute of the day. Each allotted task was given a timeframe for completion, every breach had to be justified. The mistress whiplashed Eliza with her razor tongue with each misdemeanour. Comparisons were made with Esther, who had achieved the status of near sainthood since her departure. Her recent canonisation was yet another way of grinding Eliza's spirit to dust and to ensure that she understood her place in the world.

Eliza lived in the basement kitchen. She slept on an old lumpy mattress in front of the range that was easy to pick up and store away in a nearby cupboard. It was dark and dingy. The walls away from the range were patterned with rising damp. The sound of water constantly dripped outside the window from the damaged guttering. The stench of poorly maintained drains permeated throughout. A dungeon to banish her from her masters and away from their precious things.

Eliza would lie at night remembering her overcrowded bed from home. She missed the sound of her adenoidal brothers snoring and farting in unison. She even missed the alarmingly familiar warmth of unwanted wetness. Poor Percy, the yellow stain of guilt and the smell of piss always gave him away. She longed for the smell of the baby's sweet, milky breath and stolen cuddles...

Eliza needed to busy herself...she needed to forget.

She needed the relentless tedium of routine and grind to get her through the day. It was her salvation.

Eliza cleaned, prepared fires, and blacked the grate. Black lead would dig deep under her fingernails and leech into every crack on her hands. She scrubbed until she bled.

She resented the contrast between the family's breakfast of kippers and devilled kidneys and hers of bread and dripping. She resented their idleness whilst she ran up and down the stairs making beds, slopping out their chamber pots and replenishing heavy pails of coal to their rooms.

Eliza learned that there were servants' quarters, but they were now stored with furniture and paintings. Their possessions had priority over her own needs. And then there was Nelson...

It was Eliza's duty to take him out into the garden to relieve himself. He had to be returned fully cleaned and fragrant. His little wet feet wiped clean of any soil and his little doggy bottom turd-free. She loathed this over-indulged black pug. His corpulent, flatulent body was no longer capable of waddling downstairs independently and had to be carried to and from the garden in case his little doggy heart gave out. His stubby teeth had turned black, green with age and years of being fed sugary biscuits. His breath was so rancid that no number of violet cachous could mask the vile odour. Nelson was a body that was barely alive.

Eliza took pleasure in testing the revolting canine's tentative hold of life. She would watch him struggle up the steep steps to the kitchen to see if his heart would give out. His tongue would turn blue, and his eyes would roll upwards. He would reach the point of expiration, only to revive himself by panting rapidly. He would appeal to Eliza's conscience to pick him up.

It was pathetic. Eliza knew that her father would not let a dog get so bad. He would put it out of its misery with a single shot. There was no room for sentiment on a farm, sentiment cost money and caused unwanted suffering. Better to put a bullet to its head than let it wallow in pain.

Instead, Nelson commanded a reverence and respect beyond the bounds of normality. This most treasured pug's suffering was maintained daily by being fed the best boiled, finely minced meats. He enjoyed weekly visits by the local veterinary surgeon, who believed Nelson to be a 'living wonder!'

Her dislike for the dog stemmed from her resentment that he was fed better than most people she knew. As each day passed the repugnant little pug grew more and more like the Old Cow Upstairs both in appearance and infirmity. The thought had crossed her mind that if the Old Cow Upstairs should deteriorate further she might be expected to take her to her commode and wipe her clean... Suddenly the onerous task of taking Nelson into the garden no longer seemed so bad.

Eliza hated Mondays the most. Mondays were wash days and she had to build a large fire to heat up the copper furnace. Her small frame could barely support the weight of the constant supply of heavy pails of water. Her arms would ache until Friday. She would scrub, wash, mangle and dry the washing for the entire household. All items were to be scrupulously cleaned, ironed, and returned to their owners by Wednesday.

She didn't like Fridays much either. Fridays were bashing days – days where she would bash the living daylights out of as many of the rugs and cushions as she could out in the garden. She hated how the dirt and grit would puff up and smother her with unwanted dust and detritus with two days to go before bath day.

Saturdays were dedicated to polishing the front doorstep with Cardinal Red polish and making sure the brass doorknob gleamed as well as the neighbours. Fraternising with other servants was actively discouraged, but Eliza was always willing to take the risk and use Saturdays as an opportunity to glean the tiniest bit of gossip from the servants next door. They were canny and carefully timed their other daily duties so they could clean their frontages at the same time and exchange tasty morsels of family scandal. It was prime bitching time. A time to be relished and savoured.

Occasionally a disgruntled employer would come out to observe their work and ensured that all idle chatter ceased, but they could mostly get away with an hour of stolen socialisation before being called for.

Sundays were the loneliest days of the week. They were days of hanging around waiting to go to church. Eliza bitterly resented having to sit on the Spartan pews at the back, whilst the Hamilton's sat up the front on embroidered cushions. All servants were kept away from their betters. The distinction between master and servant was always carefully observed.

Eliza would listen in earnest to the sermon. Her understanding was that God's message had been adulterated. It was now designed for her to accept contentment in loneliness and her position of servitude by the powers that be. The irony of the lack of Christian charity in the room did not escape her. It merely compounded her resentment that Sundays robbed her of precious time with her family at Berry Hill. It coloured her view of the Christian message.

Her favourite days were Tuesday and Thursdays when she would be expected to politely receive visitors and accept calling cards on behalf of the Hiltons. On these afternoons she would change from her normal greys and into a black dress with white cuffs and her hair carefully hidden by a lacy mop-cap. Eliza would look at herself in the mirror and be quietly pleased with her transformation from household skivvy to an upstairs servant, and the new-found confidence that her temporary elevation in status afforded her.

Eliza was a plain girl with pale blue eyes, straw coloured hair and a few freckles dotted randomly across her face. She had the habit of sucking in her bottom lip and wiping her tongue across her protruding teeth. It was a good, honest face, soft and pleasing, but she was not considered a pretty girl. The view from behind with her long, blonde, wavy hair commanded the anticipation of pre-Raphaelite beauty, but people were often surprised by her modest exterior when she turned around.

The shame of her hard-working hands was hidden by a pair of virginal white gloves. They had to remain spotless throughout her duties at the door. The change in uniform made Eliza feel less like a servant. People treated her differently. Some of the regular callers would even attempt to make small talk, and it made her feel a little more valued.

Even the Hilton's treated her like a different person. She secretly wondered whether they were too stupid to realise that it was the same servant that would slop out their piss pots in the morning and then would chaperone their esteemed guests into the drawing room for afternoon tea. It made her feel oddly superior. They were obviously incapable of performing the simplest tasks for themselves and had to rely on a poor country girl like Eliza.

Being 'at the door' made Eliza feel more human. If only the Hilton's would stop calling her Molly, she would feel less stripped of her identity and more like her own self.

***

Eliza was dozing off in one of the master's comfy armchairs, legs swung round and over-hanging the armrests. She knew she was taking liberties and would be in for a round of Mrs. Hilton's humiliating quips if discovered, but she didn't give a fig.

She was cross because she was left waiting up for the Hilton's visiting nephew Miles Lincoln. She had been promised that he would be back before the door was scheduled to be locked at 10.30 and it was now gone twelve.

The lack of any other live-in staff meant that Eliza would have to wait up for the inconsiderate bastard, no matter how late. She would still be expected to get up a five sharp to start the next day's work.

Eliza had taken an instant dislike to the visitor who had recently returned from India. He was a tall, bulky, arrogant man with an air of expectation and entitlement that grated on her nerves. He was the only nephew on both sides of the family and would one day inherit the house. Like the family pooch he was indulged and pampered. His every wish had to be catered for, regardless whom it inconvenienced. Lincoln was due to marry next weekend and Eliza was expected to forego her precious visit home to look after Nelson and the Old Cow Upstairs, whom the doctor considered too fragile to make the lengthy trip to Hampshire.

Eliza was just starting to doze off when she was rudely awoken by a loud banging at the door.

"Quiet Sir, please or you will wake the others," Eliza whispered through the letterbox as she unlocked the front door.

Lincoln stumbled in with no apology and insisted on frantically looking through the calling cards that were laid on a silver salver on the sideboard.

"Gammon, Rock, Usbourne, but no bloody Peterson – bastard! He still owes me money. Are you sure that Peterson hasn't called for me …you haven't lost the card, have you?" he asked Eliza who was barely containing her contempt.

"No Sir, no one of that name has called." Eliza was now desperate to lock up and get off to bed.

"You are Esther's girl, aren't you?" He reached out and touched her face.

"I'm her niece Sir. Please excuse me as I need to lock the door now and get ready for the morning. Goodnight, Sir." She hoped he would accept the polite hint and retreat to bed. She could feel him staring into her back as she turned away.

Eliza was unnerved.

She sensed that his temper was brewing and was anxious to get away. She started to walk hesitantly down the hallway.

He grabbed her firmly by the arm...

"How dare you walk away from me when I am talking to you." He held her up close to his face.

"I'm sorry sir, I thought you had finished with me." She inhaled a heady mixture of cigars and brandy.

"I don't know what gave you that idea, your aunt would never leave me alone like that." He loosened his grip on her.

"I wouldn't know about that Sir." Eliza pulled her delicate frame away and hastily made her way down past the stairs.

"Don't you dare turn your back on me!" he boomed.

Before Eliza could scream or protect herself, he had slipped his right hand across her mouth and had pinned her back to the wall in the space underneath the stairs.

Her struggle was futile. He was far too strong to shake off. His potential for violence terrified. He lifted her petticoats and pressed himself close to her. He dug his fingernails deep into her thigh, gouging out strips of her soft flesh as a warning of things to come. Suddenly a searing pain ran through her as he entered her body uninvited.

She instinctively bit down hard on the side of his hand that gagged her from screaming. He responded with a hard slap across the face.

The stars that she could see were mocking her. She lost a few seconds. Wave after wave of stabbing pains ripped through her taut body. She felt the warmth of her own blood running down her thigh and sticking to her petticoats.

Eliza tried to relax her body in a bid to stop him from being so aggressive, but nothing could detract him from his relentless, needless battering that made her question whether she would survive the ordeal.

Once he was gratified, he withdrew himself and his hand from underneath her skirts and needlessly pulled at her hair and crashed her head against the wall.

"Now I'm finished with you!" He kissed her forcefully, then wiped his mouth with his cuff.

"And remember, there is no point in telling anybody. Nobody will believe a little slut like you against the word of a gentleman. I'm about to marry into one of the wealthiest families in Hampshire and no one from this family will allow you to spread your vicious little lies and spoil things. They will make sure that you're shut up for good." He spitefully twisted her little finger until it cracked.

Anger flowed from her eyes. She chose to ignore her inner voice for calm.

Eliza immediately swung out at him with her freed hand and caught him squarely on the chin with some considerable force.

Instant regret. He returned the punch sending her over onto a table. Before she could recover, he pulled her hair by its roots and smashed her face down onto the edge of the table, splitting her lip and sending a large chip out of one her protruding front teeth onto the floor. The force from the blow ensured that the brittle tooth broke off at a distinct right-angle, leaving a noticeable gap right at the front of her mouth and a sharpness that could cut her tongue.

Her head pounded violently, and she started to see double. She was aware that her reaction had only provoked more unwanted attention.

He sought to take advantage of her position doubled-up in pain over the table, backside in the air. He rummaged around up her skirt again in preparation for a second round, only this time he really wanted to hurt her.

Eliza braced herself by holding tightly on to the table. She prayed for death. She had never known pain like it as he started again. Her screams could be heard upstairs, despite the lace napkin that he forced into her mouth.

"Miles, is that you? Is everything all right old chap?" his uncle shouted from upstairs.

"It's just Molly, she fell over and hit her face on the steps", Lincoln responded.

The new element of discovery added to his state of excitement.

"Shall I send your aunt down to help?" asked the uncle. He didn't want direct involvement but felt the need to offer his sleeping wife's services.

"No need...she's fine. She's just going off to bed."

"Send my regards to Esther," Lincoln continued, as he gave her one last painful thrust before reluctantly withdrawing. His fear of being caught in the act of violent assault by his favourite aunt narrowly outweighed the gratification of teaching the little bitch her place in the world. He didn't want to run the risk of being sent overseas again.

He quickly straitened the table, picked up the chip of tooth like some gruesome souvenir and then bounded up the stairs two steps at a time to greet his uncle on the second landing and prevent him from going downstairs.

Eliza couldn't control her shaking. She was left bloodied and with wounds inside and out. Deep in shock she stayed in her prone position until she could muster enough strength to move without collapsing. She could no longer feel the pure hatred that coursed through her veins and could only focus on the waves of pain that kept rippling through various parts of her violated body.

Her weakened legs kept giving way as she hobbled her way down to the kitchen, where she bolted the door and started to boil water. She needed to soak away the pain and the humiliation. She looked down at the newly furrowed indentations where he viciously stripped away her flesh.

What horrors had her poor aunt had to endure? She almost felt empathy. Was this the same perpetrator that nearly cost Esther her life and rendered her incapable of having a family of her own?

Did she really want her niece to suffer at the hands of the same bastard who cost her so much, or did she just want her out of the way so she could steal her baby? Or both?

10

Eliza, The North Devon Free Press, June 1890

"HORRIBLE CASE OF CONCEALMENT OF BIRTH AND CHILD MURDER...

A servant of Mr. Hilton has been charged with concealment of birth and infanticide. The mistress of the house had been suspicious for some time that her maid-of-all work Eliza Jane Barton was enceinte, but the accusation was vehemently denied. Eventually the servant confessed to her mistress that she had given birth on Saturday night and that she had thrown the child in the Taw. The deceitful wretch later confessed to hiding the body until Monday morning, when she had to do the laundry. She made a large fire under the stove of the washhouse in which she heartlessly burned the baby. Whereby, Mr. Hilton gave her into the custody of the police, where she was later examined and confined to prison.

The main witness was Eliza's mistress, Mrs. Hilton who testified.

'I am the wife of Mr. W. E. Hilton, gentleman of independent means of Barnstaple and the prisoner has been in our service for nearly eleven months. We used to call her Molly, but her name is Eliza. I suspected from a slight difference in her appearance that she may be in an interesting condition, and I offered her the services of our doctor to confirm her delicate state of health. Eliza denied that she was enceinte and refused to be seen by our physician. I told the prisoner that she should leave our service as I was not satisfied with her denial and was concerned that the reputation of the household was at stake. The prisoner seemed indifferent to my threat of dismissal. Soon after I entered her room, I found evidence that suggested that she had given birth to a child. I informed my husband to fetch my mother who returned with me to the room. We found blood stains on her bedclothes and marks on the floor. The prisoner slept in the room by herself, and it would be easy for her to conceal her condition. I questioned her further when she confessed to having a baby. She said that it was born at midnight on Saturday. She said she had no light, nor anyone to assist her through the birth. I asked her why she had not called me, and she replied that she was afraid to. She told me that the child had been born dead and that she had thrown it in the river very early on Sunday morning. My mother thought that it was impossible to throw a baby in the river without someone seeing her. But she declared that it was the truth. I did not believe the lying wretch and decided to search the premises and found nothing. I begged the prisoner to tell me the whereabouts of the baby,'

'You won't hurt me will you Ma'am?' the prisoner asked, and I explained that it was my husband's duty as a good citizen to inform the authorities of any wrongdoing. It was then that she told me the terrible truth that she had burnt the child in the furnace as she prepared the copper for the week's washing.'

Miss. Barton was given the opportunity to cross- question her former mistress.

'Did you not enter my room on Monday morning and gave me some brandy and say that nothing should come of this if I told you the truth?'

The mistress denied all knowledge of the incident.

'Yes, you did. You gave me some brandy and said it should go off quietly. You said that you thought that nobody could have a baby so quietly and not disturb or inconvenience the household any.' Mrs. Hilton then admitted that some brandy had been administered to help the girl for shock.

'You also said that your mother, Mrs. Lincoln bore witness to these events, but she found walking difficult and spent most her time confined to her bed. There was nobody else there to see the truth.'

Mrs. Hamilton whose reputation of being a respectable member of the community assured the Magistrate that her mother was there to bear witness but was too shocked and disturbed by the whole affair to attend today's session.

Mr. Carter the second witness, was the Hilton's surgeon and stated that he had been called out to the house and had examined the prisoner and found that she had given birth recently but was unsure how far into her confinement that she had given birth.

He also noted that the prisoner had been deeply upset when he questioned her about some unsightly scaring that had failed to heal properly on the top of her right thigh. The witness was then unable to continue with the surgeon's investigation, being too traumatised and weak from her ordeal.

Miss. Barton's defence was then presented to the court in the form of a written statement that had been taken shortly after her arrest.

'I wish to say that I had a dead-born baby. It was born on Saturday night at midnight. I know my baby was dead and cold when it was born. I held it in my arms throughout the night, until daybreak and I saw that it was blue and had been dead a long time. I didn't want my masters to find that I had disgraced myself and I didn't want my family to be ashamed. Not knowing what to do, I tried to throw it into the Taw, but I was frightened that someone would see me. I hid my baby in a broom cupboard until Monday morning and then I burned it in the fire until there was nothing left. I was sorry that I didn't have much time with my baby, but it was born too early, and it would never have survived.'

The evidence of the crime took barely half a day to deliver. The jury retired to consider their verdict overnight and the prisoner was found guilty of concealing the birth of her illegitimate child and discharging its body to the furnace. The prisoner was duly brought before the magistrates to receive her sentence of six months with hard labour at the assizes in Exeter."

11

Donna, May 2012 - Gran

Donna was gradually getting used to the country sounds that would rob her of her sleep. If it wasn't the pitiful bleating of the sheep, then the constant roll and rattle of tractors in and out of the hamlet would jolt her from her slumber. Her body clock was beginning to adjust from city dweller to country mode. The slower pace suited her, and she could feel her inner, strung-out coil of tension starting to slacken. She had to adjust her expectations from instant gratification to the Devonian philosophy that everything has a natural time and place.

She remembered feeling slightly patronised when Pete Tresgothick from the farm told her that she should love Devon for what it is rather than to change it. He had told her of how blow-ins from the city missed the hubbub and returned disillusioned, their romantic dreams of a pastoral idyll in tatters. He also mentioned that she had set the rents too high and that he found it hard to keep the farm going.

Donna politely informed him that her lawyer was currently investigating who was defrauding the estate. The problem was that Pete wasn't the first person to take her to one-side and brief her about the extortionate rents. She hated how she had to disclaim her involvement from the situation before they could move on and become acquainted. Despite her reputation for being a money-grabbing blow-in landlord, she was making friends and people were generally very understanding.

Donna hadn't slept well. She had been rehearsing the different ways she was going to inform Colm about her news. Her body was ready for sleep, but her brain was buzzing and up for the challenge of an all-nighter trying to second-guess Colm's reaction to the news of his impending re-introduction to fatherhood.

She played out all the possibilities. He could be overjoyed, or 'WTF!... this has nothing to do with me...!'

Her brain finally lost the battle. She had practiced all the scenarios several times over and her body finally pulled her drowsy, fucked-up mind into an unwilling and fitful sleep. She was vaguely aware of the sounds of groaning and panting in the background, but she subconsciously dismissed it as an early, dream-like, dress-rehearsal for the Big Push in a few months' time.

It was a noise that plagued her intermittently throughout the night and now that it was daylight it became louder and more regular. Sometimes it sounded like a droning heifer in pain and at other times she could hear the distinct sound of supressed yells and muted, rapid panting.

Donna got up and looked out of her window to see if she could see an animal in distress.

Nothing. Was it her phantom intruder?

She was on the brink of phoning the police again, but the humiliation of them coming down and discovering nothing for the second time was enough for her to put the phone down.

Donna decided that she was going to look outside to see if there was any visible evidence of her intruder first, before subjecting herself and her neighbours to another pantomime. She was making her way down the stairs when she could hear someone approach the house.

She sat down silently and listened. The crunch of gravel underfoot. A knock at the door.

"Morning Eliza. The door's locked, can you open up?" said the unseen man.

"Bloody hell, not them two again!" Donna said to herself as she heard the familiar grind of the crunching, squeaking latch. She thought she'd heard the last of that domestic duo and assumed they'd moved on. She was left anticipating the second round of door rattling and pounding, but instead she heard a soft, female voice with a soft West Country accent.

"Go away, I'm not feeling well. I've been sick... Come back in a while." After a few minutes of rattling the latch, he started to knock at the door again.

"Eliza, open up, it's past seven o'clock, I'll be late to feed the pigs."

"Bugger off Jack, I told you I'm not well, come back when I've sorted myself out," said the young girl feebly.

Donna realised that the action was taking place in her small hallway, it was like listening to one of Gran's favourite radio plays, full of suspense, tension, and improvised sound effects.

The young girl retched. There was a splash of vomit on the

tiles. A strong stench of puke filled the air. Donna swallowed hard in sympathy. The young man trundled off, cursing under his breath.

The drama continued for a while without Jack's interference. There was weeping, shuffling and the grating of a moving chair.

The weak, rapid panting started again. It became more and more intense. The young girl groaned as her breath climaxed with exertion.

Donna felt uneasy.

"For Goodness sake Eliza, open up," shouted Jack, pounding on the cottage door.

"Shut up for heaven's sake, you'll wake the master... Wait a minute and I'll open up," Eliza said exhaustedly. There was more shuffling and groaning as the invisible spectre opened the door.

"You look like death! What have you been doing?" said the young lad.

"I told you, I'm not well... I'm so cold Jack, will you light the fire?" asked Eliza feebly. Donna could hear the snapping of kindling and the strike of a match. She could smell the familiar odour of sulphur and burning wood.

"What's that blood on the floor?" an increasingly alarmed Jack enquired.

"I was badly sick, and I brought up some blood," Eliza replied.

"What a mess you've made, I'll better call the mistress." The young lad was beginning to feel out of his depth.

"No, Jack, please don't. It will pass again presently, honest." Eliza was interrupted by a feeble cry of a very young baby.

"What's that crying?

"Nothing."

"Eliza, have you had a child?"

"I HAVE not!" The infant let out another weak cry for attention in defiance.

"My God Eliza, what have you done? I'll better get help."

"Jack please don't say anything. You cannot believe the terrible trouble I will get in if you tell anyone. I'll do anything, please... it will be the end of me."

"Keep away from it... don't kill it!"

"I wouldn't harm it, I'm just pulling the cloth away from its mouth, so it can breathe."

"I shall fetch the master!" said Jack.

"Please, Jack...I beg of you. I've not done anything wrong... I promise!"

Donna stood up as she could hear the young man pounding the stairs. She felt a great rush of hot, black energy forcefully pushing through her, leaving her unsteady on her feet, paradoxically chilling her to the core.

Silence. No Jack, no Eliza, and no crying infant.

Donna was shaken and deeply moved. She didn't feel threatened by this historic audio replay. Her curiosity was inflamed. She desperately needed to know what happened.

The air was still chilled. She looked around. No blood, no vomit, and no fire. All sounds and smells from the scene had dissipated into the ether. There was a scrabbling at the door, it was opened with caution.

Jude's feisty Jack Russell Pipsqueak pushed her way in. The little runt made her way up the wooden stairs and straight into Donna's bedroom and started to bark and growl at Gran's wooden chest.

"What's the matter Pip? Nothing in there for you, look..."

Donna opened the chest. She was confident there was nothing to see – she had burned the contents the day before.

She looked down to find that Pip had jumped in and started to tear away at a blood-stained cloth that was feebly writhing at the bottom.

"My God Pip what have you brought in?" Donna recalled Jude's gruesome tale of how little Pip had thrashed a poor hedgehog to death in the corner of the living room, leaving a trail of dripping, chunks of scarlet flesh and spines up the wall. Donna could barely look at the anticipated carnage, but there was nothing. The stupid dog just chased its tale round and round until Donna's head started to spin.

"For fuck's sake Pip!" She was tempted to shut the stupid dog in the chest.

"Nice to see you two bonding," said Jude walking in.

"She's taken a weird disliking for Gran's wooden chest," said Donna.

"She never liked it – even as a pup. She'd make her way upstairs, growl and bare her teeth. She'd make a right fuss until we opened the chest up for her to inspect." Jude grabbed hold of the little dog.

"Are you alright? You look a bit peaky," said Jude.

Donna told her about her rough night and explained about the domestic drama that had just replayed itself in the hallway.

"That doesn't surprise me in the least. I had my suspicions about this place for years, long before I had the strange experience with Lottie... Does it bother you? asked Jude. She started to play with Pip's soft, velvety ears.

"No, not really. I'm more intrigued than scared. I'm not convinced that this place is haunted. It's like I'm witnessing a replay of events... like a recording. I never feel threatened... But the main house feels different. There's a malevolence, a presence that quite clearly does not want me to be there. THAT scares me."

"The journalist in me wants to find out more about Eliza and Jack. I think I have witnessed something of significance and my natural curiosity wants to get to the bottom of it," continued Donna.

"Who do you think they are?"

"I have a strong feeling that Eliza might be a relative. I think she's had a secret love child and is scared her parents will find out. Maybe Jack's a servant who's made the discovery and has threatened to tell the master... I would love to find out what it is all about."

"That sounds possible. Your Gran's name was Charlotte Elizabeth...Eliza is a shortened version. People would often name their children in honour of other relatives. Why don't you start by writing down the family names. I shall put the kettle on while you get dressed, and then we can look online."

Inspired by the fact-finding bug Donna and Jude settled in for a morning of detective work online.

"Right, I am just plain Donna Barnard with no other fussy second names – so no clues there. Mum was Joan Clemency Ruskin. She always hated both her names and preferred to be called Joanie. I don't know where Joan comes from, but

I remember her saying that she was named after her grandmother Clemency."

"That sounds familiar. I remember Lottie talking about her mother. She didn't have many memories of her parents. She was brought up by her grandmother. They didn't get on. I remember Lottie saying that she had made her peace with her grandmother, and she had learned to live with her ghosts."

"What a curious thing to say. Do you know what she meant?" asked Donna.

"No, she didn't explain. I assumed she was talking about whatever went wrong in their relationship. I got the impression from Lottie that there was a great rift between the pair, but your Gran never let on what the problem was. It was probably a generational thing; it couldn't have been easy a young child living with an elderly grandmother." Jude realised she had unwittingly put her foot in it.

"Thanks a lot. That fills me with confidence for the future!"

"That's not what I meant, and you know it! Things were different then – my grandparents seemed positively Victorian by comparison to my generation. You don't have to worry. When I was a midwife there were plenty of older first-time mums." Jude tried to dig herself out of the hole.

"Do you think she meant that she had learnt to live with her ghosts… real ghosts? Maybe that's why she decided to separate the house in two, so that she didn't have to deal with them." Donna interrupted Jude's reverie.

"I don't know, maybe she did. I never took Lottie literally. I assumed she was referring to her mistakes. Either way, she didn't explain what she meant. It's a bit extreme to cordon off the bulk of the house... it makes more sense that she did it to raise her income," rationalised Jude.

After an hour of searching and waiting for the website to finish buffering, Donna made a discovery.

"Bloody hell! Gran's a bit of a dark horse... she never married. I cannot find evidence of a marriage and she was born a Ruskin. I always assumed that Ruskin was her married name."

"Have you tried your mum's birth certificate? Maybe they reverted to Ruskin for some reason after she married?"

"Here we go, Joan Clemency Ruskin born 3rd of January 1941, in the parish of St. Nectan's, Devon...mother Charlotte Elizabeth Ruskin, father...left blank! No father's name recorded."

Jude took over from Donna in a bid to speed things up. Jude was familiar with the site and had picked up a couple of time saving tips along the way.

"Right then," said Jude. "This is what we have so far... Your Gran was a single parent. Lottie's parents were Charles Ruskin, artist from London and your great-grandmother was Clemency Henrietta Usbourne. Clemency was the only child of Captain Samuel Frederick Usbourne, gentleman of independent means and Susannah Frances Hill. The captain's parents were Lewis George Usbourne, and Lucinda Porter and Susannah's parents were James Henry Hill and Henrietta Bussell. No Eliza or Elizabeth's so far, I'm afraid, and I've already gone back to 1794."

"Can we look at census data?" Donna asked as they swapped places again.

"No problem. The latest available is 1911, so you need to start there and work your way backwards," said Jude as the computer went off into another five-minute buffering spin session.

"Here we go; 1911 Census... Great Usbourne House, Susannah Usbourne... (Head), widower of independent means born 1861, London. Kitty Jones...servant, born 1885, St. Nectan's, Devon. No bloody Eliza," muttered Donna. The 1901 Census proved equally disappointing with only Susannah Usbourne and a servant listed.

"1891 Census – Captain Samuel Frederick Usbourne (Head), Gentleman farmer of independent means, born 1835, Usbournes, Devon. Susannah Frances Usbourne (Wife), born 1861, London. Clemency Henrietta Usbourne, (Daughter), scholar, born 1886, Usbournes, Devon......... Bingo, got her!........ Eliza Jane Barton, servant, born 1874, Berry Hill, Devon," Donna said excitedly. "Not a relative, but a servant!"

"Brilliant. So where do you go from here?

"Normally I would go talk to the family or look at old newspapers and records. Do you have a records office round here?"

"We have one in Barnstaple, above the library. They also have a good local history society. Victoire in the Hamlet - she's very interested in local history, especially the Abbey in St. Nectan's. You could ask her to put out an alert to see if anyone knows of Eliza's family at Berry Hill. Anyway, I better get on. I shall mention your Eliza Barton to Victoire, and I'll see if she can put the word out for you. Come on Pip, let's be getting you back home." Jude gently picked up her dog.

Donna looked at Jude's beloved and realised that she reminded her of a pillowcase she had when she was little. It was her favourite toy that Lottie had given. It was in the shape of a curled up, sleeping dog with big brown eyes and floppy velvety ears. It had a long silver zip that ran along its abdomen. She then remembered the trauma of finding it on Gran's bed, head viscously severed from its body. A gift from Stephen King.

It didn't matter how Lottie tried to soothe her grieving granddaughter, she remained inconsolable. They never did discover who beheaded her beloved Belle. The injustice that the culprit remained at large and unpunished for their misdeeds left little Donna with a strong feeling of betrayal.

Gran blamed the naughty fairies who lived down at Blackwater brook and they were later blamed for many other brutal breakages that left Donna's toy box full of snapped Pippa dolls and shredded fairy wings. Gran would spin a tale of naughty pixies, jealous of her beautiful possessions they would break them before sneaking back to their magical bowers.

The last time the Blackwater pixies paid her visit they left all her favourite music cassettes scattered in a shiny brown plastic mess of tangled tape on the floor. At fourteen the fairy story didn't wash. Gran owned up to not knowing who was responsible for the macabre carnival of toy carnage and left Donna with no logical answers. It was only now that Donna realised that her Gran was talking absolute horseshit and that maybe her childhood experiences were linked to some of the other unusual happenings in the other house.

12

Eliza, Exeter Gaol, November 1890 - Shoe stringing.

Eliza still hated Sunday mornings. She was woken early by the sounds of visitors outside the quadrant shouting for their imprisoned loved ones to pass their shoestrings down. Eliza would watch from her window in fascination at the inventiveness of the visitors. Small parcels wrapped with messages were carefully hauled up to the prison windows and passed through the bars.

Some of the inmates would be lucky and get a small amount of tobacco or morsels of meat or cheese. No matter what was tied to the end of the string they were always gratefully received. The wardens turned a blind eye to the shoe-stringing. It kept the prisoners happy and quelled their thirst for dissent. They could also cream off small portions of contraband for themselves. Everyone was happy.

Eliza's fascination soon waned when she realised that none her family would ever be able to afford to come up to Exeter. On rare occasions her shoestring was requested. Some religious do-gooders would send up messages with "REPENT and you shall be SAVED!"

She was never any good at accepting religious advice from the privileged. It was just their way of keeping her in her place, belly on the ground where she belonged.

Sunday mornings would also bring the obligatorily visit to chapel. More religious do-gooders would reinforce their message of repentance and acceptance of one's lot in life with added fire and zeal. She understood how the system worked - those that had plenty wanted to keep it for themselves. They hid behind the façade of Christianity to keep those that had very little from raising themselves up to challenge them.

Going to chapel always reminded her of her stolen Sundays. Days when she should have been at home with her family. Days when she was reluctantly dragged to church to sit behind her esteemed employers.

She tried not to think of the Hiltons. They closed ranks on her as soon she produced their precious nephew's bastard. A refusal to accept that he had violently abused her was followed by the accusation that she had done away with the poor child…

Eliza was a murderous whore.

The Hilton circle of denial included the Old Cow Upstairs. Her false testimony ensured that Miles's good name was not dragged through the courts. Their considerable influence guaranteed the truth would never come out. It looked better for them if they had a wicked, wayward servant. It ran in the family; her aunt had also brought disgrace to their door.

Barnstaple's elite rallied round the Hiltons. They had been wronged and dragged through the mire because of a despicable servant. Their Christian charity was an example to all.

Her hatred for Miles Lincoln burned deep within her. It kept company with the molten ball of resentment that festered in the pit of her stomach. Wild, murderous thoughts kept her awake at night. She wanted to end it all...if only she had the nerve.

Lincoln had robbed her of the opportunity to keep her daughter. As soon as news of Eliza's troubles reached Lynmouth, Esther marched her way back to Berry Hill and claimed her prize. Eliza knew that she would never be allowed near her beloved daughter again. Her reason to be no longer existed. Eliza was still unsure whether her aunt had been a victim to Miles's depravity or whether she had been a willing accomplice. It no longer mattered. Eliza had lost the most precious thing in her world, never to be reclaimed and she had to learn to live or die with the notion that her daughter would grow up not knowing how much she had loved her.

Eliza looked round the tiny cell. Three girls cramped into a space big enough for one. She shared with Lacey and Dora, a whoring, blackmailing combo that extorted menaces from their most prestigious clients. The whores slept top-to-toe; Eliza had the top bunk.

"Eliza, someone's asking for your shoestring," Lacey called from the window.

"Tell them to bugger off. I'm fed up with do-gooders telling me that I need to repent for my sins. Tell them they need to get their own house in order before they can start preaching at me."

"She said you can Fuck Off! She's not interested in your bloody morals," screeched Lacey from the window. She relished the opportunity to tell some lardy-dah bint what to do.

"I'm not here to preach, I have something for Eliza Barton," the well-spoken woman responded, ignoring further obscenities from Lacey.

"Shift your arse Lacey, let me take a look," said Eliza, barging her way past her cellmate. She could just see the well-dressed visitor between the bars of the window. She didn't look like the other religious zealots who would dress in mourning, shrouded in black, holding their pamphlets and quoting from their Bibles.

Instead, she was dressed in a pale blue skirt and jacket and was looking distinctly uncomfortable in her surroundings. Eliza thought she would give her a chance and borrowed a set of tied laces and let them dangle in front of the visitor's face. Eliza could feel the gentle tugging as the visitor tied a small package wrapped in paper. Eliza slowly pulled the shoestrings up and was careful to make sure that she didn't lose the bundle as she gingerly pulled it through the bars and into her hands. She carefully unwrapped the parcel to discover that it was a small photograph of little Eliza dressed in a white dress and holding her precious ragdoll and a lock of her hair. Wrapped around it was a letter from Becky: -

My Dear Eliza,

How I've missed you! I hope that you have found the picture of little Eliza, which I have borrowed on your behalf. We are both in Lynmouth, as I now work for Esther in her tearoom, and I can keep a close eye on the little one. She is growing fast and never stops chattering. I will make sure that she never forgets you. I hope you are keeping well and that you know that we always believe you, no matter what. This letter was brought to you by Mrs. Lively from the parish of St. Nectan's and she has some important news. It has been arranged for her to speak to you on Sunday after church and I beg of you to listen to what she has to say. She is a very nice lady, and she wants to help. Everybody is well and sends their love.

Your loving sister, Becky.

Eliza turned to face her benefactor to thank her, but she had already marched away out of sound's reach. Eliza crumbled as she let the tears take over.

"Whatever is it? Why take on so?" asked Lacey, wrapping her arms around Eliza in a comforting embrace. Eliza showed her a picture of her little girl. It was the first time that Eliza had been proud to admit that she had a daughter and it felt like a great burden had been lifted from her shoulders.

Looking for a distraction she noticed that Dora was not in the cell.

"Where's your sister?" she snivelled, wiping the dewdrops from her nose.

"Doing tricks with one of the wardens. Mrs. Vale came for her this morning. They have an arrangement. Dora sorts her out for a small bottle of gin and other privileges when she can."

The key in the door grated and screeched as the warden opened the door. Mrs. Vale ushered her prisoner back into her cell without a hint of embarrassment.

"What you gawping at?" asked Dora.

"She's still in shock. I've just told her about you and old mother Vale!" said Lacey.

"What do you do that for? She'll want a piece of the action

too!" They both started to laugh. Dora took out a small bottle of gin and offered it to Lacey who took a large gulp and passed it to Eliza.

"Have a little something to keep you going at chapel. It'll keep you warm, and you won't give a shit what the old bastard at the front is saying!" The sisters laughed loudly together.

Eliza took a glug from the bottle. The only time she had drunk gin was when she was at the Hiltons. The hot bath and the bottle of gin failed to get rid of her little blow-in, and just made her extremely sick. The smell of the alcohol instantly made her heave, but Dora pushed the bottle back and she took a second gulp. It had a rough, dry edge to it – it was barely palatable. The small amount of gin was knocked back in a few minutes and it had the desired effect. The girls became extremely drunk on very little, their poor diets and the weeks away from the streets meant that even Lacey and Dora who were used to drinking hard, became drunk quite quickly on very little. They could barely contain their euphoria as the time approached for chapel. Booze had a depressing effect on Eliza, it merely added to her misery.

Eliza sat down on the hard-edged pew and her resentment and hatred brewed away at her throughout the entire service.

Her cellmate's strange behaviour was starting to raise the suspicion that they had been hitting the bottle. Eliza felt that she needed to distance herself from them, and she didn't want to incur a penalty on her sentence for disorderly conduct. She took a risk and left the chapel without permission, requesting a return to her cell.

Eliza was escorted into the visitor's room and was instructed to sit down and wait. She assumed that she was in trouble for leaving the service and was surprised when Mrs. Lively walked in and sat down opposite her. The gin had made her focus on her woes. She had forgotten about Becky's letter informing her of the impending visit.

"The prisoner is truly repentant for her sins. You would never know that she is a murderess, she is as gentle as a lamb now," said the warden.

"She has been convicted of concealment, not murder... you need to remember that," the visitor said curtly.

Eliza was embarrassed when the lady held out her delicate, lily-white hand for her to shake. All that Eliza could offer was her pink, cracked and peeling hand in return. The contrast between the two sets of hands was startling, one soft and elegant and the other waxy and raw.

"I'm Amanda Lively, the wife of the rector at St. Nectan's, and I have come on a mission to help you." The lady had an air of Christian purpose.

Eliza immediately recoiled her hand and settled in for another round of middle-class ideals thinly disguised as Christian values.

"Please don't waste your time lecturing me on being penitent for my sins and how if I repent before the Lord I will be received into the Kingdom of Heaven, because I've heard it all before," she said belligerently.

"I think you misunderstand me. I am not here to preach to you, that's my husband's job, not mine. I have been approached by a local family who are willing to vouch for your conduct and would like to offer you employment. If you accept, it will allow you to fulfil the conditions of your release and prevent you from entering the workhouse. They would like to offer you the position of housemaid. You would be expected to fulfil extra duties for the mistress from time to time. They are prepared to offer you eight pounds a year, which they understand is considerably less than your previous employer, but they feel that they are offering you an opportunity that no other employer would undertake. Because of the distance from your family, you will be allowed a week off every three months."

"I visited your family in Berry Hill," continued Mrs. Lively. "We talked a lot about what would be best for you. They feel that it would be better if you stay away for a while, until things have settled in the village. They are worried that if you return home, you won't be able to find work or a husband, and that you would be better off taking up this offer."

"It sounds like it has already been decided," replied a very despondent Eliza. She never thought that she would be shunned by her own family and her fragile sense of her self-worth plummeted further.

"What else do you know about the family?" Eliza enquired as she feigned interest.

"The Usbourne's have owned the estate for generations and the current occupiers have been there for just under seven years. They are of a good Christian family, the master is the brother of a former reverend of the parish, and they are prepared to take you on in full knowledge of your record. Captain Usbourne has business interests in London and spends a lot of the time away. Mrs. Usbourne is often ill, and my husband visits her on a weekly basis... she cannot get to church. Mrs. Clements is the cook who lives in the village and Parkin is the estate manager and occupies a house in the hamlet. There are various farm labourers that go in and out of the main house, but you would be the only live-in servant. I think you will find that the Usbourne's are offering you a genuine chance to make something for yourself."

"I don't know...I want to go back to Berry Hill... that's where I belong."

"Look, I am going to be frank with you. Berry Hill is not an option. The only alternative is the workhouse. I can assure you that looking at the state of you now, it would probably kill you! This offer is an opportunity to start afresh. It is not a punishment for your past. You should be thankful. Not many girls in your position have opportunities like this."

Mrs. Lively hoped that her honesty would shock her reluctant protégé back to reality.

"The arrangement is that I shall return for you next Friday at noon when you are due to be released and I shall escort you to the vicarage. You will have the weekend to rest and prepare for your new position and you will be expected for work first thing on Monday morning. I hope to see you next week. If not, I wish you the very best and that you do not regret your decision."

Mrs. Lively stood up to leave. She was not confident that she had won Eliza round but was beginning to lose her patience with the girl who was in no position to be choosy.

They parted in polite silence. Mrs. Lively was frustrated by Eliza's lack of enthusiasm and Eliza was still in shock from her family's abandonment of her. The outlook seemed utterly bleak.

To Eliza, the unusual name of Usbourne seemed familiar.

It took her back to her time at the Hiltons. She remembered

the night of the attack. Lincoln had stumbled in and shuffled through the calling cards. One of them was from Captain Usbourne - one of the many regular callers at the house. He had always behaved in a kindly way and seemed interested in how she was settling in with the new family. There was a business connection with William Hilton and had nothing to do with his bastard nephew.

The thought of the workhouse chilled her. Mrs. Lively was probably right. Eliza didn't stand a chance in that hell hole. She didn't want to wither away with consumption in some damp, dank corner of the workhouse, with her poor body gnawed at by rats. But choice was a luxury she did not have. It was Usbournes or nothing.

13

Eliza at Usbournes, December 1890 - The Blow-In

Amos Heard had whistled tunelessly all the way from the rectory at St. Nectan's until he pulled up outside Great Usbourne House. It had been a bumpy ride and Eliza's frail body felt thoroughly jolted. He helped Eliza from the cart and picked up her fraying carpet bag and handed it to her.

"I'll be off then," he said, politely tilting his cap at her.

Eliza felt protected by her anonymity. Since leaving Exeter everyone had been surprisingly kind. She had been concerned that she would be preached to by the Reverend, but he had been too busy, and they exchanged very few words.

Mrs. Lively had been particularly caring. She bathed Eliza like a child and showed concern for the trail of thick, waxy scars that had been left by Lincoln's talons. She was convinced that Eliza had suffered at the hands of some brute. She washed Eliza's short, curly hair, detangled the matted clumps and removed the head lice without complaint. Soothing balms were administered. A daughterly attachment was beginning to form.

Eliza's prison browns had been exchanged for one of Amanda Lively's old dresses, which hung loosely on Eliza's tiny frame.

A glimpse in the mirror shocked. Eliza had become painfully thin and fragile. Loose skin flopped around her belly and her saggy, wizened breasts embarrassed her. She had the body of an elderly child. She felt obliged to eat the food that Mrs. Lively had lovingly prepared, but her deprived system found it hard to tolerate even the plainest of meals and she would vomit up the repast as soon as she left the kitchen.

Eliza was saddened to leave the sanctuary of the rectory but understood that she was expected to pay her way.

The cart pulled away leaving the dark grey silhouette of her solitary figure standing out from the greens of the fields and the light greys of the sky. The wind whistled a haunting, hollow tune as it howled around the corner of Great Usbourne House, whipping up spiralling circles of leaves into frenzied mini cyclones.

Local trees were bowed and subservient to the oncoming Atlantic onslaught. They hunkered down for the storm, firmly anchored into the earth. Some appeared to be in full-leaf, until the sound of a gunshot spooked the starling laden trees into life. Great swathes of black and white dotted birds formed mesmerising patterns swirling into the foreboding sky.

Eliza watched, fascinated as the murmuration pulsed and

oscillated. The overwhelming din of several hundred starlings all registering their dissatisfaction was deafening. A startled Eliza put her hands over her ears to muffle the aural assault.

The abandoned trees looked skeletal, until one-by- one the offended birds reclaimed their places, recreating the illusion of leaves wavering on the branches. The avian symphony ceased as quickly as it started, leaving poor Eliza's ears ringing and waiting for the next assault.

Icy splatters of sleet stung against her face, and she could see on the horizon that an Atlantic storm was brewing.

Eliza decided to approach the house from the courtyard entrance and knocked timidly on the back door. A chorus of barking dogs obscured the human sounds from within. After a few moments she knocked again causing another round of the canine excitement and eventually the latch of the door was lifted,

"What are you waiting out here for? I told you to come in," Mrs. Clements yelled above the noise of the dogs.

"I'm sorry, I didn't hear you. I'm Eliza ... you're expecting me," she said, and stepped cautiously into the back lobby.

Eliza was greeted by five dogs who were eager to meet the new visitor. A large Irish deerhound stood on her hind legs and placed her paws on the newcomer's shoulders. Eliza was dwarfed by the amorous hound who towered above her and eagerly licked her face. The weight of the over-friendly resident pushed Eliza back and she nearly fell over.

"Duchess... your manners! Get down at once, before you break this twig!" Clements shouted at the dog.

"I'm sorry dear, what did you say your name was?"

"My name is Eliza Barton ... you're expecting me ...I am

the new housemaid." Eliza passed a letter of introduction to the cook.

Clements frowned in dismay. She wondered how this skinny little thing could pick up a pail of water, let alone drag it up and down stairs all day.

"There's not much of you, is there?"

"I've been ill, but I'm much better now and I'm sure I shall soon beef up!" fibbed Eliza.

"Sit down, pour yourself some tea. I'm in the middle of making pastry, but I'll get the Mrs when I'm finished." She held up her floury hands as proof.

Eliza poured herself a cup of tea from a large brown pot. Streams of amber and dark brown liquid twisted together filling her large, chipped cup full of steam. She helped herself to two large spoons of sugar and let the gritty grains grate against the spoon as she stirred and chinked against the china. She poured a small amount of milk into the steaming mixture and stirred until fully homogenised into an even golden caramel.

The hot tea radiated through her bitterly cold frame and her internal thermometer started to rise. She enjoyed every precious sip and wondered how such a simple pleasure could make her so happy.

Once Clements had finished putting the pasties together, she disappeared upstairs and re-appeared within a few minutes with the mistress. Eliza was immediately intimidated by her new employer. She walked around Eliza in silence, observing every part of her exposed anatomy. Her large, dark brown eyes had gone beyond sorrowful and made her look pained and hollowed. There was no flicker of emotion and no recognition of kindness expressed in her flawless face. Her glossy chestnut-brown hair was kept tidy in a bun at the back of her head, plain and practical with no ringlets. No room for vanity.

Each individual component of her face seemed perfect – her expressive eyes, her delicate upturned nose, high cheekbones and yet when placed together they left the observer cold.

Susannah surveyed her new maid to see if she was fit for purpose. Her latent insecurity was instantly soothed by Eliza's plainness and emaciated appearance. Her not-so-blonde curls were hidden underneath a rather plain white bonnet and her pale blue eyes and freckled face were hardly remarkable. She was pallid and old before her years.

Eliza's teeth protruded and one of them had a large chip missing, providing an entrance to the darkened hollow of her mouth. Her hands and lower arms were mottled with cracked, flaking skin. There was nothing appealing or outstanding about this forlorn, geriatric child and therefore of little threat to her fragile ego.

Susannah questioned whether Eliza would have the strength to undertake all her tasks and considered whether to abandon her Christian duties and return her to the Livelys.

But it was always difficult to find someone who was prepared to live in such an isolated farmstead and for so little. Most of the village girls sought positions at the Abbey or would migrate to the factories in Barnstaple. The Captain had been keen to recommend the worthiness of the Hilton's ex-housemaid despite the scandal she had brought to their door. He rationalised the merit of redeeming one so tainted on the grounds of fiscal prudence.

The Usbournes felt that a servant such as Eliza would be eager to keep such a position. They had discussed at length that a girl with Eliza's reputation would be more willing to undertake additional duties for the mistress to maintain favour. They would be able to offer steady employment and a good home, and this would be enough to guarantee loyalty.

"You will need to give her extra rations and her duties will need to be kept light, until she regains her strength," Susannah instructed.

"...You are expected to work under Clement's instruction. You will help her prepare meals and will also be expected to carry out general cleaning, including washing and making fires. There will be other duties that I shall need you to undertake from time-to-time ...those duties will become obvious when the occasion arises. If you have any questions, ask Clements."

"Yes, Ma'am," said Eliza. She was keen to start off positively.

"You will see little of me. I prefer my own company and I keep to myself. Please ensure that I am not disturbed under any circumstances. I shall make my presence felt should I require anything, but I rarely do," added Susannah in a crisp, curt manner.

"Yes ma'am."

Mrs. Usbourne turned effortlessly and left the room.

Eliza was immediately struck by her coldness. An air of perpetual disappointment seemed to hang around her aura like a living ghost.

"Come, I shall show you your room," Mrs. Clements beckoned.

"Won't I sleep down here?"

"Of course not. You don't want to sleep with the dogs, do you?"

"No... Oh, what will you be calling me?"

"What is your name?"

"Eliza."

"Then, strangely enough you will be called Eliza!"

"It's just that my last employers insisted on changing my name."

"Well, you don't have to worry about all that kind claptrap here."

Clements took Eliza to the servants' stairs and showed her to her room. It was away from the mistress's room and adjacent to the Captain's quarters directly above the washroom.

It was a small, plain room with a simple bed, a small washstand, chair, and a couple of shelves for Eliza's few possessions. There was just enough heat from the small fire to keep the chill off the air and a few logs to stoke it up throughout the day. Clements mentioned that it had once been a nursery and seeing no other evidence of children in residence Eliza assumed that the current owners were childless.

After a few minutes unpacking, Eliza was back downstairs reporting for duty in her greys. She was surprised that in addition to the five dogs there were numerous cats.

"The cats keep the mice down and the dogs kill the rats. The two border collies Blue and Buzzard help with the sheep and the two springers, Boss and Dottie are the master's gundogs for when he hunts. You are already acquainted with Duchess. She used to belong to the Reverend Usbourne before he died... she used to bring down deer in her heyday. Somewhere around is the Little Ruffian, but I'm sure you two will soon be acquainted. We don't bother with naming the cats, there are too many of them. If you like kittens there is always a plentiful supply in the barns that need handling before they become feral. Parkin is the estate manager, and he pops in for a cup of tea and something to eat at lunch and there's a couple of farmhands," listed Clements.

"What about the master, is he not around at the moment?"

"No, he spends most of his time up in London on business. Him and the Mrs upstairs…they don't get on. She's the one that runs this place with Parkin. The Captain hasn't been back since Verity took off."

"Who is Verity?" asked Eliza, who could sense that Mrs. Clements was desperate to share some gossip.

"Verity was our last maid, but right from the start I knew she was a wrong 'un. She took a liking to the Captain and wasn't coy about hiding it. I always thought she had ambitions well above her station and it caused no end of trouble between the Captain and the Mrs." Clements was starting to enjoy imparting her story.

"So, what happened?"

"Well, about six months ago, I noticed she was looking rather pleased with herself. I thought she looked as if she was in the family way, but she was most offended when I asked her about it. I went away for a few days to help my daughter out when she had her little 'un and when I returned Verity had gone and so had the master. When I asked the Mrs what had happened, she said that Verity had accepted a position down at the Abbey." Clements winked knowingly at Eliza.

"Well maybe she did."

"I don't think so. Lizzie my niece works down at the Abbey, and she says that there is no one called Verity working there. She never told me about accepting a new position or any plans to move on. No, she's run off with the Captain to live up in the smoke to bring up their child. It wouldn't be the first time that the Usbournes had spawned a bastard and I'm sure it won't be the last!"

"Did you see anything improper go on between them?"

"No, of course not. They were very discreet. During the day Verity and I would be working away and there would be no time for that sort of carrying on! They would have all the time in the world once I left for home. The Mrs hardly leaves her room...so anything could have happened!"

Eliza thought it strange the Captain lived in London and the mistress in Devon. It was even harder to believe that he would run off with a lowly maid. Her bitter experience proved that men like Lincoln or the Captain didn't give a fig about the likes of her. She would have to be on her guard.

Eliza took a brief tour of the house and started to assess what needed to be done. The dining room and the best room looked as if they needed her attention first and she got to task straight away.

The brewing Atlantic storm started to unleash its power. Rain whipped against the windows; branches rattled the glass, and the sounds of the tempest ripped over the peninsula.

Eliza felt safe and warm. She started to enjoy the pulses of rain violently lashing against the windows depositing sand and salt in gritty streaks upon the panes.

Eliza noticed that some of the floorboards were loose. Each careful step displaced the cut-glass decanters, making them sing musically. She started to dust one of the more fragile pieces when she heard the thud of the floorboards. Maybe one of the dogs had followed behind her.

Eliza looked...no intruder to be seen.

She carried on listening to the violence outside when she heard another thud making the glasses judder tunefully with no apparent cause. Eliza skirted around the dining table and looked behind the drapes.

Was she being followed? Still nothing to be seen. She felt uneasy. The room was giving her the creeps.

Eliza decided that she would make a start in the best room. It smelt damp and needed heat. She started to clean and make up a new fire. There was a stronger odour - a pungent, rotting rancid smell of decaying flesh. It would take an age to freshen.

She couldn't shake off the feeling that she was being followed as she fetched the dustpan and an empty bucket and started to sweep away at the ashes.

A violent gust of wind shook a dead crow down from the chimney. It landed on her hands. She cried out in disgust as the foul stench of the rotting bird hit her nose. Maggots spewed out onto her hands writhing on her flaking skin.

A haunting ripple of a child's gleeful laughter echoed off the walls. Spooked by the disembodied mirth, she quickly scooped up the rotting mass of the crow and deposited it into the fire of the range. Eliza shuddered as the bird's body was consumed by flames and she slammed the range door shut.

"What's happened?" asked the cook, as she watched Eliza furiously scrubbing her already sore hands with carbolic soap.

"A dead bird fell from the chimney and spread its muck on my hands."

"Don't do that you'll make yourself bleed. You need some goose-fat and witch-hazel on that – I'll make you up some and bring it in tomorrow."

"Thanks." Eliza carefully dried her hands on a soft cloth.

"Here, I've made you some toast, I thought you might be hungry." Clements placed a small plate of blackened, buttered toast on the table. She turned around and reached for her snack, but it was conspicuous by its absence.

"Where's it gone?"

"It's on the table, where I put it," said Clements.

Eliza looked on the table and looked towards the dogs. All but one guilty looking spaniel were asleep.

"It must have been the Ruffian. Don't worry have mine," said the cook.

Eliza relished every morsel of this unexpected gift but repeated the mistake of leaving it on the table as she poured herself a cup of tea.

"That bleedin' dog has had it again!" exclaimed Eliza.

"What do you mean? The dogs wouldn't trouble to steal toast!"

The thud of someone running upstairs.

No one to be seen.

Eliza followed in pursuit of the toast thief, but there was nothing on the landing nor down the corridor. Once more she heard a peal of giggling and was convinced it was coming from the direction of the window on the second staircase.

As she approached the window, she could just make out the tiny form of a little girl dressed in grey, face pressed up against the window looking out towards the moor. Eliza stepped closer; the girl's form became more distinct from the camouflaging effects of the exposed stone wall.

Eliza gently turned the child around to discover the impish face of the toast stealer. The child grinned and exposed her toast-blackened teeth and greasy chin. She laughed cheekily again and flung her arms around Eliza's legs and wiped her mucky face on her apron.

"Hello, what's your name?" Eliza knelt down to the little's girl's level.

Eliza was greatly saddened to see how badly neglected the child looked. Her hair was matted into clumps and her face was filthy and scratched. Her tattered food-stained dress was far too small. The odour of stale urine followed her.

"My name is Eliza, what's your name?" Eliza watched as the child struggled to articulate.

"Her name is Clemency. Will you please take the child downstairs and stop all this noise! I thought I made it clear that I am not to be disturbed under any circumstances." Susannah, the mistress, retreated into her room like an irritated hermit crab. The sound of her door slamming resonated throughout the first floor. Eliza scooped the little girl up and carried her downstairs.

"Who's this?" Eliza asked Clements, as she sat her down on the table.

"Oh, you found the Little Ruffian then. I knew it wouldn't be long before you two found each other!" The cook continued with her work.

"The mistress called her Clemency. So, who is she?" asked Eliza. The cook looked a little confused at the mention of Clemency,

"This is the Little Miss – the daughter of the Mrs and the Captain," said the cook, as if Eliza should already know.

"I thought you were talking about a bloody dog not a child!" said Eliza in desperation. "Look at the state of her... who looks after her?"

Clements deliberated before answering.

"Verity used to keep an eye out for her during the day and I always leave her some food at mealtimes. I assume the mistress puts her to bed at night, but here is no one that specifically looks after her, she just gets on with it."

"How old is this child?" Eliza was becoming increasingly angry.

"She'll be five in April."

Eliza was disgusted by the child's level of neglect. Nobody seemed to be taking any responsibility her. She was also alarmed how backward the little girl seemed. She was small for her age and seemed to point and demand for things rather than asking politely.

"Mrs. Usbourne said that she had some additional duties for her – maybe she meant that I should take care of the child?" asked Eliza, who longed to take the little waif home to Berry Hill.

"Probably. Mind you, you would have your work cut out - this one's nearly feral...she prefers the company of the hounds rather than people!"

"I'm not surprised - at least bitches know how to look after their pups! where's the child's room?"

"Across the landing from yours. Go up the main stairs and turn right."

Eliza took the child's sticky hand and wandered upstairs to find her room. Clemency soon scuttled away as they approached her bedroom and seemed to melt back into the camouflage of the stonework.

Eliza opened the bedroom door and was immediately overwhelmed by the appalling stench of an open cesspit. The child had obviously been using her room as a toilet and Eliza had to step over piles of excrement in varying states of freshness as she entered the room. Her bed linen was stained, and the mattress was soddened beyond saving. There were no toys or books in the little girl's room or wardrobes full of pretty dresses. Eliza couldn't believe the state in which the poor child lived. Even her prison cell seemed more homely than Clemency's room.

She decided to look around the other rooms and discovered a small room opposite hers which had a little bed. She took it upon herself to relocate the child until her bedroom could be cleaned.

She had no intention of clearing the mess herself and explained the situation to Clements who instructed a couple of young farm labourers to clear away the muck. She then fetched numerous pails of steaming water and bleach and washed the floors and the walls until there was no trace of dirt. The lads were persuaded to dispose of the sodden mattress and the windows were left open over-night despite the inclement weather. Exhausted after a long day's work, Eliza went downstairs and was rewarded with afternoon tea.

"I had no idea that things were so bad up there... I never have cause to go up," said the shame-faced cook.

"How did things get so bad in the first place?" Eliza asked.

"They've always been bad."

Clements recalled the fateful day when the Little Miss made her way into the world after her uncle had been pulled from the Thames...

"We thought we'd lose them both. The little one was taken to a wet-nurse in the village. Clemency was such a sickly child, not expected to live. The Mrs. was so eaten up with grief... I don't think she has ever got over it. She never took to the child."

"How was the mistress before?"

"Very quiet, but she took an interest in things. After the child was born she kept to her room, barely eating during the day and supping brandy and laudanum at night."

"And what about the child – where does she fit into all this?"

"She doesn't really," replied the cook honestly.

Clements then continued by recalling the night when the Little Miss made her return. It was about a year ago when the idle chatter between Verity and the cook was interrupted by banging at the door. Clements was resting her puffing ankles on one of the kitchen chairs, when Verity came back in and said there was something she had to attend to. The cook hobbled her way to the door to find a girl from the village of about eleven holding the hand of a much younger, bewildered looking child.

"Me Ma's ill and she can't look after this one anymore... she belongs to the mistress," the girl said as she turned to the little one.

"You're back where you belong now. There's no point in crying. This is where you live," she said to the child and kissed her on the cheek.

At first Clements refused to take her in, claiming that the mistress had no child, but the villager assured her that her mother had wet-nursed her under the instruction of the Captain and had then continued to look after her when no one came to claim her. The Captain continued to pay for the child, but never indicated when they would take her back.

The cook looked at the little girl and she could imagine

how the Mrs looked when she was young and realised that the older girl must be speaking the truth. She remembered how she looked on the night of her birth - a sickly wee thing. Clements had assumed that child had soon met with her maker. No one ever spoke of her. Verity and Clements were wary of asking questions about the babe in fear of upsetting the masters.

Before Clements could ask them both in, the older girl ran off and hiked herself onto the back of a cart and was quickly out of sight. Clements picked up the child and placed her on the kitchen table.

"What's your name darlin'?" she asked, but the child made no answer.

"What are we to call you?" She put some spittle on the corner of her apron and wiped the little girl's mouth. The stunned child continued to gawp silently at the cook, as if she spoke in a different language. The child was handed over to Verity, while Clements ventured upstairs to inform the Mrs.

She quietly knocked on the door so as not to startle her jumpy mistress. There was no reply. Clements could hear her speaking,

"Leave me alone... Why won't you leave me alone? I need peace for goodness' sake!"

"Ma'am. Something has turned up that needs your urgent attention!" Clements peered through the keyhole.

She saw the mistress at her dressing table looking and talking to her reflection. Clements knocked one more time before entering, shocking her nervy mistress back to reality.

"Clements, I thought you understood that I do not like being disturbed," Susannah snapped.

"I am very sorry, but something urgent has turned up that needs your immediate attention."

"Let the Captain deal with it." The mistress glared at the cook from her reflected image.

"I'm afraid the Captain is still in London, and this needs your attention now. Someone from the village has left a little girl downstairs for you. They said she is yours and they can no longer look after her."

All colour drained from the mistress's face, and she stared at herself in disbelief that yet another ghost from her past should revisit. Clements could see that she was visibly shaken and faltered as she made her way to the door. Susannah descended the stairs slowly, with some considerable trepidation.

She was initially relieved when all she could see was a little pauper girl sat with her back to her. There must have been some mistake... a fraud. One of the villagers must be trying to extort money from her husband.

It was only when Verity turned her around to face her mother that Susannah recognised the very image of herself as a child. Her knees buckled. Her dress billowed out and deflated back again like a squashed concertina.

Susannah knelt in front of the child for ages waiting for something to happen. The child stared at her mother in silence, her gaze transfixed on the familiar brown eyes, challenging her to respond.

She was unnerved by the deep penetrative stare of the little girl but was unable to engage with her. No tidal wave of maternal love. She felt nothing. The sight of her own daughter left her cold.

The child was frightened and in awe of the scary looking

woman. She tried to reach out towards the lady. The child knew from experience that she could melt the heart of anyone if she wrapped her arms around their neck and snuggled them.

Susannah instantly recoiled from the threat of intimate contact and placed the little girl's arms back firmly by her side.

"I am your mmm......" She couldn't bring herself to say the word.

She took a deep breath and focussed more on the precise wording of her introduction.

"I am Mrs. Usbourne ... You are to live here."

Susannah was not her mother. She was merely her unwilling carrier from oblivion to existence - no more, no less. She had long convinced herself that the child had perished. No one had spoken of her, and she had failed to ask after the child. A convenient spiral of self-deception and denial.

The Captain had kept his distance since his exile to the new wing of the house. They barely spoke and he rarely corresponded from London. The novelty of looking at her newfound daughter was already waning, and she decided to get up and carry on with her day.

"The child will need to have some supper and a bath before a suitable bed can be found for the night. Verity, I expect you take charge of the child, as Mrs. Clements has her hands full. I shall write to the Captain tomorrow and see what he has to say about the matter," Susannah instructed.

The forlorn child was not used to being rebuffed and made a dash for the door to reclaim her playmate. She soon realised that she had been abandoned and was at the mercy of the scary lady who had just rejected her appeals for affection. She instantly burst into torrents of inconsolable tears and rapidly worked herself up into a violent tantrum - just like Susannah did when she was a child.

"For Heaven's Sake will someone please stop that infernal noise!" Susannah said impatiently. The noise cut like a knife. Each heart-felt scream sliced through her head. The familiar kaleidoscope of colours started to cut a pathway across her eyes.

Philip was in the room. She wondered what he would make of the return of her long-lost daughter. It struck her that it would be just like him to bring her back from the dead as punishment. The child was unnatural... menacing. Her purpose was to haunt and torment. A reminder that Susannah had chosen to live rather than depart with her twisted brother. She was a ghost-child... a phantom...her torture.

14

Eliza, December 1890 - The Night Terrors

The night was no friend to Eliza. Fitful sleep punctuated by vivid re-enactments of violence. There was little distinction between reality and the other realm. Often, she would wake up cowering in a corner of the kitchen. Pitch black and breathless. The kitchen knife eagerly poised to plunge deep into her tormentor.

He was her under-the-bed demon, lying-in-wait to strike at a stray arm or leg. He would sink his carefully manicured nails into her pale skin. He would plough deep furrows of delicate flesh, leaving a trail of bloodied, rucked-up matter in neat little rows of exposed white and red. The self-inflicted grooves on her arms and her legs were a testament to the intensity of the horror she felt on a nightly basis.

The spectre of Miles Lincoln was soon displaced by the

horror of Eliza failing to nurse a cold, blue baby. It was damp, waxy, and smelt of her. It wouldn't breathe, no matter how she rubbed its chest and blew her warm breath into its tiny lifeless mouth.

Blind panic. This little mite was never going to draw its first breath. What could she do with it? Where could she hide it? The mortal fear of discovery was always enough to wake her.

That was never enough to stop her remembering how the poor child had made its way into the world. The trauma of being alone with only a slug of rum to numb and a wooden spoon in her mouth. She never remembered her struggle to pull the child from her body. Hands tightly round its head and a fumbled attempt to unwind the thick, gelatinous chord from its squeezed throat. The hollow feeling of guilt never diminished.

Eliza's first night at Usbourne's was no exception.

This time it was the twisted image of Esther and Lincoln together at a train station. They were eloping. Eliza stood there staring in disbelief. A small child brushed past. It was the Little One running towards her new parents ready to start a future without her.

The train pulled out of the station with the new family on board. She screamed with all her strength. No sound came out.

She tried again; her throat taught with effort. Eliza sat bolt upright, panting breathlessly. Her surroundings were unfamiliar. Where was she? Panic started to overwhelm her. Was she back at the Hilton's?

No this was her new room... in the safety of her new masters. Children giggled outside her room. Two sets of shadows passed by her door. Eliza grabbed the dressing gown and left for the chill of the passageway. She looked past the clocks in the hall to see if the infants were hiding between the statuesque timepieces.

Nothing to be seen. They giggled playfully again. Still no one. An icy blast brushed past her. A servant girl, clad in grey approached. She lovingly rocked and swayed a swaddled child. She hummed in a random, soothing lullaby.

Her pale, drawn face was written with purpose. She had a round gaping hole in the middle of her forehead. She teetered towards Eliza on the brink of collapse. The fragile nursemaid beckoned towards Eliza, encouraging her to take the infant from her.

Once the child was exchanged the servant stumbled backwards between two of the clocks. Eliza tried to pull her back, but the servant melted into the background of the walls and faded from sight.

Eliza sat bolt upright and was still in bed. She could just about make out the outline of the window and the chair in the corner of the room with her clothes on.

Only glowing embers were left in the grate. A child giggled. The patter of little feet flashed past the bottom of her door.

She wrapped herself in the hand-me-down dressing gown and left the warmth of her room for the coolness of the passageway. The oil lamp flickered a ghostly luminescence along the hallway and down the stairs.

Clemency was not in her room. She strained to listen for the child, but all she could hear was the haunting symphony of wind and rain lashing against the rattling windows.

Eliza carefully searched the passageway and between the clocks. They unnerved her. The shrouded sentinels guarded the mistress's door. Each one seemed to have a presence - a dormant personality waiting to reanimate at any given moment. Eliza didn't trust them. She crept past them to go downstairs.

The dogs were fast asleep in front of the range. She could just about see their individual shapes from a sea of black and white fur. Only Duchess stirred to growl lazily. Eliza reached down to pat the head of the elderly guard and surveyed the kitchen at floor level to see if she could detect the missing child. She noticed that within the sea of black and white there were patches of chestnut brown and pale pink flesh.

"The dear of her!" Eliza whispered to herself as she moved closer to the pack. Clemency was sleeping soundly with her little pink arm wrapped around one of the spaniels. She sneezed quietly as some of the spaniel's fur tickled her nose and another dog gently licked her ear in response.

Eliza wondered how many nights the child had slept within the protective warmth of the pack. She carefully lifted the little maid without her waking. With care, she placed the child into Eliza's bed and they both soon drifted away into a safer sleep.

Eliza woke with a start.

The numbing sensation of pins and needles prickled her dangling arm. She tried in vain to re-animate her numbed limb, and she realised the child was no longer in the bed.

Dream or reality? Eliza couldn't distinguish. She didn't trust the surreal machinations of her troubled psyche. A deposit of silky, chestnut hair was left on the pillow…

15

Donna, May 2012 - The Records Office

Donna had been waiting in a queue for the records office for at least ten minutes and was surprised to see so many local enthusiasts gathered in the foyer. She was even more surprised to find that the queue seemed to consist mostly of slightly over-weight women.

Finally, the doors were opened by an extremely slender, well-presented middle-aged woman sporting a brightly coloured lanyard dangling from her neck along with a pair of spectacles suspended by a string of amber coloured beads.

"Welcome everybody, do come in and take a seat – it's so super to see new members!" she said in a super-enthusiastic tone.

Donna peered down to the gaudy pink and magenta lanyard

to discover that her supervisor for the day was Xanthe from Supa-Slimmers Weight and Fitness Club.

"Records Office?" asked a slightly embarrassed Donna.

"That door immediately to your left," replied Xanthe. The Supa-Slimmer Supervisor studied Donna's physique and was just about to enquire whether she should reconsider, when Donna put her finger to Xanthe's glossy coral-coloured lips.

"Sshhh! Pregnant not fat!" whispered Donna as she brushed past.

"Cheeky cow!" thought Donna, who was over-playing the pregnancy card, as she didn't look any different. She entered a quiet room where half a dozen or so local history buffs were busy flicking over well-worn index cards.

"Can I help at all?" asked a rather tall, baby-faced man with a hint of Scottish lyricism.

"Yes please. I'm researching two things. The death of a distant relative and any information on a local servant around 1890 -1892."

"What parish?"

"St. Nectan's." Donna wondered whether he was an old looking young-man or young looking old-man.

"We hold copies of the parish records on the right. If you have the servant's name, I can locate the appropriate tray of index cards when you have finished."

"Eliza Barton, originally from Berry Hill, but she worked in Usbournes near St. Nectan's."

Donna realised that none of the records had been digitised. She was due to meet a certain Mr. Algernon Potts from Georgeham at one for lunch and was worried that she hadn't allowed enough time. Victoire had come up trumps with her enquiries at the local history society and one of its members had suggested contacting her neighbour who was looking into his family history from Berry Hill. After a brief exchange of emails, they had arranged to meet up for lunch to share their findings.

Donna placed her bags down at the table and started her search for the parish records. Her internet research on Susannah Frances Usbourne had come to a halt when she couldn't find an entry for her death or a registered will. Donna theorised that if she could locate the will, she could see what proportion of the estate had been left to Lottie and thereby deduct the full extent of her own inheritance. She was determined to resolve the whole estate debacle as soon as she could.

Initially, the rows upon rows of ox-blood leather-bound records were overwhelming, and Donna had no idea where to start. She found several volumes relating to St. Nectan's.

Donna knew that Susannah died around 1950, because Joanie remembered her scary great-grandmother and thought she died when she was about ten or eleven. Donna selected two volumes – 1940-1949 and 1950-1959 in case Joanie had misremembered her dates.

Joanie rarely spoke about the time she lived with Lottie and Mrs. Usbourne. Donna had the impression they were not happy times and that her childhood really started after the nasty old woman passed away. Donna scanned the names from 1948-1949 in the first volume. Luckily for Donna there were not too many entries – although the parish of St. Nectan's was the largest in Devon, it was sparsely populated.

Her first search, as expected, yielded no deceased Usbournes. Much to Donna's frustration and surprise the second volume also proved to be fruitless. Donna took the third, fourth and fifth volumes out, yet still no mention of the name Usbourne. It should be a name that stood out. Donna double-checked again and again and concluded that she had been as thorough as she possibly could, and that Susannah was not registered. She was puzzled. The death failed to appear either on the on-line digital archive or the hard copy at the records office. She decided to enquire at the desk.

Stuart the archivist patiently double-checked the entries and could offer little insight into the lack of records. He thought it was highly irregular for a record to be missed on both a local and a national level and that maybe she had died overseas. Donna decided to cut her losses and hoped that Eliza would prove to be less elusive. The search for Susannah had already taken over an hour and she had little information to exchange with her co-researcher.

Donna retrieved her allotted long-box of well-thumbed index cards. They had been carefully arranged in alphabetical order with listings of publications, dates, column number and micro-fiche identities. She breathed a sigh of relief when she found Eliza after a few moments of searching and made note of the dates and numbers. It didn't take her long before she was flashing through the microfiche of the late nineteen century until she got to June 1890: -

"Horrible Case of Concealment of Birth and Child Murder.........."

Donna was shocked. She suspected Eliza had a baby but failed to consider for one moment that she was a murderess. She took a sharp intake of breath and continued scanning for information.

"Barnstaple – not Usbournes - the crime took place in Barnstaple - WTF!" mused Donna to herself.

Her eagerness to skip to the end was overwhelming, but she knew she needed to soak up every detail to get her story straight before meeting with Mr. Potts. Much to her relief she discovered the incident had been grossly sensationalised for local consumption and realised that poor Eliza had served a six-month prison sentence for concealment. It was clear that Eliza had no legal representation, no advocate or family to speak up for her. It was evident that there were no reliable, unbiased witnesses or even solid proof of a birth or murder. Eliza had no real case to answer. Donna instantly felt overwhelmed with empathy for the unfortunate teenager.

Donna looked at the time; "13.05. Shit!" she said to herself, and hurriedly packed away the micro-fiche and her notebook. She thanked her archivist angel and hurried off hoping that Mr. Potts would not reprimand her for her tardiness.

Donna had arranged to meet her mystery genealogist in the square outside the library. The benches were full of people scoffing their hurried lunches in the sun before returning to work. She managed to squeeze onto an already crowded bench and searched through her bag for something to take the edge of a low blood-sugar sickie feeling that she wanted to fix before meeting her mystery man. She broke open the bag of toffees and surveyed the square.

There were a couple of bouncy teenage lads who were annoyingly loud. She wondered whether she should point out to them that if they stopped listening to music and removed their earpieces, they might be able to communicate without shouting.

There was a grey, abstract sculpture representing the nuclear family which was thickly splattered with white and purple pigeon shit. The colourful excremental display hung in chunky waterfall formations. Donna found the feral bird's preference for shitting on the ideal family a little ironic.

There were the usual groups of office workers huddled round each other in a circle of fire, zealously sucking at tiny stumps of Marlboro.

There was a middle-aged tall guy propped up against a wall, struggling to grapple with his opened 'Guardian', trying and failing to look composed and in control of the unruly newspaper.

Donna continued to search for her retired gentlemen and noticed a smartly dressed elderly man in a tweedy jacket and hat with a large Tupperware lunchbox on his lap. He was obviously looking around for someone. He pulled out a pocket watch from his waistcoat, tutted and decided to open his lunchbox. Donna got her bag of toffees out as a means of an apology and started to walk over to meet him.

Just before she could introduce herself, an elderly woman rudely pushed past and scolded the old man for not waiting for her in Marks and Sparks, as instructed. Some of the golden wrapped nuggets spilled onto to the pavement in the unexpected collision and Donna bent down to quickly gather them up. It was then that she felt a gentle tap on her shoulder.

"Donna Barnard, I presume?" enquired Guardian man, as he carefully placed his newly conquered, folded newspaper triumphantly under his arm.

"Umm, umm yes," stuttered Donna as she body-scanned the surprisingly youthful and not-so-unattractive man.

"Algie Potts, pleased to meet you. I bet you were waiting for some crusty old, toffee eating geezer, weren't you?" he teased charismatically.

"No, not at all, I was..."

"You were just approaching that poor hen-pecked old sod over there. I saw you armed with your bag of Werthers, and I thought I'd come and rescue you before falling foul of the barging battle-axe...I just didn't make it time!"

"What made you think it was me?" Donna was still visually assessing the new potential.

"Easy... look - the office Cancer Stick Brigade over there, the Teenage Mutant Tinnitus Turtles over there, the Plastic Flavoured Sandwich Appreciation Society and then you."

"And what mythical secret society do I belong to?" asked Donna, who wasn't sure whether she should be flirting at this early stage of introduction.

"I'm not sure yet. Let's try lunch and I'll see." Algie was reluctant to reveal his Single and Flirtatious Over-Forty membership card so early in the proceedings.

Donna wasn't familiar with Barnstaple and was happy to follow Algie's recommendation of having lunch at Georgia's. He took the lead and escorted Donna through a couple of narrow, old-fashioned back streets with over-hanging Tudor-style buildings and cobbled roads.

The route took them across the High Street and through an indoor panier market full of craft stalls. Donna couldn't resist the warm waft of vanilla fudge and insisted on going into the shop to purchase a bag of crumbling confection perfection. They watched in fascination as the confectioner poured the molten, fudgy mass onto the cool of a marble slab, then scooped and folded the shiny caramel lava between two oblong spatulas to lower the temperature for several minutes, before spreading it evenly over the slab.

They cut across rows of stalls filled with hand-knitted curiosities, scented candles and an embarrassed looking mobile phone case seller who had obviously booked his stall for the wrong day. The under-employed stallholders all waited in anticipation, but were disappointed when Algie veered to the left into another back street.

Georgia's courtyard restaurant was tucked away in a corner with tables haphazardly strewn across the cobbled square. The cafe was devoid of any other diners, and an eager waiter sprinted out armed with a couple of laminated menus. Donna decided to err on the side of caution and opted for a lemon and ginger tea and a cheese toastie, while Algie ordered a cafetière and a club sandwich. They exchanged pleasantries and potted histories. Algie explained that he was from local stock, but had moved away to go to uni and had recently returned after getting divorced and jacked in his career in computing to rescue a much-loved Devonshire village pub.

"Anyway, enough about me, let's talk about Grannie!" said Algie eagerly.

"Well, I don't know a great deal about her. All I know is that she worked as a servant for my great-great-grandmother at Usbournes in 1891, and I just wondered whether you had any other info that would help with my research."

"Why are you so interested in some poor old servant who worked for your family?"

"It's complicated, but I started some research about my family and the history of the estate, and Eliza Barton's name kept cropping up. I was hoping that you may have some additional background that might help. Are you sure she was your Gran – it was a long time ago." Donna was keen to avoid talking about her spectral visitations at this stage in case her flakiness put him off.

"I don't think we have the right Eliza - Gran was born around 1888. I think you're talking about her mother, who was also Eliza Barton," suggested Algie, pouring himself a cup of steaming coffee.

Donna referred to her notebook.

"That's not right either, according to the 1891 census she was born in 1874 – that would make Eliza only fourteen when she had your Gran."

"That sounds about right. My great grannie was exceptionally young when she had my Nan. She was the black sheep of the family. My Grannie Eliza was adopted by her great-aunt Esther when she was little and was brought up in Lynmouth away from her family in Berry Hill. The only stories we have are from her aunt Becky. The two old dears lived together until Becky died in the early seventies and then Gran moved in with us until she popped off a few years later."

"Wow, so we are on the right track then. So, what do you know?"

"Becky was great-grannie Eliza's younger sister. Eliza disgraced herself by having a tumble-in-the hay with her childhood sweetheart and ended up producing my Gran..."

"...and what happened to the sweetheart?"

"He died before Eliza found out she was in the family way. He got caught in a threshing machine. It was incredibly tragic... he was only a young lad," Algie said wistfully.

"That's awful." Donna started to write down the new findings.

"The family were struggling farmers and couldn't afford to keep the baby and she was taken to live with Esther and her husband. Becky later went to work for them in their tea shop in Lynmouth and Gran didn't find out that she was adopted until she got married."

"What happened to Eliza senior?" Donna was keen to keep the conversation focussed on her Eliza.

"She went into service to help the family out financially and at some point, she fell out with them. According to Becky, Esther ensured that mother and child were kept apart, and great grannie Eliza was squeezed out from her inheritance by her brothers. The last time Becky heard from her she was struggling to find work locally and had left for London. The two sisters were very close and always kept in touch and then suddenly Eliza stopped writing. Becky went up to the big smoke several times, but she found no trace of her and was convinced that something bad had happened. It troubled her throughout the rest of her life."

Algie was already starting to regret the club sandwich, which was making a bid for freedom by spewing its contents all over the plate. Not wanting to seem a slob, he opted for cutting each sandwich half into quarters in the vain hope that he would not end up wearing its contents on his shirt. Donna chuckled to herself as she observed her companion struggle for control of his lunch. She too had struggled with many unruly sandwiches and had deliberately ordered a more modest creation in a bid to avoid any potential for public humiliation.

"She just disappeared without a trace?" Donna too was

starting to struggle with the molten cheddar elasticated strings oozing from her toasty.

"Becky visited a few addresses from different parts of London. Eliza was obviously struggling because the lodgings became more and more dilapidated. Her last known address was a real den of inequity and Becky often upset herself wondering what kind of life she had to live to get by. She never forgave her brothers or Esther for turning their backs on her sister." Algie finally managed to master his luncheon.

"Do you have any idea when Eliza was last in contact with Becky? asked Donna.

"Sometime at the end of the century – my mum might know. She has boxes of Becky's and Gran's old letters that she hasn't had the heart to throw out." Algie placed the last bite of his troublesome sandwich securely into his mouth.

"This mystery has plagued our family for decades and now my dear old mum is knocking on a bit it would be good to finally find out what happened," added Algie.

The journalist within Donna was becoming twitchy and she instinctively knew that there was a story of interest waiting to be unearthed. It wasn't the right moment to tell Algie about Eliza's concealment conviction. She wanted to sift through the evidence and assess all the implications. Donna restated to Algie that she was only at the preliminary stages of research and promised that when she had anything more solid she would contact him.

Much to Donna's surprise she was enjoying her lunch with her new fellow messy-eater friend and was happy for the meeting to drag on longer. They'd exhausted the possibility of any new discoveries about Eliza, and she really didn't want to divulge anything too personal. The conversation started to dry up.

Donna decided to quit whilst she was ahead, but needed a get out clause...

"Oh bugger! I better be heading back to give the girls a hand clearing up after lunch. I'm sorry, but I better get a move on," said Algie and he insisted on paying the bill. Donna was used to paying her way and insisted that she should pay.

"OK. Here's the deal - you pay for lunch, as you did invite me in the first place. But if you don't think it too cheesy, let me invite you over to my gaff sometime," Algie suggested as he blushed a little. He was never any good at asking women out and started to cringe inwardly.

Why had he use the word gaff? Gaff wasn't a word he would normally use... or cheesy. What the hell was he playing at?

"Yeah, o.k. that would be nice. I'll try and glean some more info beforehand," responded Donna. She found Algie's bashful mutterings quaintly endearing.

Donna watched as he rummaged through his jacket pocket for a business card for The Dog and Lamppost in Georgeham.

She stared at the black and white cartoon of a smiling West Highland Terrier cocking his leg and pissing on an old-fashioned streetlamp.

"What's this?" asked Donna, who wanted to double-check he wasn't some weird dog-pee fetishist.

"That's my pub. The Dog and Lamppost. That old lamp is outside the pub and that's my Mum's old dog."

"Fine. I'll email you as soon as I have some news for you," said a relieved Donna, as she carefully filed away the business card.

"Oh, and have you decided which mythical secret society I belong to?"

"Not yet. We definitely need that second meeting!" said Algie in a less embarrassing attempt to send out the right signals.

Algie and Donna made their way back to the library square, which was now empty except for the Circle of Fire smokers who were back with newly lit cigs dangling from their mouths. They both hesitated awkwardly whether to be very English and politely shake hands or go Continental and air kiss on the side of the face. After a mis-matched clash of noses, the clumsy, awkward teenagers bid farewell.

Algie wandered off in the direction of the car park, but Donna hung back for a while. She wanted to see what kind of car Algie drove.

"Please, not a Big Man Wanker car! Please not a Big Man Wanker car!" Donna's ever-present internal narrator sprang into action as she crossed her fingers. Much to her relief Algie drove past in a re-conditioned olive coloured Mini Countryman with newly restored wooden batons.

"Thank fuck for that!" continued her narrator, who was always suspicious of men and their status symbols. The Countryman symbolised a man who was comfortable with himself, a little quirky and not bothered whether he could break the sound barrier on the motorway.

"Nice guy...tick! Sense of humour...tick! Intelligent...tick!

Treats women as intellectual equals...double tick!!

Available...treble tick!!!" she listed.

Donna made her way back to Gertie and caught a glimpse of herself in the wing mirror. She hadn't dressed to impress. Her messy mid-brown curly hair was pinned down by a couple daisy hair clips at the side of her head. Her floral, brightly coloured summer dress was partially camouflaged by a large mustard cardigan and her over-sized leather satchel hardly projected sophistication.

She looked closer. Her smudged mascara gave her panda eyes. Her teeth were crossed with dark red lipstick lines and a disgusting film of yellow stringy cheese. She dug away at the plastic-like substance with her tongue but found that it had adhered firmly and required a stiff gouging out with her fingernail to prise it away. Her cheese-mining efforts provided enough time for her enthusiasm and positivity to melt away into a spiral of self-doubt. Her internal saboteur decided to go into to overdrive.

"Middle-aged frump... tick!

Look like I need to be in a care home...tick!

Emotional baggage... tick!!

Listens to dead people... double tick!

Up the duff... treble tick! And on, and on, and on...

16

Donna, May 2012 - Donna and Jude

Lottie's old deck chair creaked and strained as Donna plonked herself down unceremoniously without caution. The ancient relic from the 1940's made an alarming ripping sound and Donna could feel the blue and white stripy fabric rip fruitily beneath her buttocks, holding her hostage until she managed to prise her lower body from captivity.

"For fucks sake!" she muttered angrily to herself, as she struggled to close the unwieldy artefact. She failed to appreciate that the threadbare fabric was only tenuously holding together and assumed that its destruction was due to the size and weight of her arse rather than the age and general wear and tear of the cloth.

She had been trying to read a copy of 'Fifty Shades of Grey' that Jude had lent her, but she couldn't keep a straight face and kept giggling to herself wondering what lessons in love Jude had picked up from reading it. It was the kind of book that Joanie would have criticised for portraying women as needing to be sexually dominated by men, whilst paradoxically liberating women from the shackles of sexual taboos. Donna inhaled deeply and wiped her watery eyes, as she realised she was still missing the old girl and that all her recent distractions were only temporarily filling the void.

The washing machine beeped loudly to signal the end of the wash cycle and she decided to make use of the warm, breezy air to dry out her sheets before Jude's scheduled visit. Donna's newly super-human enhanced sense of smell was responsible for her constant state of queasiness, and she discovered the source of the new aversion was her favourite washing detergent. She had found on numerous occasions that the slightest hint of fragrance would have an instant effect on her ability to contain the contents of her stomach. The last straw came when she stood next to a fellow Persil user whilst queuing for stamps. The gentle waft of the offending fragrance instantly connected Donna's olfactory sensors to her super-sharp gagging reflex and resulted in her immediately throwing up a whole carton of Ribena on the Post Office floor. The violent purple explosion came with no warning or time to prevent the splattering of vomit on the shoes of the mortified pensioners waiting to collect their pensions. Once they had been assured that she wasn't pissed or carrying some highly contagious virus, the queue of be-splattered O.A.P.s seemed very understanding and one kindly old lady offered to escort her back to Gertie.

Donna searched high and low for a brand whose perfume failed to turn her stomach and found the only one that didn't provoke an immediate gastric explosion was a specialist hyper-allergenic, non-scented brand that was twice the price of the others. She had spent the last two days washing every piece of clothing, towels, tea-towels and bedding that she could in a bid to suppress her newly acquired talent for projectile vomiting. The lack of added fragrance ensured that the freshly dried and aired washing smelt of farmyard animals, which ironically seemed preferable to the scent of 'ocean breezes' and partially digested food substances.

Donna piled the damp and neutral smelling white sheets into her wicker wash-basket and carried it out into the front garden. It was a beautiful sunny morning, warm without being too hot and sufficiently breezy to dry the bedding before the end of the day. It didn't smell too farm-yardy, unlike yesterday when an inconsiderate neighbouring farmer sprayed his field with noxious, super-shit which obliterated the coco-nutty smell of gorse and the delicate aroma of hedgerow flowers, replacing it with a powerfully pungent piggy-ness that one could almost taste. Despite Donna's aversion to strong smells, the eau de Pig-Shit didn't make her gag for England, and she managed to get through the day without incident.

Donna started to peg the sheets neatly to her Grannie's old washing line. The tide was changing, and the breeze was transitioning from gentle to boisterous. She struggled to contain the billowing sheets as they puffed up and blew around like sails. The whole heavily laden line swung precariously in the wind and the line creaked under the strain. A peg snapped away from the line, liberating one end of a newly washed sheet and Donna just managed to catch it before it collapsed onto the ground draping the crisp, white fabric onto the newly cut grass. She brushed away the thin blades of green and yellow and re-pegged the rebellious sheet firmly back onto the line. Donna was on automatic pilot, drifting off into a replay of her meeting with Algie, carefully reconstructing every minute detail and potentially embarrassing word or action, picking apart every syllable of the meeting and analysing the content for hidden meaning.

She was staring abstractly across the valley when she noticed a servant girl immediately the other side of the sheet staring back at her. There seemed to be a moment of recognition. Donna could see that the girl had seen her as she smiled back, revealing a badly chipped tooth at the front of her mouth.

"Eliza?" said Donna to the girl. But she had already gone. Donna looked again to find Jude's concerned face staring back at her.

"How long have you been there for?" asked a shell-shocked Donna.

"Just a few seconds. Whatever's the matter? You're looking very pale." Jude escorted Donna back indoors.

"I just saw her!"

"Who, for heaven's sake?"

"Eliza! I have just seen Eliza. I KNOW it was her and I'm not going mad!" said an excitable Donna. Jude took a few moments to pour Donna a glass of water before replying.

"Look, I know some weird stuff has happened since you moved in, and I know that there is something strange about this place, but are you sure you weren't daydreaming? You looked pretty spaced out!"

"No. I know what I saw. I was just re-hanging a stray sheet back on the line and there she was staring back at me. She was solid, she was there! She saw me, she smiled at me and then she was gone!"

"What did she look like?" Jude wasn't sure whether Donna had genuinely seen something strange or if she was enduring some form of bizarre hormonal hysteria.

"She was wearing a light grey dress, an apron, and a mop-cap. She had dark blonde, just-above-the-shoulder wavy hair. She was quite plain with bluey-grey eyes and freckles on her cheeks. She had sticky-out teeth, a broken front tooth, and dry-chapped lips. She was so young …just a kid. It had to be Eliza."

"OK. Say if this is a visitation from your Eliza, what now? What do you want to do? You can't let this blast from the past keep exciting you like this. The stress will make you ill." Jude was in mid-wife mode.

"Nothing! I don't want to do anything! She's harmless and I'm convinced there's purpose to this whole experience."

"It's just my friend Eddie has a young niece who might be able to help. A kind of spiritualist. She's supposed to be very talented."

"You've got to be kidding me! A spiritualist! Never! I find it hard to believe that a down-to-earth person like you would have anything to do with anything so unscientific and flaky! Anyway, who's Eddie? Your special gentleman friend?" she added, in a bid to shift the unwanted focus of attention back to Jude.

"Not quite," said Jude sharply, who was obviously a little rattled at the suggestion of a man in her life. "Do you feel up to taking Pip for a walk today? I've got something I want to show you. The fresh air will do you good."

"Of course! I just need to change out of these shorts, and I'll be ready." Donna realised that the zip from her denim cut-offs now needed a safety pin to bridge the chasm between fabric and flesh and she'd be better off with a pair of old cycling shorts and her favourite Bob Marley t-shirt.

Much to Donna's surprise the 'walk' involved scooping Pip into the back of Jude's Yeti and a short drive to the church.

"What colour is this supposed to be?" asked Donna as she hiked herself out of the car.

"St. Nectan's brown. Look all around you. Local cars are all a deep shade of St. Nectan's brown - cow shit, sheep shit, bird shit and mud. You can always tell a blow-in car by whether it's clean or not! You watch, it won't be long before Gertie loses her beautiful orange glow and starts sporting the local colour!" laughed Jude, as she released a very excitable Pip into a small flock of carrion crows. The crows had been picking away at some indistinguishable, brown-furred roadkill that had been festering away for a few days. A manic circle of black, buzzing flies zig-zagged over the putrid stodge and Donna watched in disgust as Pip rolled over and over in the rotting carrion. Jude ignored her beloved's revolting raptures, but she was mildly amused by the look of revulsion on Donna's face.

"Nothing that a quick dunk in the stream won't put right!" Jude said as she filed past the church gate.

Disgusted Donna from Devon followed her neighbour into the church grounds and stood in awe as she gazed up to the spire which towered above her, altering her visual and vestibular perspective. She instantly felt off-kilter but realised that her Crocs were sinking into a muddy patch and were responsible for destabilising her. After liberating herself from the mini-quagmire and scraping off the black-green tar-like substance, Donna started to wonder what Jude had dragged her out for.

"What are we doing?" asked Donna curiously. Jude beckoned her over to a secluded, over-grown corner of the graveyard that had been neatly cordoned off by a set of dangerous looking black wrought-iron railings. They passed through the barely hinged gate.

"These are your ancestors! Your lot thought a lot of themselves. Even in death they needed to be separate from the rest of the riff-raff!" Jude teased. It was obvious that nobody had tended the graves for decades. The lichen covered monuments were splitting and cracked, many of the epithets were hard to decipher. The one exception was that of Charlotte Elizabeth Ruskin, 2001. Lottie's grave had been well-tended, and a wilting bunch of wild flowers had been lovingly placed on the site. It was only then that Donna noticed that Jude was carrying a small posy of yellow roses.

"Have you been looking after Gran all these years?" asked Donna, who suddenly realised that Joanie wasn't the only aching gap in her life.

"Of course! I couldn't let her sit here looking unloved and unkempt like the rest of her family." Jude passed the posy to her.

Donna was touched by Jude's care and dedication to her long-neglected Grandmother and was hit by a brief wave of delayed grief leaving her feeling bereft, vulnerable, and embarrassingly tearful. Jude shuffled around the pocket of her jeans until she found a clean tissue and a small piece of folded paper.

"Look at these. I scribbled the names and dates of all the gravestones. Notice anything unusual?" asked Jude. Donna scanned the list in Jude's wobbly handwriting. The usual suspects were there – Samuel Frederick Usbourne, the Reverend Austin, several Lewis's, and a Lucinda.

"I'm not sure what you're getting at," puzzled Donna.

"Well, who's missing?" Jude pointed through the list of names individually. Donna re-examined the ancestral roll call.

"Ah! Susannah! Susannah is not here. My archive angel must have been right. She must have died overseas." Donna was enjoying the distraction from being emotionally challenged.

"I'm not so sure. I remember Lottie telling me about her grandmother. Susannah was a known recluse. She never left the house. I suppose now you would call her agoraphobic. Your Gran said she felt really trapped because there was no one else to look after the old lady and I think that may be why Lottie never married or moved away. So, I think it's highly unlikely that the old lady left the confines of the house, let alone travelled overseas."

"What are you suggesting?" asked Donna.

"I'm not really suggesting anything. Maybe Susannah's records have been lost."

"So why isn't she in the family plot?"

"Well don't forget this is the family she married into. Maybe she was buried with her birth family, or she was cremated. It might be an idea to focus on trying to find her will. Susannah may have filed it with a local solicitor, or she may have kept it in the house. Lottie was well-organised, and never seemed to throw anything away, so it maybe in with Lottie's old correspondence."

"Possibly. I've not got round to sifting through Lottie's papers yet. I've been putting it off ... there's just so much of it. Most of it is probably rubbish and needs burning," said Donna with an air of dread. The thought of having to wade through boxes of her dead Gran's ancient private papers failed to thrill her, but she knew that she would have to tackle them at some point.

The conversation was interrupted by the sounds of puffing and panting, as an over-zealous Pip had started to dig away at one of the other graves in the compound. Jude hurried over to stop her beloved from desecrating one of Donna's ancestor's final resting places. The grave was kept separate from the other Usbournes with a more modest monument than the others. A mortified Jude watched on as Pip crapped on the grave of Captain Samuel Frederick Usbourne, who looked as if he was being ostracized beyond the grave by his embarrassed predecessors. The message on his grave was brief and to the point; "Here lies Captain Samuel Frederick Usbourne." There was no date or any other inscription that would indicate his relationship within the family or any other tribute to wish him well in the afterlife. Jude picked up her pooch and tried to cover Pip's statement on Donna's ancestor with some old leaves.

"I wouldn't bother, Jude, it looks like Susannah and the others didn't think much of the poor captain either!" remarked Donna as she observed the distance from the rest of the Usbourne clan and the economy of sentiment of his epitaph. "I wondered what he did to deserve this level of post-life rejection?"

They made their way back to the car. Donna got a whiff of festered road-kill and decided that she didn't want to be in the car with Jude's smelly old dog and take the risk of seeing her scrambled egg breakfast again and she opted to walk home.

Jude started to drive past Donna when she slowed down and opened her window: -

"I forgot to ask. How did your meeting go with Mr. Potts? Did you find out anything interesting?"

"Yes. He doesn't like Werther's!"

17

Eliza, Christmas 1890

Clements had been impressed with The Twig so far. Unlike her predecessor, the child didn't need to be told what to do. She was naturally industrious, and she had a way with the Little Miss that Verity could only aspire to.

On reflection, the cynical cook had seen through Verity's thinly disguised willingness to look after the child. It was another way of getting noticed by the Captain. He was very fond of his only offspring and was inclined to be generous with those who treated the child kindly. Clements suspected that the openly ambitious maid had been amply rewarded for her troubles.

The cook was particularly impressed with how plucky Eliza had fought hard with the mistress to gain permission to use the household accounts in the town. It gave her the means to purchase clothes and toys for her new charge.

The Twig had been warned that the mistress wouldn't

be happy with the interference of a lowly servant, but Eliza's skills of negotiation and her determination won through. The newly acquired purchases had been delivered just in time for Christmas and the expected arrival of the Captain. It was easy to see the look of sheer joy on Clemency's face when she was presented with her new possessions and the excited child had spent the morning with Eliza trying on her dresses and playing with her new doll. The child had been bathed and her hair lovingly wrapped in rags to make her hair curl. It was hard to believe the transformation from sullen and neglected pauper child to the excitable little girl that was eagerly waiting for the return of her father.

"Oh, Susanna's a funny old sow, sow, sow,

Susanna's a funny old sow, sing la, sa, fa ral de ray,

Susanna's a funny old sow..." sang Eliza as she prompted Clemency to snort like a pig, and attempt to whistle her part through the gaps in her teeth.

"Susanna's a funny old sow...." they sang in unison as Clements returned from the pantry with a bowl of lard.

"I wouldn't let the Mrs. hear you two singing that, she won't like it!" advised the cook.

"Why?" asked Eliza.

"It's her name...Susannah," laughed Clements.

"Never... how can someone with such a pretty name be so..."

"Susanna's a funny old sow, sow, sow!" sang a very giggly Clemency. She snorted and laughed so hard that a little trickle of blood oozed from her nose. The scarlet nasal eruption didn't deter the Little Miss from singing her new favourite song and was only stopped when she unwittingly danced herself into the emerald-green skirt of her mother.

"Please explain yourself," demanded the Mistress.

"Nothin' ma'am. Just a silly song that I used to sing to my brothers and sisters when they were little," Eliza replied cautiously.

"Susanna's a funny old sow!" interrupted Clemency, and she started to blow raspberries at her mother. Mrs. Usbourne knelt to meet Clemency's face and spitefully pinched both the little girl's arms until she squealed. Eliza felt helpless as she witnessed the poor child's face twist with discomfort. She fought against her overwhelming urge to free the child from the grip of her persecutor, but didn't want to place the child in further jeopardy.

"How dare you mock me! What an ungrateful and unruly child! If I should ever catch you singing that song again…I will put you into the poor house with all the other disgusting little street urchins… where you belong. Do you understand?" Her jawline bulged with the contortion of her anger.

Clemency stared back at her mother's wide, manic eyes in silent defiance.

"DO. YOU.UNDER. STAND. ME?" Her jaw continued to knot and twist in response to the ghost-child's silence.

"Yes Mrs. Usbourne," muttered Clemency, who could no longer bear the pain of her mother's grip.

The child was released and hurried away from the kitchen to disappear once more into the background of the house. She was determined not to cry in front of her bully and remembered why she didn't stay in the warmth of kitchen for too long during the day. The mistress didn't need to say anything to her servants. Both were shocked at her overbearing behaviour but felt constrained by the necessity of employment not to say anything to defend the child.

The unusual jovial mood of the house had been broken. A return to an unnatural quiet was the only option. Susannah walked past the becalmed servants keeping a steady gaze in their direction to ensure that they understood. She left the deafening silence of the kitchen and once more retreated to the sanctuary of her solitude without any further distractions. Clements and Eliza exchanged knowing looks and continued with their chores - too scared to follow the Little Miss in case they fell foul of her mother's temper again.

"She's always a bit touchy when the Captain's due back... Whatever have you done to your lip?" whispered Clements. Eliza paused, moistened her protruding teeth with her tongue and realised that she could taste blood where she had bitten her lip.

"I need a chicken for the Captain's supper. Go sort out that cocky bugger that's been pecking the feathers out of the hens. Make sure you drain it properly... the Captain likes his flesh white," instructed the cook in hushed tones.

Eliza was happy to escape the heavy mood of the house and grabbed her shawl and woolly hat and proceeded across the yard to the paddock. The cold instantly slapped across the warmth of Eliza's face, and she noticed that her nose and bitten lip were already losing sensation. The frost gripped grass crunched glassily under her boots, and she could barely see the gates to the paddock through the dense fog as it rose eerily up from the ground. It swathed the landscape in an uneven, oppressive opaqueness.

All sounds were deadened. Even the overwhelming noise from the starling tree was sufficiently muted.

Eliza stumbled a few times on the uneven, icy ground as she chased her chosen victim for slaughter. The young cock had been a menace, bullying and pecking the backs of the other chickens. His fate had been decided and he was destined for the pot. The big fat bird started to cluck and flap manically. She stopped chasing and coaxed the nervy bird with soft tones and the pretence of corn in her hand. The creature came close enough for her to grab. She seemed to charm the sparky bird calm and was able to place him mesmerised and inverted against her thighs, supporting his weight before the final snap and twist.

"Right, you little bugger, this will teach you for pecking at my girls!" She pulled the neck of the bird firmly and sharply downwards. Pressing her knuckles into the vertebrae, and by bending the head back and stretching the neck, she dispatched the poor creature with a calmness and efficiency that her mother would have been proud of.

Hardened by the regularity of this necessary evil, Eliza no longer felt any guilt. She waited a few minutes while the bird flapped its wings and opened and closed its beak as its nervous responses grew weaker and weaker. The now flaccid bird was devoid of life and Eliza decided to finish the job back in the yard.

The deceased was strung up by its feet on a washing line and Eliza scattered some straw and sand on the ground in preparation for the ensuing bloodshed. There was little point in using a bucket. The harvest was always scattered over a wide terrain, and it was easier to sweep the mess up when the body had emptied. She stood behind the bird and slit its throat with a sharp knife, and watched as it rained a fine spray of ruby onto the golden straw. She wiped her bloodied hands on her apron and watched until the gory shower ceased.

Eliza stood back to admire her own craftsmanship. One cocky, aggressive bird despatched and emptied with little fuss or commotion. It wasn't the first time that she had aided a living creature from existence to oblivion and she was sure it wouldn't be the last.

The post-slaughter mess was swept up with ease and shovelled into a wheelbarrow. The evidence was squeakily transported over the road and dumped onto the compost heap in the paddock.

Eliza heard the haunting tones of a child quietly weeping in the direction of the yard. The mournful sobs penetrated the dense swirls of fog, weaving pitiful lamentations through the air. She dashed across the road without caution. The child's cries were instantly drowned out by the noise of two startled horses rearing up in front of Eliza, and the clatter of a carriage grinding to a sudden halt. Eliza instinctively brought her arms up to shield herself from the imminent impact...

But the horses just managed to swerve away and stopped, panting heavily. The driver jumped down and started to shout at Eliza for her stupidity. Too shocked to care, the man's words failed to make an impact and she was soon listening to the soothing, gentle tones of the Captain who had emerged from the mist.

"Are you hurt? Did you not hear us as we approached?" He was alarmed by the sight of blood dashed across her apron and the red streaks upon her face.

"I am so sorry. I thought I could hear the Little Miss in distress. I thought she may have followed me out here and was frightened... I didn't think to look!" Eliza felt dazed but was counting her blessings that she was still alive.

The Captain cast a stern look to his driver and the torrent of abuse ceased. Eliza was escorted back to the safety and warmth of the kitchen and discovered that Clemency was sitting on the table waiting for her to return.

"We need some hot water...Molly's hurt herself!" ordered the Captain. Clements threw him a puzzled look. Why would he be making a fuss over the Twig.

"I'm Eliza, sir, not Molly," corrected Eliza.

"And she's just slaughtered your supper!" added the cook.

"So, you weren't hit by the horse?"

"No sir... just a drop of chicken blood, that's all." She rinsed the streaks of red from her hands and changed her apron.

"And who's this little princess? Is this my little Clemmie? How tall you've grown!" he said, turning his attention to a very impatient little girl. Clemency craved her father's attention. She reached out and clung to the Captain's neck and snuggled her face into his.

The Captain pulled a small paper bag full of chocolate drops from his coat pocket which were eagerly received.

"This little one doesn't seem to be upset - you must have heard someone else." The Captain watched with delight as his daughter stuffed small pieces of chocolate into her mouth. Eliza explained to the cook about the incident on the road.

"She's been here for the last few minutes. She crept back in not long after you left for the paddock. Come with me," said

Clements. Eliza followed her back into the yard and across to the paddock, and they stared into the opaque mist.

"Listen!" whispered Clements. They both stood and listened to the haunting sound of sobbing penetrating through the otherwise masking effect of the dense fog.

"Who is it?" said Eliza, who was spooked by the ethereal sobs.

"I'm not sure. I've often thought I've heard mournful sounds out here, only to find that it's a calf separated from its mother. But this is different. The last few months I've heard these terrible heart-breaking sounds. I can't work out where they come from... "

They returned to the warmth of the house.

It felt different now that the Captain was in residence. The constant threat of Susannah's temper looming from above or her thudding down on the kitchen ceiling for attention instantly abated. Clemency was happier and spent the whole afternoon sitting with her father while he read the newspaper. Even the cook seemed more contented now that she had a master to cater for.

After a reasonably harmonious supper between man and wife, Eliza presented them with a tubbed and scrubbed daughter, who was eager for the Captain to see her new bedroom.

Susannah failed to be impressed either by the child's willingness to please her father or by the return of her prodigal husband. The duration of a chicken supper was just long enough for her to excuse herself and she left to spend time in the company of herself and the mirror. She knew what he'd really come back for, and she wasn't impressed...and neither would her brother be. Phillip's ghost-child had lured her errant husband back to the fold and she was now bracing herself for the inevitable consequences of his return.

In her eagerness for her father to see all her new things, Clemency took him by the hand and attempted to mount the stairs in twos. She dragged the Captain into her room, closely followed by Eliza. They found that it had been ransacked by the hand of some unknown assailant. Her bed had been turned upside down and the contents of her drawers were strewn across the floor. A dismembered china doll crunched grittily underfoot. The doors of the new wardrobe had been flung wide open, revealing the shredded contents still hanging on silk-padded hangers.

"Not again!" exclaimed the Captain, as he looked at his distraught daughter.

Clemency's eyes filled with tears. Determined not to cry in front of her father, she turned and ran back down the stairs. Eliza had noticed a small puddle of warm fresh piddle where the poor mite had been standing.

"Has this happened before?" asked Eliza in disbelief.

"Many times...as soon as her possessions are replaced, they are ruined again. I have no idea why she does it," said the Captain disappointedly.

"Surely, you don't think Clemency has done this. She was so excited this morning when they were delivered and she's far too little to reach the clothes in the wardrobe ...and the drawers are too heavy for her pull out!" Eliza realised that she was speaking above her station.

"Who else do you think would do such a thing?" he snapped.

Eliza remembered the earlier confrontation between mother

and child. She recalled the manic look of hate and the unnecessary spiteful grip of the mistress as she intimidated the poor child. In that one moment of excessive vitriolic display, Eliza could see her potential for harm. She needed to keep her mouth shut and decided to seek out the accused instead.

She discovered the child under Clements voluminous skirts, heaving and shuddering to control the power of her emotions. The cook pointed downwards to her skirts and whispered.

"Up to her old tricks again?... I knew it wouldn't last!"

"You knew this would happen. Why didn't you warn me?"

"Temperamental, just like her mother!" said the cook. She pointed to her head indicating the familial tendency for madness.

"I AM NOT like my mother!" yelled Clemency indignantly, revealing her hiding place under the skirts. "She did this, not me!"

Eliza bent down to the child's level. "I'm sure Mrs. Usbourne wouldn't do such a thing to all of your beautiful things... would she?"

"I said my mother, NOT Mrs. Usbourne, stupid! She would never come into my room... she's too scared!"

Eliza looked at a wide-eyed Clemency and judged wisely that there was little point in pursuing her current line of enquiry and would get more sense out her in the morning.

"Come on then, my little Miss, off to bed!" Eliza reached out for the child. Once her safety was assured, the mischievous imp was coaxed from the sanctuary of the skirts and was happy to be carried.

"You're being played!" mouthed the cook to Eliza. "You

know exactly what you're doing little missy!" thought the cook as she watched the child grin knowingly over Eliza's back.

Clemency refused to sleep in her own room and was offered the little room opposite Eliza's for the night. It had been an emotionally exhausting day and it wasn't long before Clemency drifted off to sleep. Eliza watched as the frown on her face melted away, leaving it unmarked by the trials of the day and back to her normal cherubic state.

18

Eliza, December 1890 - Christmas Day

The tension in the Usbourne household was unbearable. Clemency had whipped herself into a state of mischievous excitement and was in trouble for removing the silks from the ancestors faces. The defiant child had refused to reveal to her mother the whereabouts of the missing silks and was left for hours standing face to the wall until she relented. Both mother and child were embroiled in a bitter battle of wills, with no one prepared to acquiesce to the other. Eliza had witnessed this battle play out several times over the last few days and was rather hoping that with the Captain's arrival a temporary truce would ensue. Eliza's hopes were soon dashed when she heard the defiant tones of a little girl digging herself in for the long-haul.

"I told you silly, it wasn't me!" exclaimed Clemency.

"How dare you speak to me like that! You find those silks this instant!"

"Find them yourself! I've already told you that I don't know where they are. You really shouldn't be so stupid!"

"Well, you will have to stand facing the wall again, until you remember where you have put them."

Susannah forcibly placed Clemency facing the wall, slammed the door in her usual customary glass-rattling manner, and left the child to soak in her own remorse for the duration of the afternoon. After an hour or so the young child looked over her shoulder to see if she could make good her escape. She was just about to abscond when she noticed the pure white of her mother's eye flicker through the keyhole.

"Don't you dare defy me! Will you never learn?" the keyhole-eye shouted sternly, and the little girl turned back to face the wall. She was resigned to another wasted afternoon pointlessly staring at the grey.

The Captain decided to remove himself from this domestic battlefield and retreated to his study until the hostilities had ceased. His involvement would only enflame the situation and he did not want to interfere between the feuding combatants. Eliza had to fight her instinct to check on the child. She knew that the mistress would be keeping watch and she could ill-afford to upset her employer and risk losing her job.

Clemency continued to huff and puff throughout the duration of the day, arms folded and feet repeatedly kicking away at loose bits in the wall. Her mother continued to stand guard at the keyhole watching for the slightest hint of insubordination. She took a sadistic pleasure in robbing her daughter of her liberty, even though it was Christmas day. After four and a half hours of fruitless stalemate the child was in a state of obvious distress. She kept crossing and uncrossing her legs and quiet tears rolled down her face. The delicious smell of the Christmas goose wafted up from the kitchen, tormenting the little girl who had forsaken food in favour of staring at the wall. Her stomach felt hot with hunger and churned with discomfort every time the range door was opened to baste the bird. She was determined not to break first.

Kick, kick, kick! The sound of the child's boot against the wall dug deep into Susannah's brain, irritating her to the point of surrender. The hallway clock continued to tick monotonously... each single tick dripped lazily from the clock face getting slower and slower. Both mother and child were on the brink of capitulation, when a loud crashing noise startled the entire household. The noise was enough to stop the mistress's vigil and to prise the Captain from his quarters. They rushed to see what the commotion was all about. Eliza mounted the stairs, fearful that Clemency had somehow managed to pull one of the long-cased clocks on top of her. She discovered all three Usbournes outside Clemency's room listening to the racket.

The Captain took charge and entered the room. Once more a scene of utter devastation revealed itself to disbelieving eyes. The wardrobe had been overturned and smashed against the floor, leaving splintered wood and ripped clothes on the floor. Clemency's Christmas presents were left vandalised. A new ragdoll lay beheaded amongst the rubble of a broken China tea-set. A spinning-top was left bent, spinning irregularly on the floor and a newly hacked rocking-horse gently rocked in the corner. Shredded pages from Clemency's new books floated down from the ceiling like over-sized confetti littering the floor with unread fairy tales.

"I told you it wasn't me!" shouted Clemency.

"So, who's responsible for this wanton act of vandalism?" asked the Captain.

"I've told you before... my mother!"

"How dare you! I was watching you in the hallway, how can I possibly be in two places at once?" responded the Mistress savagely.

"I said my MOTHER, not you!"

Susannah felt relieved by the fact that the ghost-child had exonerated her in front of the Captain.

"So, who is this mother of yours?" Susannah replied sarcastically, happy to see the child visibly squirm in front of her father. Clemency tried to pluck an explanation out of the ether.

"Verity of course, stupid! Who else?" said Clemency incredulously. She waited to gauge the reactions of the adults.

Eliza watched with interest and witnessed the effect that Clemency's words had on her parents. The mistress immediately stormed out of the room, once more slamming the door. The Captain turned pale and immediately instructed Eliza to lock the room and see to the child. He was genuinely shocked and seemed heavily burdened by his daughter's revelations.

Clemency smiled. Her campaign was over. Divide and conquer was her successful strategy and she had managed to drive an unstoppable wedge between her parents. At last, she was the victor!

CHRISTMAS NIGHT: -

It had been a difficult day and Eliza was happy to lay it to rest. It was Little Eliza's birthday, and she wasn't there to celebrate. One of many missed birthdays and Christmases that she would endure without her daughter. Eliza missed her family too, but the thought of Christmas without the little maid was enough for her to want to remain at Usbournes for the duration of the holiday.

Eliza had hoped it would be a happy time, but the day had been marred by the mistress's unreasonable behaviour and the child's constant challenge to her mother's fragile authority.

The Captain had disappointed. Her once dashing hero failed to live up to the figure of fair play. He failed to intervene in the twisted relationship between his wife and child. He was failing his only daughter.

The strength of Clemency's wilful defiance was beginning to re-shape her opinion of her new charge. Eliza remembered how shocked she had at first been at the child's seemingly backward behaviour. She ran wild and unchecked throughout the house grabbing food and saying nothing. The child clearly wasn't deaf as she always responded promptly to a call for food. After a few days of the child behaving like a savage Eliza started to wonder whether she was hiding behind the safety curtain of silence. Clemency managed to get her own way perfectly well without the effort of speech. Frustrated by Clemency's mutism, she asked directly why she wouldn't speak. She was surprised when the child replied: -

"Because I don't want to, silly!" with a broad West Country accent.

That instant the child seemed wiser, and Eliza eventually coaxed her from behind the wall of silence with a bag of lemon drops and hours of patience. Yes, the child antagonised and pushed the limits of peace and equilibrium within the household, but Eliza found it difficult to stay cross with her for too long.

Eliza had just got into bed, nearly burning her foot on the heated brick she had placed there to warm the sheets. The hot brick thudded heavily on the floor as she skilfully kicked it out. She had checked underneath the bed to make sure that it was vacant. Her irrational fear of the under-the-bed-demon still needed to be reassured. She had double-checked that there was a lamp on in the hallway in case Clemency embarked on one of her night-walks. It was only when the ritualistic checking and re-checking had been completed that Eliza could settle comfortably for the night.

As she lay listening to the soft tick of the hallway clock beat out its lazy rhythm, she saw the familiar passing shadows of Clemency's feet glide past the bottom of her door. She waited patiently and she heard the twist of the doorknob and the creak of the floorboards as the child filed past her bed.

Eliza always pretended to be asleep when the child cuddled up behind her. She waited for the little girl to whisper in her ear, "I'm cold, can I get in?" But tonight, the child remained eerily silent.

Unusually, Eliza heard the key turn in the lock and the child seemed more heavy-footed than usual. The feather-light child seemed to make more of an impression and the other side of the bed dipped significantly. Instead of Clemency's gentle snuggling, Eliza could hear the heavy breathing of the Captain.

His warm breath prickled against the back of her neck. The uninvited lightly kissed the smoothness of her shoulder. She hoped that if she lay there pretending to be asleep, he would understand her subliminal message and leave in a gentlemanly manner. But he stayed.

She started to panic inwardly as she could feel his excited body rubbing slowly and rhythmically up and down her back. She could hear his breath rise and fall as his heaving became more punctuated with increasing pleasure. She remained rigid and composed, hoping he would satisfy himself without further intrusion. As he placed his hand across her mouth an image of Miles Lincoln's face flashed before her eyes. The memory of his vicious depravity came rushing back. The intensity of the physical pain that he caused made her body shudder.

Rather than fight and risk being half-murdered, she decided to lay passively and hoped that Usbourne would be more merciful. The Captain interpreted Eliza's passivity as a signal of acceptance, and he gently pulled her onto her back and continued in earnest.

He did NOT hurt her.

He was NOT wanted.

She STILL felt violated.

Eliza breathed a sigh of relief when he climaxed and rolled off her. She lay there praying he would leave, but he soon started to snore indicating that he was there for the night. Eliza eased her way out of the bed and started to put her clothes on in the dark. She didn't know what she was going to do or where she would go, but she needed to escape.

"What are you doing?" asked the newly awoken voice from the darkness.

"I'm leaving."

"Why?"

"Because of what you've just done!"

"But you knew this would happen one day. It's part of your duties to my wife."

"I thought you meant that I was to look after your daughter... not YOU!"

"We chose you especially. We thought you understood why you were here!"

"SHE knows about this?"

"Of course!"

"I would never agree to such a sordid arrangement. WHAT do you think I am?"

"You're unemployable! One bastard and a prison sentence served for the concealment of another. No one else would risk such an enterprise...You nearly ruined the Hiltons!"

"I nearly ruined the Hiltons? If it wasn't for them and their bastard nephew, I wouldn't be here!"

"What's Lincoln got to do with it?"

"What do you think?"

The Captain understood this implication and realised that he wasn't the only one to have taken advantage of Eliza. Lincoln was known to be a dishonourable bastard who never paid his gambling debts and had a reputation for being free with other men's wives. Usbourne didn't view himself in the same light at all. He was an upright gentleman of independent means and a doting father and husband. He was charitable and looked after all that was in his care. This was clearly a misunderstanding.

She should have realised that his nightly visitations were part of their contract. He offered a good home and employment and in return she was expected to lie with him when required. A simple, mutual contract of business. Nothing more...nothing less. Quid pro quo. An expected and unexceptional part of her duties as a servant. She had made a mistake. She had got it wrong. He wasn't like Lincoln...Lincoln was a bastard.

Eliza, taking advantage of the lull in hostilities had finished dressing and was starting to pack her bag.

"Well, you are free to go. You probably won't last long in the cold of the night across the moor."

Eliza continued to pack, eager to escape the Usbourne madness.

"Where will you go... the workhouse?"

"I don't know...I don't care. I just want to be away from you and Lincoln and the whole bloody lot of you!"

The threat of the workhouse reignited a deeply held fear in Eliza. She had heard terrible stories from her fellow inmates about how hard it was to survive. Many had opted for a life of crime and the risk of prison.

"I'd rather freeze to death on the moors than stay with you!"

Eliza understood she could easily perish out in the freezing December fog.

"Why not stay? Am I not a good man to work for? Have I not provided you with a good home and food on the table? Stay. If you look after me, I promise I will look after you."

"I don't want to be yours or anybody else's whore, thank you very much!"

"Well, what do you want?"

"I want a quiet life. A husband... a family. I want to have a simple, normal life without the likes of you fucking me and my life up just because you can!"

"If you stay, I will look after you. I'll make sure you're safe I'll protect you..." The Captain was interrupted by a manic knocking on the door and the fragile voice of a frightened little girl.

"Eliza, Eliza, please help! I've got blood!"

Eliza opened door and discovered Clemency, smothered from top to toe in blood, holding out her dripping hands in desperation and fear. Eliza picked up the swooning child, whose nose was still violently pumping viscose red liquid. She took the child back to her bedroom only to find the bed was sodden with the child's blood and realised this was more serious than just a simple childhood nosebleed. The Captain followed them both down into the kitchen.

"Get a cold cloth from the sink." She desperately tried to stem the flow of blood by pinching hard on the poor child's delicate little nose.

"Ice...I need some ice. In the garden, find some ice, NOW!" she added with a deepened sense of urgency.

The master ran bare-foot into the yard and brought back a bucket of frozen water. He got a toffee hammer and started to hack away at the hardened contents, breaking it into shards. Eliza wrapped some in a flannel and applied it to the child's face. The coldness roused her from her stupor and Eliza tilted her face forwards. Clemency started to cry as her face started to ache with the ice and the loss of blood leaving her nose.

"Shush! Calm now. Everything is going to be fine. Try and breathe gently through your mouth and try not to panic. The ice will make the blood stop. I need you to be brave for me. I am going to put this little piece of ice up into your nose. It will sting a bit, but it will stop the blood."

Eliza saw that both parents were now looking on helplessly. She tilted Clemency's head back and gently inserted a small shard of ice into the child's nostril. She repeated the action on the other side. Clemency lay entranced on Eliza's lap as she felt the ice plugs go up her nose. The ice quickly melted, but Eliza reapplied the little plugs until the bleeding eventually stopped.

Clemency could barely keep her eyes open, and she looked strikingly pale underneath the streaks of pink and crimson. Eliza delicately wiped the child's face with a cold sponge.

"I'll stay with her down here for tonight. She'll need a doctor in the morning," said Eliza.

Her urge to flee had now subsided. The mistress said nothing and retired back upstairs. The Captain gently kissed his daughter, placed a blanket over her and wrapped Eliza in a shawl.

"Don't touch me... I'm staying for her not you!" she said firmly.

"Of course!" replied the grateful master.

19

Donna, June 2012 - The Rottweiler

Donna couldn't believe that she was on her way to being late to meet Algie Potts for the second time. She had spent half of the morning burning some of Lottie's old bills and other superfluous correspondence that dated from the 1950's. It was obvious that by 1951 her gran was the only bill payer, which correlated with Joanie's claim that her great gran died around 1950. However, her death certificate and will remained elusive. Over the course of three days, Donna had sorted and burned over eleven large cardboard boxes of outdated ephemera. She was now beginning to understand the smugness that feng shui practitioners felt went they purged their homes of all their unwanted crap. Donna's newly acquired feeling of self-righteousness was only tempered by the fact that she had yet to venture into the main house to conduct another thorough purging of all unwanted artefacts.

The second half of the morning was spent trying to work out what to wear. Donna was no fashion style-icon and was desperately trying to put together an outfit that satisfied two important criteria. Firstly, it should fit! Although Donna still didn't look four months pregnant, many of her clothes were beginning to look a little stretched and unflattering. The lumpy sack-of-potatoes look was not a good one and was not exactly the answer to her flagging self-confidence. Secondly, it had to be an improvement on her last effort. The middle-aged, frumpy, eccentric bag lady look had failed miserably.

Admittedly, she had dressed comfortably and safely to meet what she thought was a toffee-sucking, geriatric genealogist. She had not expected the Guardian-reading, middle-aged, tall bloke with a good sense of humour, whose company she enjoyed. She was rather hoping they would strike up a friendship.

Anyway, she spent far too long weighing up the pros and cons of each garment combination and had decided on her comfy black skinny jeans, with elasticated waistband, and a blue and white stripe nautical themed long-sleeved t-shirt, which was suitably baggy round the abdomen. She fussed and preened her hair like an over-fussed peacock until she was vaguely satisfied with the result. After spending nearly three hours carefully rejecting umpteen outfits, deliberating over her use of make-up, and fussing with the same annoying few strands of hair that never stayed in place, she finally stood back to admire her morning's work in the mirror. She realised that she had opted for her usual favourite outfit and looked no different from normal.

"Victoria Beckham, eat your heart out bitch!" she said to her diminishing sense of self-worth.

Gertie wasn't playing ball either. The bloody engine wouldn't start and Donna was in danger of flooding it. The starter motor repeatedly churned, coughed, and spluttered like a bronchially challenged smoker just after the first ciggy of the day. Donna decided to let the car breathe for a few minutes, while she opened a letter from Canada that Daphne, the post lady, had just popped through the window.

"Dear Ms. Barnard etc., etc., cut to the chase... the deposits from the Usbourne estate have been deposited into an account in the name of Mrs. Susannah Usbourne, England. We understand that the account was opened in 1951 by the account holder and we are currently trying to trace the whereabouts of the said Mrs. Usbourne and shall be writing to her in due course... etc, etc."

"Bloody hell! Why had Lottie never closed her Gran's old bank account?"

She bundled the letter into her battered handbag and attempted to encourage Gertie back to life. The temperamental VW relented and started without a hitch... just in time for Donna to get stuck behind Tresgothick and a flock of sheep being transferred from one paddock to another. A further setback of fifteen minutes.

"Come on you walking kebabs... get a bloody move on!"

The farmer came out to hurry the stragglers up and spied his new blow-in landlady.

"Bugger, bugger, bollocks!" She tried not to notice her neighbour, but his usual direct approach of knocking loudly on Gertie's side window meant there was no escape. Donna wound the window down and waited for the usual dig about the rent.

"Not such a good crop of lambs this year... mostly singles. I don't 'spose you've heard any more about the rent yet, have you?"

"I'm sorry Mr. Tresgothick."

"Call me Rob," interrupted the farmer who appreciated the value of being on first name terms with the landlady.

"I'm sorry Rob. I don't like to pass the buck, but I'm no wiser than you," Donna said in her most sincere 'this is not my problem yet' voice that she could muster.

"It's just that I've received another letter this morning with yet another rent increase! I'll have to give it all up at this rate... not worth the trouble."

Donna felt a horrible sinking feeling as he started a long diatribe about his profit and loss ratio and that he'd be better off working at Sainsbury's, selling produce rather than supplying them. She nodded politely and practiced all her polite non-verbal vocabulary, until he noticed that his flock were starting to go down into another lane.

"Look Rob, when my solicitors have sorted out this mess they will be in touch, and we can re-negotiate terms. Ignore the letter, it doesn't come from me," she said, as Gertie pulled away down the main track.

It wasn't that Donna lacked sympathy, but they had this conversation every time she bumped into him, and she had already told him to stop paying until it had been resolved. Donna was starting to wonder whether he was just fishing for information. After all, he never offered any proof that he was paying any rent to anyone, and his persistence seemed unnecessary.

Gertie and Donna were over an hour late. They had got stuck behind numerous 4x4s towing caravans on the A39, and a poor parker had straddled a car over one and half spaces outside the pub. It meant that Donna also had to park Gertie on an angle, consuming more of the limited parking space that they would normally require.

Donna double-checked in the mirror, no dangling nasal hair, no crusty bits in the corner of her eyes and no lipstick lines on her teeth...yea, nearly normal!

The Dog and Lamppost was a picturesque, whitewashed pub, set in a picturesque, whitewashed village. The ivy clad frontage looked the same as the business card – sans pooch. Donna could hear the general hubbub of conversation filtering through the air as she nervously approached Algie's 'gaff'. The door was opened by a couple of holiday makers who were leaving to take their photos outside of the pub. It was now the tail-end of lunchtime with a few tourists finishing up their ploughman's lunches and a couple of crusty old locals eking their pints out in a dare to see who could wind the landlord up the most. Donna surveyed the surroundings, eagerly looking for a familiar face.

"Hi! Is Algie around?" she asked the pretty barmaid.

"He'll be down in a minute. Are you Donna?"

Donna nodded as she observed the competition. Feeling outclassed by the youth's fresh-faced appeal and general wholesomeness, Donna ordered a ginger presse and a packet of ready salted.

"He'd given up on you. He's been sitting here like Billy No-Mates all lunchtime. He thought he'd been stood-up!" The girl had a soft south London accent.

"What's he like to work for?" asked Donna in a bid to stretch out the conversation.

"He's a tight, miserable old git with wandering hands!"

"Really?" Donna was starting to regret the lunch date.

"No, silly – he's lovely! Oi, Dad, get a move on. Your new lady friend is here!" she shouted up the stairwell. Algie thumped down the stairs. He nodded towards Donna but was immediately accosted by one of his customers.

"Will the inconsiderate bastard who has parked their orange VW across two parking lots, please move and turn off their lights. A disabled driver needs to park up!"

Donna visibly shrank with embarrassment as she picked up her keys and trundled off to salvage her pride. The original bad parker had left, exposing Gertie's slanted positioning which was preventing a blue badge user from finding a space. Donna re-parked and ensured that the lights were off and apologised profusely to the waiting car. Back inside, Algie was sitting at a table in the conservatory with a pint and Donna's drink.

"I'm so sorry. I parked across the bays because it was the only space available."

"Please don't worry. I'm sorry if I'd embarrassed you... I was just joshing. My regulars expect me to be deliberately obnoxious!"

"Oi, Pinky and Perky, isn't it time for you two to sod off?" he shouted at two old codgers who were waiting for Algie to pick on them for making their pints last an hour and a half. The red-faced remnants from the cast of 'Last of the Summer Wine' smiled as they middle-fingered Algie in unison and left.

"Don't worry, they'll be back at five!" Algie split open a packet of crisps and started nibbling.

"I'm sorry I'm so late."

"Don't worry about it. It's been heaving. Just as well you weren't here."

"Your lass is a bit of a joker. Told me you're a tight git with wandering hands. I was seriously beginning to have second thoughts about our meeting."

"Chloe, what do you think you're playing at showing up your poor old dad in public?" he said to the girl behind the bar. Chloe left the counter and came over with an order pad.

"Just doing my job. You were placed on this Earth to embarrass your children and I was placed here to show you up for the smooth-talking bastard that you are!" She kissed him affectionately on his slightly receding hairline.

"This is Chloe - my youngest by five minutes. Sophie my FAVOURITE daughter is still at uni, where this one should be, had she not decided to drop out two months before her finals!"

"I keep trying to explain to him that it's called a tactical withdrawal. I screwed up this year with a couple of dodgy essays... at least if I re-sit my final year next year, I can still salvage a 2.1. It also means I don't have to share my graduation glory with Soph this year!"

"What were you studying?" asked Donna.

"Events management and hospitality at Middlesex."

"And your sister?"

"Sophie's just finished her BSC in Chemistry in London...she's the clever one!"

"Same as my mum. She was a research scientist. I was always seen as a bit of a dud! Studied English and got into journalism." Donna remembered the childhood pressure to take up the sciences. Joanie never really approved of her daughter wasting her time at university studying English, and her inverted snobbery against the arts and humanities was responsible for Donna's second-class citizen complex.

"I didn't know you're a journo!" exclaimed Algie.

Donna explained about the trajectory from her aspiration to be a serious current affairs journalist writing for one of the leading newspapers, down to writing columns in a local newspaper about the shocking lack of commodes out on loan in her district and the price of parking outside the library. Donna always hated reviewing her career. The surprising lack of peaks and surplus of troughs served as a testament to why she should never have tried to juggle a successful career and child-rearing without a complex network of support...or a willing partner. Donna had accepted her part in letting Colm's ambitions and children take precedent over her own career. No one forced her to relinquish her rights to a flourishing career. It just was the right thing to do. She just didn't bargain on Joanie instantly filling the gap that the children left when she split from her wandering husband. She just managed to stop herself short of explaining that her chances of a career revival were slim given her current situation and diverted attention back to lunch.

"So, what's on the menu?"

"Anything between two slices of bread at this time of the day, I'm afraid. Chef's gone home for the afternoon."

They deliberated over the plethora of exotic fillings that were on offer and then both decided that you couldn't go far wrong with cheese and pickle. The two new recruits from the Messy Eater's Society managed to consume their booby-trapped sandwiches with only the lightest smattering of oozed brown pickle juice that conveniently dribbled onto their fingers and was discreetly cleaned up in the general process of consumption. Dining pride was left intact, and they could both boast with internal smugness that they weren't wearing their own leaked luncheons.

A vertically challenged older lady burst through the doors struggling with two R-chive boxes and made her way to Donna and Algie's table.

"Watch out here comes the Rottweiler!" Algie said affectionately.

The boxes were plonked down in front of them and Algie stood up to kiss the mildly agitated pensioner before she could introduce herself.

"You'd think that being nearly eighty-four someone would offer to carry these boxes for me!" exclaimed the woman in a rich, fruity voice.

"No way are you eight-four!" exclaimed a genuinely surprised Donna.

"This tough old bird is my mother, Elin." Algie kissed his tiny mother's cheek. Elin rose on tiptoes to thump her son affectionately on the bicep and then offered the same hand for Donna to shake.

"Donna Barnard, please to meet you."

Donna could feel the Rottweiler weighing up her potential, as Elin started to compare Donna to her ex-daughter-in-law. Donna seemed polite and friendly enough, but she was quite plain, middle-aged with no sense of style. Nothing compared to Natasha. She always thought that Algie was punching above his weight with that one. Natasha was beautiful, vibrant, and ambitious...too ambitious perhaps. Natasha was always impeccably well-turned out. You wouldn't catch Natasha wearing slacks in public. Natasha was perfect. Natasha was the daughter-in-law to be proud of... until she dumped her beloved son with two teenage girls to look after... No, plain, dumpy Donna might just do.

Donna looked at Algie and Elin and wondered how this mismatched pair could be related. How could a resident from the Yellow Brick Road give birth to Hagrid's lovechild? How could this sparky octogenarian look twenty years younger without looking like mutton?

Elin was exceptionally well-groomed with short, choppy-cut, salt and pepper coloured hair and discreet make-up that gave her a fresh glow. Most old ladies in Donna's experience were either snaggled-toothed hags with thick hairs growing out of their chins, or so caked in powder that every crease and line was so well-defined that the markings could be picked up by satellite. Her dress-sense also reflected the perfect balance between making the most of herself without trying to compete with her grand-daughters. No, Elin had got it completely sussed in one neat package without any complications. She really didn't look eighty-four.

Algie made the tactical error of leaving Elin with his new friend while he put the kettle on.

"Such a shame about Algie and Nat splitting up...isn't it?"

Donna was surprised at Elin's forthright approach to assessing the situation between her son and a potential new female.

"I didn't know them as a couple. It's not something we've spoken about." Donna was beginning to understand why they called her the Rottweiler... she had gone straight for the throat and wasn't about to let go.

"Have you slept with him yet?"

"Excuse me?" Donna nearly spat out the of the last of her ginger presse. "I think you've got the wrong end of the stick!" She wasn't used to such a direct line of enquiry. "There's been some misunderstanding. I'm only here to do some research on your grandmother."

"Shame! I think you should! He's a nice boy, he deserves to be happy," said Elin, transforming from a Rottweiler to a doe-eyed Spaniel.

Donna didn't know whether to be flattered, embarrassed, or insulted.

"Gran! Did I just hear you right?" said Chloe. "You can't say that to Donna...they've only just met! I'm very sorry Donna." She hoped Gran hadn't put her big foot in it.

"Forget it... it's not a problem. What's in these boxes?" Donna remembered some of the uber-embarrassing and cringe-worthy statements of Joanie's.

"Algie told me about your research, and I thought I'd let you have a look at these photos and letters of my mum's and Aunt Becky's. You must promise me that you will look after them - they're very precious to me. Apart from a couple of jars of ashes, they're all have left of them," said Elin in a much softer manner.

Elin took the photo's out first and introduced her dead relatives to her son's new 'friend'. She shuffled through various ragged edge sepia snaps.

"This is my mother about the age of three. This is a family portrait outside the tea shop they had in Lynmouth. And this one is of Becky and..."

"Eliza, that's my Eliza!" interrupted Donna. She instantly

recognised her laundry girl and felt a quiver as the hairs on her arm bristled.

"That's funny, she hasn't got her broken tooth."

"That's a picture of Becky and her sister Eliza at Barnstaple fair. What did you mean about a broken tooth?"

"I saw a picture of Eliza as an adult and she had a broken tooth at the front." Donna felt a little guilty about telling a white fib.

"Could we have a copy?" asked Elin. "This is this only faded picture I have of her."

"I tried to get a copy from the records office, but they wouldn't let me because the picture was so fragile." Donna added a little grey to her fabrication. She was a useless liar and hoped that Elin couldn't see through her thin veneer of deceit. Luckily, Algie arrived with a tea tray and plonked himself down on a chair.

"Right then ladies, who's for tea?"

"Actually, I've changed my mind. I'd better be off. Countdown will be on soon. It's not quite the same since the delightful Des left, but I still don't like missing it!" Elin said in a hurry. She couldn't be dissuaded from leaving and Algie didn't try to stop her.

"Remember what I said." The doe-eyed spaniel directed a look at Donna.

"I promise I will look after them for you. Thank you for bringing them over."

"That's not what I mean," said Elin, temporarily relapsing into Rottweiler mode.

"Message understood!" responded Donna, who would have

said anything to get rid of the threat of Elin going for the jugular again.

Donna breathed a sigh of relief when Alfie's canine mother drove off in her shiny red car.

"I'd better be going too," said Donna, who was worried about outstaying her welcome. "Thanks for an entertaining lunch."

Algie walked Donna back to her skilfully parked Gertie.

"I hope my delightful mother didn't say anything inappropriate when I was making tea." Algie could tell by the smirk on Donna's face that something of an embarrassing nature had been divulged.

"You may as well tell me. If you don't Chloe will...she's my ears and eyes when I'm out back."

Donna reluctantly recounted her conversation with the Rottweiler.

"I am so sorry! I cannot apologise enough for my mother. She really shouldn't be allowed out in public without a muzzle!"

He realised that if he didn't use this opportunity to say something now, he probably never would. Despite her lack of tact and diplomacy, Elin had paved the way for Algie to ask Donna if she would be interested in taking their acquaintance further.

"Would it be so bad if we did get to know each other a bit better?"

"In what way?" asked Donna with a mock coyness.

"Well, you know, if we should go out together, go for a meal, catch a film maybe, you know that kind of thing," he said, reverting to an awkward teenager mode.

"Algie, are you asking me out?"

"I guess so. I mean yes. I am asking you out!"

"Good! But there is something you need to know." Donna decided to confess.

"I'm not interested. We both come from fucked up marriages and we are both grown up enough to accept we both have pasts. So, unless you are some kind of cyber lady-boy ... I'm not interested!"

Algie stuck his fingers in his ears and started to "la, la, la."

Donna refrained from telling him about her little blow-in from Canada. What was the point? After a couple of dinner dates, he'd probably get bored and start looking for a much younger, more attractive, and more amusing model. She would be back in the junk yard with all the other broken bits of scrap.

20

Algie and Donna, July 2012 - Billy No-Mates

Date Number One; The Records Office.

When Algie the neo-pubescent clumsily asked Donna out, he had hoped for a conventional food and alcohol-based affair, with the vague possibility of having his new playmate stay over for a grown-up sleep-over. He didn't bank on a session at the records office rooting around like a truffle-obsessed pig trying to snuffle out precious nuggets of information on his long-lost great grannie. He wanted something less... research-y.

The developing picture of dear old great-grannie Eliza was a complex one. Finding out that she had two illegitimate offspring and had been tried for infanticide by the time she was sixteen was frankly a bit of a turn-off. The gentlemanly side of Algie felt it was inappropriate to push for an amorous conclusion to the afternoon, but his more passionate side felt bitterly disappointed that after several years in the barren wasteland of his love-life, he still wasn't going to get his leg-over.

Date Number Two; The Restaurant.

Algie had planned a sophisticated evening wining and dining Donna at some swanky restaurant in Ilfracombe.
Unwitting mistake number one: - Ordering a bottle of overly- expensive bottle of Chianti.
Algie sold the same wine for a fraction of the price down at the Dog, but he was determined not to let the 625% mark-up spoil his evening. He tried desperately to disguise his resentment at being ripped-off and attempted to pour some of the ruby coloured nectar into Donna's glass. He then had to mask his further disappointment when Donna politely declined on the grounds of having taken some unspecified medication.
Unwitting mistake number two: - Ordering spaghetti vongole.
Algie's pining for his favourite Italian dish over-rode his need to remain suave and sophisticated. Although Algie truly relished every mouthful of the sweetly fishy, garlicky combo, he failed to appreciate the splashing of the silken orange sauce that left his best white shirt resembling a Jackson Pollock masterpiece.
Unwitting mistake number three: - Washing his best white shirt in Persil.
Donna, sensing Algie's embarrassment decided she would be helpful and leaned over to brush away some of the spaghetti juice with her napkin. With one potent in-take of breath, the

smell of Ocean Breeze immediately connected with her supersonic gagging reflex and sent her running off to the ladies to rid herself of the twisted torrent of undigested carbonara and garlic bread. She returned to the table looking pale and pasty rather than pale and tasty and was definitely not up to a night of passion.

Date Number Three: - The Return of Billy No-Mates.

Algie kept looking up at the bar clock. Yet another half an hour had ticked past the agreed rendezvous time. It was starting to look as if Donna had finally owned up to the fact that she wasn't interested in any form of liaison - dangerous or otherwise. Her phone was going straight to voicemail and her landline was permanently busy. Determined not to serve punters on his only night off, Algie secreted himself into a cosy snug away from the general hubbub and merriment of the bar. The evidence was beginning to stack up for a no-show. In fact, the whole affair seemed to be doomed. He started to weigh-up the evidence.

Passion killer number one: - The records office. Who in their right mind would insist on a first date at the record office? He knew that Donna's interest in his long-lost relative was the catalyst for their friendship, but he was beginning to suspect that she was way more interested in Grannie Eliza than him...

Passion killer number two: - Grannie Eliza. The discovery of his teenage infanticidal great grannie was enough to dampen down any normal red-blooded male's libido, and he was no exception.

Passion killer number three: - That bloody bottle of

Chianti! He was convinced that his constant carping on about the wretched price was the real reason why Donna declined to drink that night. She probably thought he was a cheap-skate.

Passion killer number four: - The vongole. He knew deep down that he was very likely to end up wearing his favourite Italian food on his new white shirt, and that he ran the real risk of looking like he needed to be in a care-home. He should have realised that fishy garlic breath was a real turn-off, and unlikely to promote uncontrollable, passionate snogging.

So, Algie was beginning to paint a picture of himself as a carping, tight git, who couldn't look after himself and was probably only a few years away from being abandoned by his daughters and put into a home for the permanently bewildered. He had a murderous grannie and a vicious canine mother. She had already sunk her teeth deep into their nascent relationship and throttled any real chance of them getting together with one misplaced comment. No wonder Donna wasn't interested. He finished his pint and resigned himself to the fact that he wasn't really cut-out for this dating malarkey. Perhaps he'd be better-off spending his time with his long-lost soul-brothers Cleggie and Compo, making his pint last for two hours.

21

Eliza, Wednesday 29th July 1891 - Salvation

The short journey from the village down to the quay was a hazardous one. The steep incline from the cliff top to the cobbled slipway made Eliza feel that she was going to slip off the edge of the world into the void. The appeal of a dark, safe place was very alluring. Free from the shackles of servitude, free from the madness of the Usbournes and free from the child that she was now carrying. The Captain drove the cart precariously down to the public house and tethered it to a post. He promised he wouldn't be long; he was only going to pay off a debt from the previous night's cards. She knew that he would be persuaded to stay for a drink and another game. The old proverb about a fool and his money aptly described the Captain and the familial tendency for addiction. He was only supposed to be taking her down to the village for some purchases for cook, but he had used the trip as an excuse to meet up with some of his cronies and hangers on.

The sun was trying to poke through the wisps of mist and mizzle. It was trying to be a nice day, but somehow all of nature's efforts seemed inadequate and worthless. Eliza failed to be captivated by the scale and beauty of the scenery. She was not impressed by the array of coppers, rusts and ochres that weaved their way through the contortions of the stone. The intricate geometric lines seemed beyond nature, as if crafted by a draughtsman, but nothing could impress her today. All the colours had been sucked out of the landscape leaving only the greys. All beauty and meaning was lost.

Eliza was burdened by an oppressive blanket of melancholy that was wrapped around her so tightly that she could barely breathe. She dismounted from the cart. The judder encouraged the child to kick and grind, but she was no longer in awe of the movements of the unborn. The deserted environment provided Eliza with the opportunity to free herself from her burdens. She passed by the custom house which was now empty and boarded up. She managed to slip unnoticed past the window of the public house and could see the captain surrounded by locals who were happy to free him of his wife's money and abuse his name when absent. He was going to take his time – a pewter jug in one hand and two more lined up. How generous his friends and associates could be when they could see easy pickings.

Eliza stood at the water's edge. The tide was beginning to recede. The gentle waves rippled across the stones. The water, not yet fully warmed from the summer splashed coolly over her ankles. She remembered how relieved she had felt when the

Captain swiftly departed from Usbournes after Clemency's night of terror and the disappointment when he returned but a few days later. She now noticed how he looked at her when she served the food and how he would brush her hand with his when she removed his plate. Determined that he would not interfere with her again, she ensured that her bedroom door was locked securely. This proved no barrier for the determined one, who could easily poke out the key and open the door with a new one from the other side. His attentions were mercifully brief, but habitual. He somehow seemed dependent on the nightly charade of creeping into her room uninvited - the pretence to gain her interest and affection and the consolation of climaxing when she proved unresponsive.

The sea was up to her knees, rapidly soaking deep into the cloth making her skirt more weighty and less buoyant. She felt a magnetic pull into the horizon as the waters slowly rose to her waist. The conversation with her masters from the night before rang clearly through her consciousness. Arrangements had been made. She was to stay on at Usbournes until the end of the summer. She was to return home and have the baby back at Berry Hill from whence it would be quickly deposited at the Foundling Hospital in London, where the Captain still had some favours owed. She was expected to return soon after and take up the 'arrangement' prior to her confinement and so the whole process could begin again and again and again, until her broken body could conceive no more or her broken spirit invited her to the madhouse. She could see the future of umpteen little bundles being spirited away to some unknown destiny and her empty body left savaged and hollow.

She could now feel the waves push at her chest. Her body's

lack of symmetry pulled her downward and the weight of her water-logged clothing proved a cold, comforting, sinking feeling as she was pulled under. Wave after wave washed over her. The purifying waters started to wash away the stains. It washed away her tears as she remembered poor Sam. It washed away the strawberry stains from her apron and the blood that she had on her hands. It washed away the unwanted taint of Lincoln and Usbourne that stayed in her body. She felt purer. She felt saved and happy to meet her maker. She was determined to have her daughter's face as her last memory as she sank her face happily beneath the sea.

In her preoccupation, Eliza had failed to notice Amanda Lively and her servant arriving on yet another fruitless mission for the Temperance Society. She failed to see their quick exit when they were heckled and cajoled out of the public house or their worried faces when they spied a woman deliberately walk into the sea to let herself be claimed by it its dark waters. So singular was her purpose that she failed to hear their cries for help or notice them wading into the sea. The first that Eliza realised she was not alone was when she was rudely deprived of her salvation and pulled back from the grey and into the light. Deprived of her watery demise, Eliza coughed and spluttered as she was dragged back to the shore. Eliza's determination to end her life was met with equal determination from the women to prevent her from committing a mortal sin.

"Why ever would a girl do that to herself?" questioned the servant innocently, as she loosened Eliza's stays.

"You can see why," answered her mistress, as Eliza's rotund abdomen burst out from the confines of her underwear. Amanda took her shawl from her shoulders and placed it over

Eliza's shivering body. The commotion had alerted the fisherfolk who lived in the end two cottages, and Eliza was soon plied with small sips of brandy. Amanda started to protest at such a practice, but quickly gave up on the grounds of the liquid's medicinal application. The shock of the alcohol placed Eliza's frail body into crisis, and she started to convulse. Eliza's body shook violently as Amanda cradled her in her arms. She was still happy to go. She didn't want to be saved. She didn't want the infiltration of air that was sweeping through her body, filling her lungs and fuelling her heart and brain. The air sucked out the moisture. It sucked out the cleansing power of the water and in its place it left behind the taint and the stains. She could feel her body's instinct for survival wrestle with her dire need for release and despite the frailty of her frame, her body emerged as the victor. The shaking subsided, she started to breathe, and she returned re-burdened.

***

Eliza had an awareness of being back in her bed. She had the urge to purge the bitter and salt from the sea and was violently sick in a bowl that had been considerately placed by the side of her bed. Through her blurred vision, she could see the moving shape of someone sitting close to her.

"Mrs. Lively?"

"No, it's me. She left ages ago. She left after she took the Mrs. to task – there's going to be one almighty row when he gets back!" exclaimed the cook who couldn't hide her misplaced delight in the drama.

"So, who did that to you?" asked the cook, as she spied the pregnancy that Eliza had cleverly concealed from her.

Eliza closed her eyes and rolled over away from her gentle inquisitor.

"It doesn't take much imagination to work out what's happened. When will you girls ever learn? Anyway, I'm glad you're alright. I've got to go. My mother's on her way out, so I won't be around for a few days. Listen, you look after yourself. Don't let them push you around. Let them sort themselves out for a change. Things won't seem so bad in the morning."

"Clemency – who will look after Clemency?"

"She will stay with me; she can play with my grandchildren. Its best she's kept out of the way for a bit." The cook gently squeezed Eliza's limp hand and left to be at her dying mother's bedside. An exhausted Eliza slipped back into a deep sleep.

When she woke, she could hear a storm brewing between the mistress and the Captain. It was the dead of night and the echoes of the mistress's displeasure ricocheted round the house. Eliza had never heard the Captain raise his voice in anger before and she knew that she was its cause. She listened at the door as Susannah threw her ill-will down the hallway in his direction.

"Your wanton disregard for the virtue and safety for those in your care nearly cost Eliza her life!" she screamed at her husband.

"I don't understand why you are suddenly so interested in the wellbeing of our servant. It didn't trouble your conscience where the other one was concerned."

"The other one had a name, which conveniently escapes you. Or is it because you cannot bear to be reminded by your part in her downfall?"

Eliza could see through the crack in the door that the Captain was squeezing the mistress's thin white throat within his hands; "We agreed that we would not discuss that issue any further. What is done is done! I shall advise you for your own well-being that you should refrain from any further discourse on the matter, otherwise I will not be responsible for my actions!" He could feel her throat crunch and gurgle beneath the strength of his large, strong hands. He forcefully pushed his mortified wife backwards and she seized the opportunity to free herself and slam the door in his face. She hurriedly locked the key and counted her blessings.

The Captain stormed into the study and poured himself a large whisky. It wasn't long before he returned to vent his anger in the direction of Eliza. She lacked the energy for flight. The will for survival left her days ago – there was little that could frighten her now. Her indifference left her defenceless and vulnerable as he pushed the key through the hole and unlocked the door with ease. He burst into her room and for the first time he didn't want to bed her.

"What possessed you to do such a thing? The whole of St. Nectan's now knows of your condition. God knows whether they have associated me with this mess. Was it beyond you to keep to what was agreed?"

"I agreed to nothing! If I had been given a choice I would rather die than to live a life as your whore, bearing your bastards. My flesh creeps when you touch me. The thought that a part of you lives within fills me with revulsion. Each time it kicks it reminds me of how it got there!"

The Captain was not in the mood to take her

insubordinations. He pushed her against the wall and held her by her throat.

"I promise you, if you continue, I shall squeeze every last drop of life from your body!" He felt the crack of her throat as he started to squeeze.

"Go on then! Kill me! I don't think much of your promises. You promised you'd look after me, you said that everything would be alright. It would give me great pleasure for you to put an end to me knowing that you would swing for it!"

He fought the desire to rob her of her life. He saw a reflection in the mirror of himself towering over the deathly pale, heavily pregnant Eliza, with his large hands tightly squeezing her tiny throat. The image shook him from his savagery, and he desisted from his murderous path. He was not prepared to risk his life and reputation for this worthless specimen. His gentlemanly code would be violated if he killed her. It would leave his reputation in shreds, his daughter an orphan and his financial affairs far from being in order. He was not prepared to give her the satisfaction and sully the good name of Usbourne.

Brazened by her liberation, Eliza spat directly at his face and opened the door for him leave. He wiped himself and made a bid to exit. Eliza held her hand out for the key, which he willingly gave to her. Defeated by both his wife and his mistress, he planned to get even more drunk and then skulk back to London in the morning. She pushed him out of her room and quickly re-locked the door, safe in the knowledge that she had both the keys in her possession.

Completely broken and dispirited she climbed back into bed, only to realise that the lower part of her nightgown was soaked through. A familiar dull, persistent ache had started in the small of her back and she could feel her belly tighten. She no longer trusted her masters with her welfare and feeling decidedly feverish and unwell she remained secure under her blankets. She drifted in and out of consciousness as the fever took hold. One minute hot and beaded with sweat, then shivering with the cold and trying to bury herself further under the blankets. She was aware that she was not alone. She felt the feminine presence of someone watching over her, but through the haze of fever and pain she could not decipher who her guardian angel was. Eliza languished in pain for many hours puffing and panting. She tried to remember how her mother coached her through the birth of her little maid.

Eliza could hear the dawn chorus spark up, igniting a cacophony of sound as the light of the morning started to flood the room. Through her blurred vision she was aware of someone leaning over her and she could just make out a round mark or wound in the middle of her forehead. Eliza tried to focus, but clarity of vision left her with an empty room. She knew she had to get up as Jack would soon be knocking at the door to collect the swill. She managed to haul herself from her bed and noticed the blood and mess that she left on the sheets. She bundled it all up and chucked it in the empty wooden blanket chest at the foot of her bed. As Eliza swathed herself in her dressing gown, she realised that her bulging stomach had dipped a couple of inches and she was hit by another wave of pain emanating from her tightened belly. She rocked to and fro as she panted through the discomfort. She hoped she could get to the washroom downstairs before the annoying farmhand appeared.

She was half-way down the stairs when she hit by another

wave of pain. She stopped and quietly panted her way through, wary of drawing attention of the master. There was a banging at the door.

"Morning Eliza. The door's locked, can you open up?"

"Go away, I'm not feeling well. I've been sick… Come back in a while."

Eliza stood hunched over the banisters as she could hear the latch rattle. Jack was obviously in a rush, and he started to knock at the door again,

"Eliza open up, it's past seven o'clock, I'll be late to feed the pigs."

"Bugger off Jack. I told you I'm not well. Come back when I've sorted myself out." She could feel yet another gut-wrenching pain pulling away at her body. She vomited loudly and the mess hit the floor. Eliza couldn't contain herself anymore and she started to cry. She shuffled over to the chair, and she started to pant with increasing intensity. She couldn't help but groan with exertion and she continued to rock. She wanted to avoid all this. If only bloody perfect Amanda Lively hadn't turned up and pulled her from the sea. She didn't ask for salvation. If it hadn't been for her, she would be oblivious to all this.

Then suddenly it happened. The baby's head started to push its way from her body. She tried desperately to pull it out, but she couldn't get a firm grip. She was now sat upright on the slate floor pushing back on her outstretched arms. She grabbed and pulled as she tried to heave the child away from her. Like slippery soap the child was hard to grasp and in a frantic bid to birth the child she covered the infant's face with her hands. At last, it was over, it had been born. She wiped its face with the bottom of her dressing gown and wrapped the tiny mite in a tea towel that she grabbed from the table.

"For goodness' sake Eliza, open up." The irritating lad was now pounding loudly at the door. In her panic she placed the child in the washing basket and covered it loosely with a cloth.

"Shut up for heaven's sake. You'll wake the master. Wait a minute and I'll open up." She managed to shuffle and groan her way to the door and let the persistent lad in.

"You look like death! What have you been doing?"

Eliza was hit by another wave of pain and fever.

"I told you I'm not well ... I'm so cold Jack, will you light a fire?" She wrapped herself in a blanket. She watched him light a fire in silence as she focussed on containing her pain.

"What's that blood on the floor?" asked Jack in a growing state of alarm.

"I was badly sick, and I brought up some blood."

"What a mess you've made, I'll better call the mistress." He started to realise that this should be dealt with by another woman.

"No, Jack, please don't. It will pass again presently, honestly." Much to her dismay the child offered a feeble cry.

"What s that crying?"

"Nothing... Probably a cat in the garden or something."

"Eliza, have you had a child?"

"I HAVE not!" The infant let out another feeble cry for attention.

"My God Eliza what have you done? I'll better get help."

"Jack, please don't say anything. You cannot believe the terrible trouble I will get into if you tell anyone. I'll do anything, please... it will be the end of me."

"Keep away from it...don't kill it!" Jack said agitatedly as he witnessed Eliza approaching the wash-basket and pulling away at the covers.

"I wouldn't harm it, I'm just pulling the cloth away from its mouth, so it can breathe." The child's colour had started to change to an alarming shade of purple.

"I'll fetch the Master!"

"Please Jack – I beg of you. I've not done anything wrong; I promise!" As he ran up the stairs to sound the alarm, Eliza thought she could see the outline of a woman sitting on the stairs, but Jack just rushed straight through the phantom silhouette.

22

Eliza, July 1891 - The North Devon Free Press - Vile Wretch

"VILE WRETCH, STRIKES AGAIN...

Eliza Barton, a former servant of William Hilton, Barnstaple was tried and convicted of concealment and was committed to gaol last year. She is said to be a native of Berry Hill and already has an illegitimate daughter somewhere in that direction. It was stated at the time that there was not sufficient evidence to secure a conviction of the capital charge of infanticide, but she served a sentence for the concealment of birth and the unlawful disposal of an infant's body in the furnace of her masters. The prisoner was warned by the presiding judge that had she been convicted of child-murder she would have surely hung. But neither the pangs of remorse, nor the warnings of the judge have proved sufficient to deter this hardened criminal from refraining from this vile course of action and now stands accused of repeating the offence within the brief space of a year after her liberation from prison. After serving her sentence Barton was taken into service by Captain Usbourne with the benevolent view to her reformation.

It is strange, as it is true that this same Eliza Barton is responsible for a similar act of barbarity, with circumstances, if possible, still more atrocious. The perpetrator of this heinous crime has since been re-arrested for an incident equally disturbing in its brutality and lack of humanity.

Yesterday morning, Mr. Mitchell, surgeon to the parish of St. Nectan's, was sent for in great haste, to attend an urgent case at the farmstead. He promptly obeyed the summons and found on his arrival, that the servant had been that morning delivered of twins, and was now in a deplorable state, requiring urgent medical assistance.

This guilty wretch had strangled one of the infants and had attempted to strangle the other. This vile creature had not been entirely successful in her bidding and the pitiful subject of her unnatural cruelty survived for an hour after the surgeon's arrival.

Of course, before an inquest, our information may be subject to correction, but we firmly believe that we are substantially correct in our statements. The discovery of this appalling crime was made by Jack Parkin, a young farmhand, who came to the house prior attending his stock. He discovered the woman doubled-up with pain. She said she was ill, and the lad questioned her further when he observed some alarming appearances on the kitchen floor. The detained accounted for it by stating that she had vomited some blood and she would soon be better. Parkin was furthered alarmed by the feeble cries of an infant. He discovered the poor child, close to death secreted in a wash basket and wrapped in a common tea towel, struggling for breath. It was at this point that the farmhand called for the master.

The second child had already expired and was discovered in a wooden blanket box at the foot of the accused's bed and bore striking red marks upon its neck, as if pressed between a person's fingers, the eyes protruding from their sockets. The other child that clung dearly to life also bore the mark of violence around its neck and soon expired. We understand that this monster of all mothers is doing quite well and evinces little concern about her atrocious conduct. A Coroner's inquest will be held tomorrow when a searching investigation will take place."

23

Eliza, August 1891 - The Inquest, Day One

Susannah pushed back the off-white lace curtains and observed the rabble down below. The inconsiderate throng had set the dogs off and she could barely hear her own thoughts. It was the wretched Coroner's fault. He had been due back from Exeter the day before, but owing to delays had adjourned the hearing to the morning. 'Unforeseen circumstances' had delayed this nightmare by a further four hours and now the sound of mass impatience was beginning to twist her nerves.

There was nobody else to help in the house. Clements had taken the ghost-child with her to tend her soon-to-be-ghost mother and Eliza, whom she had grown to depend upon, had been carried away to the Lively's by her oh-so-gallant husband. She assumed that the Captain was somewhere in the house, but she had neither the curiosity nor the inclination to seek his company. If it hadn't been for Parkin senior, there would have been no one to lay out the bodies in the parlour and she probably would have had to attend them herself. The notion of laying out her adulterous husband's dead off-spring filled her with horror and the thought that they lay there in her home ensured that she remained securely in her own room.

Susannah had received notice that the Coroner was on his way, and she needed to extract herself from her room to testify. As she was considered a pivotal witness there was no way to avoid this necessity to speak in public. She took one last look at herself in the mirror and pulled up her high-neck lace collar to hide the streaks of scarlet and purple bruising on her recently throttled throat. She hated her husband, but she was determined that his recent diabolical conduct was not going to drag her reputation through the mire.

The impatient jury and local spectators started to bang loudly at the door. She had no intention of letting them into her home before the coroner had arrived, and she expected her husband to open the doors. Susannah's fear of the public overcame her natural fear of the dead and she ventured into the parlour to satisfy her morbid curiosity as to what his bastard children looked like. Anyone with an ounce of empathy would have been deeply moved by the pitiful sight of the two tiny open caskets and their delicate contents, but Susannah could only view them in the context of her own losses. She had lost a life that worked for her limitations - a quiet life of solitude with few demands made upon her. She had lost the person who had removed her burden to attend to her husband's basest needs and the person to whom she could delegate her parental duties.

The infants had been laid with care and were swaddled

in white crocheted blankets that had been procured from the trunk containing their half-sister's baby clothes. Both were small, with the male child significantly smaller than his sister. The female child had a pretty rose-bud pout which was spoilt by the dark red crusting from her flared nostrils. They would have been considered bonny babies were it not for the pallid blue hue of their waxy looking skin and the dark purple marks around their necks. Susannah gently stroked her own sore neck and the thought raced through her mind that maybe hers was not the only throat that had been violently squeezed by the hands of her husband. Both babies were at peace now, but their fragile frames suggested a violent demise at the hands of an unknown perpetrator. Susannah felt chilled that she too might have been laying in a casket waiting for the coroner if she hadn't escaped to the safety of her room.

On the arrival of the Coroner, Mr. John Babbage Esq, the jurors and witnesses were led into the dining room by the Captain.

The proceedings were swiftly opened and the jurors introduced. Babbage informed the jurors that the object of the inquiry was to ascertain whether the infants were born alive, and how and by what means that they had met their deaths... whether by natural cause or by violence. If by the latter means, by whom was that violence committed.

"I have no doubts that you may have heard many reports touching upon the subject of this enquiry, but I must impress upon you the duty of divesting your minds of every scrap of gossip or innuendo that you may have heard or read on the subject and to concentrate upon giving a true verdict based upon the evidence alone. If you are satisfied from the evidence that violence has been perpetrated by the mother of the offspring, then it is your duty to place her in such a position as she might be put on trial for the offence, however painful this might be to your sensibilities," directed Babbage.

"I am duty-bound to divulge the contents of a letter sent by Captain Usbourne, charging me with dereliction of my duty as Coroner. He is threatening to report my conduct to the Home Secretary. I would like to point out that this is the first time in my experience as a Coroner that such a charge has been made against me or such a threat held out. I would like to apologise wholeheartedly for any inconvenience caused by my inability to attend the initial enquiry, and that Captain Usbourne is at liberty to take the course that he thinks proper. For the record, I was attending my duty at the General Quarter Sessions of the County in Exeter. When I telegraphed to him that his presence was required to attend this hearing, the Captain responded that he was suffering from an indisposition and would be unable to attend. I am pleased to observe that a change of heart has resulted in the attendance of the said Captain."

Susannah was listening to the proceedings and was sure that the Captain had remained at the farm, despite not seeing him. She quickly shuffled out of the way back to the kitchen when she heard that the jurors were to inspect the corpses. It didn't take long for the men to look at the bodies. There wasn't much to observe and they soon made their way back to continue the hearing. Jack Parkin was sworn in as the first witness.

"I am Jack Parkin, farmhand to the Usbourne estate and son of Jake Parkin the estate manager." He recalled his movements and conversations with Eliza to the jury, while nervously looking up at his father, who stood firmly by his master's side.

He could feel Usbourne's eyes boring deep into him. In a well-rehearsed fashion, he explained how he found the servant in a very poorly way and how she denied that she had a child, despite the sound of cries coming from the direction of the washing basket.

"She had her hand across the face of the infant. I grabbed her other arm and told her that she was not to kill it. I said so because I thought she was pressing on it. It was then that I decided to fetch the master."

"And how did your master react when you informed him of the event?"

"He was frightened sir and so was the mistress. Eliza had the little one on her lap and under the mistress's direction I took it from her and placed it on the kitchen table. I then moved the cloth from the child's face and saw its head. It made me sick to the stomach and I had to go out to the yard for a minute or two. When I returned, I heard the mistress question Eliza about whether she had had another child. She said yes but didn't think it would live long. I saw the child... I'm not sure which one, but I saw it move. The master picked Eliza up and took her to her bedroom. He then told me to saddle a horse and he rode back to St. Nectan's to see if he could get a medical man."

"And who was that medical man?" asked Babbage.

"Mr. Mitchell Sir," replied the young lad, who was then happy to step down.

Mr. Mitchell was then summonsed to testify to the jury. Mitchell raised his eyes to the ceiling to signify his presence and formerly identified himself in front of the coroner. The young surgeon looked distinctly uncomfortable as he closely scanned every face of the gathered crowd. He noticed how relieved Jack looked after delivering his version of events. He also saw the confidence on Parkin senior's face now that his close alliance with the Usbourne family had been preserved. He studied the Captain and his wife who now stood united together, their eyes staring intently on the medic who was now about to make his first inquest of importance. He knew he bore a huge responsibility and that his testimony could send a woman to the gallows. He also knew that there was more to this situation than had previously been revealed and understood that the power of his testimony would make others in the room nervous. His strong faith earnestly governed his need for the truth and justice, and he was determined to deliver his findings in the most impartial way possible.

"Last Wednesday, Jack Parkin arrived at my surgery to advise me that my help was needed urgently. I was told that a young servant had secretly given birth and was in dire need of medical attention. We went directly to his house where I found that his servant-girl had been confined with twins. On entering the bedroom, I found Eliza Barton lying on her bed with her bedclothes on. She was faint and in a semi-conscious condition. I observed a male child lying in a blanket box at the end of her bed. He was wrapped in bloodied sheets. I took the child, but he had already passed. A woman – Mrs. Parkin was also in the room holding the female child in her arms, wrapped in a tea-towel. The child was breathing and crying weakly. There was bleeding from her mouth and nostrils and her eyes were open and distinctly blood-shot. On the lower part of the front of the child's neck I noticed a bruise about the size of a two-shilling piece extending to the left side of the windpipe. My attention was then directed at Eliza Barton who lay in a half-conscious state. Her pulse was weak, and she was in need of stimulants, which I administered. I satisfied myself that she had been recently confined."

The young medic paused for breath. He didn't need to look at his audience to realise that they were hanging on his every syllable and word. The morose crowd stood like children morbidly listening to one of Grimm's darkest tales and he could feel their revulsion as he continued.

"I then directed my attention to the female child, whom I feared would not be long for this world. I ordered a warm bath and tried to administer some sustenance. The child became weaker and weaker... and soon expired. I continued with the mother for a further five hours, until I estimated that it was safe for me to leave. When she had regained full consciousness, I asked her where she had had the child and she told me that she was delivered of a child in the washroom. I then questioned whether she had given birth to the other child there, and she replied that she was unaware that she had delivered a second child. She said that she had been taken ill in the early hours of the morning and that she had given birth in the washroom, and then had to answer the door to let the farmhand in. She also made some communication to me with regard of the paternity of the children, but that is of little value."

Mitchell realised he had probably divulged too much and could see the fury brewing in the Captain's face. Mrs. Usbourne looked as if she was about to swoon.

"Why do you believe that the paternity of these poor unfortunates is of little value?" Babbage questioned.

"The very fact that they both expired at such a tender age leads me to believe that their paternity bears no relevance to this case Sir." The young physician tried to back-track unconvincingly on his statement.

"Would you be willing to write the name down for me to examine?" enquired the coroner.

"Yes Sir," responded Mitchell reluctantly. He realised that he had no real option other than to divulge the children's paternity. He scribbled down his evidence, carefully folded the paper and passed it directly to Babbage. The silence within the room made Susannah's head reel. She sensed that her secluded little world was about to implode.

Usbourne stood there in defiance, silently repeating the mantra of "Lincoln is a bastard, I'm not like him!" over and over again in an endless whirl of pathetic self-justification. Babbage unfolded the paper and then stared intently at the newly unified Usbournes. He cleared his throat in an exaggerated fashion and requested that Mitchell should continue. He left the spectators in little doubt as to the identity of the father of Eliza Barton's children.

As Mitchell proceeded with his medical evidence of the infants' post-mortem, Susannah spied Mrs. Lively and her maid-servant outside the kitchen window. They were trying to push their way in through the crowd of spectators. Susannah realised that they should be prevented from entering at all costs. She alerted Parkin senior, who immediately left the kitchen to apprehend the unwanted visitors. When his polite refusal to let Mrs. Lively enter was met with an impassioned demonstration, he gently pushed the reverend's wife back into the road and informed her that the evidence was too gruesome for a gentle woman such as herself, and that she would be better off back at home. Mrs. Lively persisted in her bid to enter the farmstead, but was forcibly led out by one of Usbourne's gamekeepers, bundled into the back of a cart and escorted from the estate. Parkin returned to the proceedings and apologised for interrupting the surgeon.

Mitchell continued. "I proceeded with the post-mortem on the female child, and I found that her windpipe contained a quantity of frothy, bloody mucus, and its inner surface was somewhat congested."

"Can you account for the existence of this appearance on the inner surface of the throat?" questioned Babbage.

"I am of the opinion that such an appearance might have been caused by the external bruising."

"Without interrupting your statement, can you form any opinion as to whether it was produced during life?"

"I believe that this injury could only have been inflicted whilst the child was still alive. The effusion of frothy mucus would not have been produced post-mortem. I continued with my examination and found nothing abnormal in the abdomen, but I did find a quantity of extravasated blood, and the vessels of the interior of the head presented the slight appearance of congestion." Mitchell sensed that the Corner was about to ask the most pertinent question of the enquiry so far.

"Now, Mr. Mitchell, what in your opinion was the cause of death?"

Mitchell bit his lip as he mulled over the evidence and the potential consequence of his words. He hesitated before replying somewhat reluctantly.

"From the healthy state of the internal parts I consider that the child lived for some time, but from its otherwise puny condition would not have survived for very long. I believe that the external injuries on the throat were sufficient to cause the child's death."

The jury and spectators muttered to each other and started to look around for answers.

"Is there any possibility that these injuries could have been caused during the process of self-delivery?" asked the coroner.

"It is possible that the marks on the neck might have been produced in attempts at self-delivery, but not probable," Mitchell replied with a heavy heart.

"Thank you for your testimony Mr. Mitchell. I would now like to call upon Mrs Susannah Usbourne to testify before the jury."

The instant the coroner summonsed Susannah her pulse raced, her heart thumped loudly, and she experienced the distinct feeling of faintness. Her vision started to blur, and her thoughts became muddied and confused. Susannah had no intention of telling them what they wanted to hear. She wasn't going to be judged to satisfy their twisted curiosity. It was none of their business. Susannah looked at the Captain and felt a rush of power push through her body. She realised that she could destroy him. Her knowledge could ruin him and place him before a judge testifying for his life. But this wasn't the only secret that bound them together and she was canny enough to understand that he too could incriminate her for her past deeds. She loathed the outside world much more than she loathed her husband and she didn't want to give them the pleasure of seeing him publicly ripped to shreds. She rubbed her sweaty palms deep into the folds of her navy-blue dress and felt her knees buckle under the strain as she moved towards the coroner. She was handed the bible in preparation to take her oath.

"I never take an oath!" she exclaimed and pushed the family Bible back firmly towards the Coroner.

A shocked gasp ran round the crowd.

"Upon what grounds ma'am?"

The Coroner was dumbfounded. Susannah paused while she reconsidered her options. She remembered the many visits paid by the Reverend Lively and their involved discourses on the importance of truth and justice. His visits were not wasted. She had been a willing pupil but now she was going to pervert his teachings to satisfy her own needs.

"Because we are all commanded by our Lord in both chapter five of St. Matthew and chapter five of the Epistle of James to 'swear not at all'. To do so would be against a sacred commandment."

In his twenty-five years of service, Babbage had never experienced such an uncompromising witness and was especially vexed that this lack of co-operation should come from a woman.

"May I clarify your position? Are you are refusing to be sworn in on the grounds of religious principle?"

"I am!" she replied victoriously.

"Under these circumstances I cannot take your evidence. You may go for now but let me assure you that I am not yet done with you! I now call Captain Usbourne to testify."

Usbourne was admiring Susannah's boldness and resolved to follow her example. He could prove to be equally uncooperative and belligerent. He had no case to answer - after all, he wasn't Lincoln, Lincoln was a bastard...

"Your name Sir?" said Babbage.

Usbourne was still inwardly chanting this mantra as he replied: - "I am Captain Samuel Frederick Lincoln of the parish of St. Nectan's." He spluttered: - "I mean, I am Captain Samuel Frederick Usbourne of the parish of St. Nectan's!"

"You don't seem very sure of your own person Sir!"

"I am Usbourne. Anyone in this room can testify to that," he replied testily.

The Captain felt humiliated and was even more determined not to give satisfaction that afternoon.

"Then, will you please be sworn in for this hearing."

"I will not. Like my wife I am a man of religious principle and I concur with her opinion that one should not swear at all. It would be of no use anyway, as I am in a deeply agitated state and would prove to be a useless witness. I know nothing of any relevance to this situation and therefore it suits no purpose to repeat it."

"Are there any circumstances in which you could be persuaded to testify?"

"No, I'm afraid not."

The Captain could sense his tactics were beginning to weaken the resolve of the Coroner, who was anxious that the proceedings should not go beyond five o'clock. Consequently, the exasperated Coroner decided to adjourn the hearing until ten o'clock the next morning.

The gathering filed out in frustration. Those that they suspected were in the know were not prepared to divulge their secrets. It was a shocking affair, the like of which St. Nectan's had never seen before. Those poor babes. To what evil had they been subjected in their brief and tragic lives? Some had heard that the little slut had done this sort of thing before and had only narrowly escaped with her life then. Others speculated that the Usbournes were as guilty as Hell and that's where they would end up when they stopped hiding behind their blessed principles. There was much tutting and scratching of heads, and many continued the debate over a few hearty pints of ale down at the Quay.

The Captain waited until the horde was out of earshot. He poured himself a large brandy and one for his wife. His hands visibly shook as he poured the chestnut-coloured fluid from the delicate crystal decanter. He dripped a few drops of laudanum into Susannah's glass and decided to make his peace with the woman who could have so easily had tied a noose around his neck.

"Nothing has changed!" she stated as he passed the peace offering. "When this debacle is over I never want to see you again. Is that understood?"

Usbourne failed to grace his wife with an answer and sullenly left the room. Susannah could feel the laudanum course through her body, spreading warmth and bliss through every vein and capillary. The heady mixture of alcohol and opiate gave her the resolve to go back to her room and deal with Phillip's disappointment.

24

Eliza, August 1891 - The Inquest, Day Two

Amanda Lively was the first to arrive for the second day of the hearing. She was determined not to be man-handled again, and appeared with her husband's burly manservant, who could equal the brute strength of Usbourne's gamekeeper. She needed to know that Eliza was innocent. She needed to know that her charge had been wronged and that the perpetrators of her abuse should be exposed, with justice served. And yet, there was a nagging doubt in her mind gnawing away at her good-will. She truly wanted to believe that Eliza was incapable of performing such a terrible crime, but how could one girl be so very unlucky? Why would the good Lord test the poor child so?

Her husband had advised her to stay away from the hearing and to let justice take its course. He didn't believe in Eliza. He had seen it all before. Young girls free with their services and quick to complain when they had to pay the price for their wantonness. He had witnessed umpteen illegitimates struggle for life in the workhouse, and he had heard the disturbing tales of new-born babies found writhing in the privy or being stifled with a surreptitious pinch of the nose and the covering of the mouth. He had seen girls like Eliza before and whilst he commended his wife's devotion to the needy and the downtrodden, he wished that she wouldn't become so involved in the troubles of her protégés. This one could leave her heart-broken and destroy her faith in human goodness.

The previous day's hearing had caused a sensation in the village and many more people arrived to hear the next instalment of the proceedings. Parkin had even found some opportunistic pedlar trying to sell mock broadsides of Eliza's hanging, with gory details of the murder of the twins and her last words on the scaffold. He ripped a sheet from the hands of a passer-by and tore it to shreds. The crude description of the children being slain by the hand of their vile and murderous mother revolted him, but there were many in the crowd who were happy to part with a penny for this sensationalised fiction.

When Babbage arrived, he wasted little time and called the first witness of the day – Mrs. Parkin. The estate manager's wife reluctantly stepped forward and was sworn in with little fuss.

"I am Matilda Parkin, dressmaker and wife of Jake Parkin, estate manager of Usbourne's. My son Jack informed me that Eliza had had a child and that my assistance was required. I entered the farmhouse to find Eliza sitting in the washroom with a poorly baby on her lap. 'Eliza what have you done?' I asked and she told me that she had had a baby - come before its time. I told her I knew that she was enceinte some weeks ago, but she said her stays were bad and that she needed some new. I offered to measure her for some new ones, but she snapped at me and told me I would have to wait until she had some money. Eliza was in a bad way and the Captain carried her upstairs to her room while I followed. Her bed had been stripped and the sheets were badly bloodied and bundled into a blanket box. I noticed there was some weak movement and when I pulled back the sheet, I found a tiny little scrap of a thing. Mrs. Usbourne had entered the room, but soon left when the Captain picked the child up and passed it to me. He told me to give the child to its mother. I then went downstairs to fetch the other child. When I returned, I saw the Captain had taken the first child away from Eliza – it was dead. 'What have you done to the child?' he asked Eliza, but she said nothing. She turned over and drifted off to sleep. We placed the dead child at the foot of the bed, and I comforted the other."

Her testimony was briefly interrupted by a tearful villager who could no longer contain her emotions and was sent out of the room to spare her further distress.

"Please continue Mrs. Parkin," said the Coroner.

"It was at that time that Mr. Mitchell the surgeon showed up. He looked at the dead baby and then he examined Eliza. He took the little girl and instructed me to fetch some sugared water and to prepare a warm bath to see if he could revive the child. As I prepared the babe, I removed the cloth that covered its face, and I noticed a bruise on its neck. The baby's eyes were wide and startled and it was bleeding from the nostrils. When the baby seemed a little more settled, we tried to give it some food, but it could not swallow. The child died not long after. I am proud to say that I have born and baptised thirteen children, but I have never seen a new-born in such a deplorable state as this one!"

"Thank you, Mrs. Parkin for the satisfactory way you delivered some very unsavoury evidence, under very difficult circumstances. I now wish to inform the jury that my clerk has confirmed that the Law Procedure Act of 1854 makes provision for witnesses with conscientious scruples. This law enables the said witnesses to give evidence without the need to be sworn in, thus bypassing the need to compromise their sensibilities. It is my belief that the testimony of Mrs. Usbourne is indispensable to the enquiry and should be taken without the need to be sworn in. However, should the witness refuse once more, there would be no alternative but to commit Mrs. Usbourne for contempt. I would therefore now like to call forward Mrs. Susannah Usbourne," summoned the Coroner with an air of triumph.

Susannah's faced blanched at the prospect of having to testify. She believed that she had done enough to thwart the Coroner and to avoid standing before the rabble. She released the arm of her husband and once more took to the centre of the room.

"You are here to give evidence concerning the death of the new-born infants in your home last Wednesday. Please step forward to take the oath," the Coroner requested firmly.

Susannah swallowed hard; her parched throat could barely articulate.

"I refuse to take an oath!" she muttered under her breath.

"The Law Procedure Act confers the power and responsibility upon me on behalf of Parliament to accept your evidence without being sworn in. I can accept your solemn declaration as a suitable substitute. May I remind you that you are bound both by honour and the laws of this land to comply with this request and failure to do so will result in your arrest for contempt. I hope I make myself perfectly clear on this account." Babbage was more than happy to settle the score publicly with this uncooperative female.

"Perfectly," she responded tersely. She braced herself and stepped forward to make her declaration, unsure of which direction she was about to take.

"I Susannah Frances Usbourne do solemnly, sincerely, and truly declare that the taking of any oath is, according to my religious belief, unlawful, and I do also declare that I am the wife of Captain Samuel Frederick Usbourne of the parish of St. Nectan's. I reside in Great Usbourne House, of the same parish. I have a domestic servant named Eliza Barton, who came into our service in December last year."

"Were you and your husband aware of Eliza's past history?" enquired the coroner.

"Yes, we were. We took her on as an act of Christian charity with the idea that we could encourage her reformation."

"Please can you clarify what Eliza's past was… specifically?"

"Yes Sir. Eliza Barton already had an illegitimate child living with family in the North of the county and she had already been convicted of concealment and served six months in prison."

Susannah knew that this would titillate the local gossips. The spectators reacted audibly with many stating that this confirmed the rumours percolating through the village were true… she was a baddun and she would surely hang for this one!

"Please calm down and let the lady testify. It has taken me a whole day and an Act of Parliament to encourage this witness to give evidence and I don't want to stop her now!" Babbage pushed his round spectacles back onto his pudgy nose.

Susannah did not like being teased in such a manner and would have walked away, but for the threat of conviction.

"I frequently questioned her about being in the family way and each time she denied it. About two months ago I begged her to tell the truth. I promised not to divulge her secret. I said that I would consider taking her back once the child had been born. I implored her not to allow such a thing to happen in my house as happened at the Hilton's in Barnstaple, but she continued to deny her state. She claimed that she was dropsical. I believed her right up until last Wednesday when I was woken early by the shouting of our young farmhand Jack. He told me Eliza had had a child in the washroom and that I was needed. All my fears were confirmed. I knew she would bring disgrace and scandal to the sanctuary of our home and here we are now!"

"I went downstairs and discovered Eliza in the washroom with a little bundle bound in one of my tea towels twisted up at one end. I reproached her for having deceived me. I told the lad to take the bundle away from her and he placed it on the table. He unwrapped the child, but its appearance was so unnatural that it made the poor boy sick, and he had to go into the yard to relieve himself. I became unwell with a headache, and I ran upstairs to tell my husband that Eliza had had a baby, and that judging by its appearance she had tried to murder it. The Captain rushed downstairs to see what was amiss and soon returned carrying Eliza, shortly followed by Mrs. Parkin.

Mrs. Parkin noticed something unusual in the blanket box and discovered there was another child. It was even smaller than the first and had been placed in bloodied sheets. It was a fine boy. There were no marks on it, but it had a strange bluey, purple colour. I said it looked as if she had tried to suffocate it under all those sheets. The Captain picked the child up. I could not bear to look at it, so I left the room. Shortly afterwards I was informed that the child had died. I was not surprised. I went back to my room. I was feeling too ill to wait for the doctor. That is all I know."

Susannah finished abruptly, hoping that she had given just enough to satisfy the Coroner.

"Thank you Mrs. Usbourne. I live in hope that your testimony was not too traumatic and that you still have your religious principles intact!" remarked Babbage, somewhat sarcastically.

Much to Susannah's relief she was able to return to her husband's side. He gently squeezed her arm in appreciation, but she instantly recoiled from his grip, making him fully aware that there had been no change of heart at all.

"I am of the belief that the testimony of Captain Usbourne is also of the utmost relevance to this hearing, and I would like to recall him to make a declaration," called Babbage.

The Captain made his way to the centre and once more refused to take an oath on religious grounds and garbled his declaration. He felt foolish. Everybody in the room knew who he was. He had played cards with most on the jury or at least had been drinking pals with them at one time or another. The whole affair was ridiculous. None-the-less he reluctantly made his declaration.

"I do solemnly declare that on the morning of Wednesday last I was rudely awoken by farmhand Jack Parkin and my wife and told that Eliza had been delivered of a child that morning."

"Were you aware that your servant was likely to give birth?" interrupted the Coroner.

"No Sir, I was not. It was a total shock!"

"That is not so!" cried Amanda Lively from the crowd.

"I can assure you that IS so!" retorted Usbourne angrily.

"Do you have proof that Captain Usbourne was aware of Eliza Barton's condition? Did you speak to him personally about the situation?" Babbage asked Mrs. Lively.

"No Sir."

"Then may I remind you that your comment is surplus to our enquiry, and that as such I may charge you with contempt should you continue to interrupt the testimony of Captain Usbourne."

Amanda was about to respond, when her burly manservant took the liberty of stepping in front of her, allowing Usbourne to continue.

"I went downstairs to find Mrs. Parkin speaking with Eliza, who was very ill. I carried the servant upstairs and we discovered another child close to death suffocating under some sheets in a blanket box. I picked the child up and passed it to Mrs. Parkin who gave the child to its mother. Mrs. Parkin went to fetch the other child. I had to look away ... I'm not comfortable with women's affairs and I felt uncomfortable as a gentleman being in her presence. When I looked back at mother and child, I saw that the baby was dead. I asked Eliza what she had done to the child, but she said nothing. Mrs. Parkin returned with the other baby, and we placed the dead one at the bottom of the bed. It was then that I left to fetch the surgeon."

"Were you at any time left alone with either of the children?" enquired the coroner.

"No, I was not."

"That is all!" Babbage instructed.

"I would now like to address the jury. As I stated at the beginning of this hearing; the object of this enquiry is to establish whether the infants were born alive, and by what means these children met with their deaths. It is your duty to establish whether they died by natural causes or by violence. If it was by violence; by whom was that violence committed. Please pay careful attention to the evidence that has been presented before you. I would particularly like to commend the quality of evidence that has been provided by Mr. Mitchell, the surgeon, which is of scientific value. I now dismiss the jury to consult their verdict on this case," Babbage concluded.

The jury filed into the dining room leaving the spectators at a loss of what to do with themselves. Some left believing that there was too little time left in the day for a verdict, others remained to deliberate and analyse the evidence that had been presented. For those that remained their patience was rewarded, for after only twenty minutes the jury resurfaced ready to deliver their verdict. The Usbournes were hastily extracted from their respective boltholes and the throng reassembled in the kitchen. The kettle barely had chance to boil, and the jury had little time to sup the generous bounty that had been provided in the deliberation room.

The Speaker for the jury took to the centre of the room.

"Have you reached a unanimous or a majority verdict?" asked Babbage.

"A unanimous one sir! We the jury have found that both the twins born to Eliza Barton died violently at the hands of their mother. We therefore deliver a verdict of WILFUL MURDER against ELIZA BARTON on both infants."

Amanda Lively cried out; "How so? How can you possibly find her guilty? She has no case to answer. The children were born too..." but she was silenced as her manservant bundled her out the room for her own safety.

"Eliza Barton will be taken to Barnstaple borough prison as soon as she able to travel and will be transferred to the county gaol at Exeter at the earliest opportunity. I now hereby formerly close this hearing," Babbage declared.

His chubby fingers shuffled his papers, and he removed his glasses from his sweating, puffy face. He left the room leaving a vacuum of authority and creating a space for others to pour scorn over the whole sordid affair. The audience eventually drifted off back to their own lives, the house was cleared of its unwanted visitors, and the Usbournes left alone to fill the void.

"Satisfied?" Susannah asked Usbourne.

"Most definitely!" But his satisfaction was short lived.

"Good. Then you can leave." Susannah loosened the wedding band from her finger and placed it on the table. The Captain understood there was no point in demonstrating his dismay and duly followed his wife's example and placed his wedding ring by the side of hers.

"What of the child? When am I expected to see her?"

"Take her to London with you." Susannah saw the opportunity to be rid of the ghost-child as well as her husband.

"I think not. My house is no place for a child. She is better off with you in the country."

"I see. In other words, you don't want your daughter curbing your debauched lifestyle and once more I must take up the responsibility. Very well, I shall not step in your way. Just be sure to inform me before you visit, so I may avoid your company."

"What about Usbourne's?" said the Captain. "This estate has been in my family for generations. I can't just walk away."

"You should have thought of that before you gambled the lion share of your fortune away. It is my money that has maintained this property and my management that has kept the bailiffs from the door. I see no reason why you should feel aggrieved at my living here with your daughter. The property will stay in the blood line - I shall not sell."

Usbourne conceded without further discourse. Susannah was victorious. She had finally won the bitter matrimonial war and as victor she claimed the estate as reparation. Admittedly, she would rather that custody of the ghost-child had been given to the father, but as with all peace deals, compromises had to be made.

"I can only hope that you never bring trouble to my door again and that at some point your failings will catch-up with you."

Susannah left the room freed from the burden of having to deal with her husband again. Phillip would be pleased with her for finally shaking free of her spouse, although a little disappointed that the ghost-child was to remain as an unfortunate reminder of their disastrous marriage.

Usbourne waited for his wife to vacate the room before

scooping up the twin bands of misplaced vows and broken bonds. He placed them into his pocket. He knew the value of gold and even when his chips were down. He would be able to raise a little capital and pay off some debts. He had never felt the true owner of Usbournes. It had never been intended that he should inherit the estate and it never truly felt like his. He now realised it was Clemency who was destined to inherit the land of his forefathers. He was just a temporary caretaker, a subordinate who was never up to the task. No matter what; he had unfinished business to conclude in town and the sooner he could track down the scoundrel the quicker he could conclude his affairs.

25

Usbourne, August 1891 - The North Devon Free Press - Horse Whipping

"LOCAL PROFESSIONAL HORSE WHIPPED!...

On Friday last, a serious and unprovoked attack was committed upon a respected member of our local community. Mr. Charles Robert Mitchell, of the parish of St. Nectan's was set upon by a person who has resided for several years in the same parish as a gentleman. The incident has stimulated a great deal of interest, both from its novelty and the position of the parties involved. The assailant Mr. Samuel Frederick Usbourne, of Great Usbourne House, St. Nectan's and his victim Mr. Mitchell, surgeon of the same parish were both recently witnesses in particularly gruesome case of infanticide. Eliza Barton, the woman charged with the said offence was a household servant of Mr. Usbourne and Mr. Mitchell was the surgeon that attended the woman and her infants. As far as we can ascertain, the evidence was unequivocal and implicated no one else beside the unnatural mother.

Considerable excitement has been produced by this savage and unnecessary assault, by the intelligence that Mr. Usbourne had been escorted back from London by Superintendent Rottenbury by train and later brought before the magistrates. A considerable crowd greeted Usbourne on his return to the county, in a style usual with the populace towards persons who have transgressed the laws of public decorum and gentlemanly conduct. The prisoner has made it crystal clear that he has no intention of denying the charge and has already admitted to having horse whipped the surgeon. Mr. Usbourne was also desirous for the public to know that he had not gone away out of cowardice, but to ensure that all his financial affairs were left in order, as he has a sick and suffering wife at home whom he was desirous to relieve.

Charlie Alcott, a lad of thirteen, son of John Alcott, butcher, from Bideford was the first witness. Charlie testified that he was in the market, when he was approached by the defendant and requested that the lad run an errand for him to which his father consented. The boy was instructed to go to Mr. Mitchell, who was staying at his parent's house in the town and tell him that a man had been hurt by a piece of timber falling upon from the Old Custom House. The defendant also requested that the boy keep the errand a secret. The lad was given sixpence for his troubles. The lad ran directly and delivered the message as instructed.

Mr. Charles Robert Mitchell was the next witness who collaborated that he had indeed received a message from the lad to *attend the accident. The surgeon thought it strange at the time that he should be approached at his parent's house in Bideford as he normally resided in St. Nectan's. he questioned the boy who stated that he had been asked to run the errand by a gentleman. He immediately abandoned his affairs and left to attend the accident. It was during his travels that he was attacked from behind with repeated and violent blows to his body and head. At first the surgeon could not see his attacker but was able to swing round and saw that it was Usbourne. The surgeon protected himself as well as he could from the attack and was offered refuge from the assault by a Mrs. Hockings who was able to slam her door on the assailant. It is reported that Usbourne continued to whip the door for some time. The victim has stated that he has not exchanged any words with his attacker since the inquest and that the attack was perfectly unprovoked. The prisoner also had a large deerhound with him, which was also used against the surgeon. Mr. Mitchell sustained several blows to the head and was covered in blood and bruises. Mrs. Hockings was called and collaborated with the victim's testimony.*

Mr. Usbourne testified that he was responsible for the attack, that he had thrashed the scoundrel and left town to arrange for funds for his wife in case he was incarcerated and fully intended to return under his own volition. Mr. Baker, who represented the prisoner stated that Mr. Usbourne had openly admitted responsibility for the assault, one that on reflection he deeply regretted that his feelings should betray him, but he had acted under great excitement. Baker stated that the prisoner had been under a great deal of stress, as a household servant had been delivered of two children in his home and that an inquest had proven that they came to their deaths by violent means. The mother of the children had been committed upon a charge of wilful murder and will stand trial at Exeter in due course. Mr. Mitchell was the surgeon that had been called upon and his evidence included spurious charges against Usbourne had been made by the servant, which had been calculated to cause damage to Mr. Usbourne's character. Mitchell's conduct ensured that these falsehoods had been made public, without the prisoner having the opportunity to rebut them. The prisoner is also of the belief that said findings were then talked of around the town by Mitchell, consequently despoiling his good name. Whilst his client could not justify the assault, he hoped that his testimony accounted for the exasperation that he was feeling when the assault took place. Mr. Baker also stated that there was no evidence to imply that the assault was of a very violent nature nor had Mr. Mitchell been injured or laid aside thereby.

After much deliberation the jury came forth with a verdict of GUILTY OF AGGRAVATED ASSAULT WITH MITIGATING CIRCUMSTANCES and was fined £50 and was bound over to keep the peace."

26

Donna and Algie, June 2012

It was early in the morning – super early, ridiculously early and Donna was already awake and troubled. She was wrapped in Algie's old multi-coloured striped dressing gown, knees up under her chin, arms closely hugging her legs staring at a peacefully slumbering Algie, who was blissfully unaware. What the feck had she done?

As if her life wasn't complicated enough, she had gone and made things even more stupidly complex and now she was going to have to deliver the bombshell.

Poor Algie, he hadn't done anything wrong... in fact the very opposite! He was kind, considerate and amusing. She really hadn't banked on being so willing to be seduced by this charming and quietly passionate man who was now wrapped in the cosy blanket of false security.

The evening didn't have the most promising of starts. As usual, Donna's unique perception of time meant that she was dramatically late for her rendezvous at the Dog. All day her inner saboteur had been whittling away at her self-confidence, and she had been debating whether to phone and cancel. The hot topic of today's self-destructive narrative was how to slip into the conversation that she was in the family way with her bastard ex-husband's child. This would surely blow the whole relationship out of the water long before Algie had the chance to put the boot in. He was bound to drop her anyway and telling him about junior Barnard would just provide him with the ammunition that he needed. He could get himself out of an awkward situation without having to be the guilty party.

She had been mentally shaving off layers of reasons as to why he was going to dump her. Now there was nothing left but a puny, brittle toothpick of self-worth.

No, she'd better get out of this before she vested any more time and emotion into this doomed relationship that would probably leave her feeling vulnerable and wretched. All she had to do was to select her method of rejection and deliver the elbow-bomb ASAP before anyone got hurt.

She had considered phoning, but there had been a thunderstorm the night before, shorting out the power and killing the landline. She couldn't believe that a simple storm could rip her from the twenty-first century and zap her back in time by a hundred years, just by a simple flash of lightening. It wasn't the first time it had happened, but it always took the telephone company a few days to rectify the fault. The storm had also hit the local mast and robbed her of internet and mobile connection. Jude said she would have to get used to it, as it was one of the many pleasures of living on a remote Devonian peninsula that frequently enjoyed tempestuous weather.

Donna knew she couldn't keep the poor man hanging on forever, and she never thought much of those who were prepared to give someone the flick via the 'Dear John' method. There was only one thing for it. She would have to meet him as planned and deliver the news in person. If only she could have a stiff drink before-hand to supply the courage she so clearly lacked. Being pregnant wasn't all that it was cracked up to be. No booze, no brie, no picking up cat shit – ok that one wasn't so bad, but the whole romantic glowing mum-to-be bullshit had started to wear a bit thin.

Then there was Eliza to consider. Like a moth to a flame, Donna had become strangely obsessed by the plight of this enigmatic young infanticidal mother who had started to take priority in her research. There was always the chance that Algie might request that Eliza's letters should be returned if she decided to dump him. She might never find out what had happened to the poor unfortunate servant if she severed ties with her great-grandson.

Donna decided to open the envelope that her angelic archivist had handed to her earlier that afternoon. It contained copies of local newspaper reports revealing Eliza's second brush with the law. She sat engrossed, devouring every scrap of evidence and every sensationalised syllable of text. She was mortified beyond belief when she discovered that her great-great-grandfather was probably responsible for the poor girl's second fall from grace.

The feeling of ancestral responsibility hit her hard. The thought that one of her relatives had abused this poor young maidservant affected her deeply. Her pride for the Usbourne-Ruskin-Barnard clan was soon abandoned and replaced by ancestral guilt and a very real need to make amends. Donna needed those letters, if she was to discover Eliza's fate...

She had to talk to Algie immediately and explain her situation. She hoped he would be gentlemanly enough to allow her to finish her research. Donna grabbed her bag and her keys, and in the rush forgot her mobile.

Once more Gertie was a temperamental old cow and once more the heavens opened, and the sky fell in. The journey was slow and hazardous. The mid-summer storm had caused a few minor landslips and the road was full of bracken and large stones. The tangerine dream made slow progress and Donna could feel that the poor old girl beginning to labour. She limped past Barnstaple and eventually ground to a halt near Braunton. It took two hours for a rescue service to arrive and deliver the bad news: - her beloved VW was looking critical and was going to need intensive care and life-saving surgery.

After an emotional farewell and a desperate search for a taxi, Donna arrived in Georgeham completely soaked through, emotionally fraught and four hours late. Her emotional state was further heightened by the pub door being bolted. She had to bash loudly for Chloe to open.

"Are you alright Donna... you look a mess!" said Algie's perfectly wholesome daughter, helpfully.

"Don't ask! Is your old man still around?" Donna tried to sound casual and emotionally calm.

Chloe pointed to a secluded corner, where Algie, Compo and Clegg were slowly supping halves and playing bagatelle on an old, battered board that had been a part of the pub's general decor for over sixty years.

"Donna, you've surpassed yourself this time! You're only four hours late!"

Algie tried not to sound too annoyed and gently kissed her cheeks in continental fashion.

"It happened again!" exclaimed Donna. She showed him the envelope stuffed with the scandalous press cuttings. Algie looked at Donna, as if she had just spoken Swahili.

"I can honestly say I have not a clue what you are going on about!"

"Eliza! She was prosecuted a second time, this time with twins. And to cap it all, my great-great-grandfather was the bastard responsible for putting her in the family way!"

Algie's insecurities about Donna's interest in him were confirmed. She WAS only interested in his mad, sad, infanticidal great-grannie and not in his maddeningly attractive middle-aged body after all!

He said:- "Sorry Algie for being so late! Sorry for making you look like Billy no mates again and for making you sit with Compo and Clegg etc, etc, etc."

Algie's new best friends took offence at this and decided to bugger off back home to their long-lost wives.

"Oh my God! Algie, I'm so sorry. I got delayed and I couldn't phone because my landline is fucked and then Gertie died."

"What happened to Gertie? In fact, who is Gertie?"

"I think it's something to do with her carburettor or maybe the gearbox. I don't know, but it sounded pretty serious and expensive!"

"You're talking about your bloody van, aren't you?" Why

didn't you say that you'd broken down? I could have picked you up."

"I couldn't find my bloody mobile. I had to find a phone-box and they are as rare as hen's teeth and then I thought that I may as well call a taxi and save you the bother."

She hadn't actually thought about calling Algie for a lift. Algie made Donna a hot drink while Chloe finished closing and left to meet her new boyfriend.

"I honestly thought you had stood me up this time."

"Silly sod! It's not my style." Donna was trying to think of the nicest way to drop the e-bomb, when she started to shiver from being cold and damp.

"You'll catch your death staying in those clothes. Whip them off and I'll shove them in the tumble."

Who would have thought that the immortal words 'whip them off and I'll shove them in the tumble' would have been the words that would melt her resolve?

No clever one liner. No carefully rehearsed lines of pseudo-sophistication and no pointless big romantic gestures...

***

Donna woke to find herself protectively spooning Algie. She wondered how she could have been so easily and willingly lured into bed. She had finally met someone half-way decent, and now she was planning to treat him the same way that Colm had treated her over the years. She had never classed herself as one of the fuck 'em and chuck 'em brigade, but that was now exactly what she was contemplating. She got up and stared down at her naked forty-five-year-old body. Suddenly remembering that he had never seen her naked, and not wanting to spoil the mystique or frighten the poor guy, she reached for his old dressing gown. The last thing she wanted was for him to see her fatty middle-aged body before being dumped.

It troubled her that she might be ending something that had the promise of being interesting - something that might last. She decided to get dressed, but her attempt to put her clothes on quietly and unobtrusively failed miserably as she stumbled and knocked a glass of water all over the peacefully slumbering Algie. He woke with a start and grumbled loudly.

"What the hell was that for?"

He noticed that his new playmate was preparing to leave, and that it was very early in the morning.

"I'm sorry Algie. I think we need to talk."

27

Eliza, Berry Hill, March 1892

Eliza had never experienced a storm like it before. An almighty crack came from the leaden sky and flooded the countryside with dazzling blue-white light. In an instant an unnatural amount of cold spring rain was deposited upon the unsuspecting village. Semi-transparent sheets of liquid glass melted into large pools of bubbling, muddied water. From her vantage point she could see the villagers in the High Street scurrying around for temporary shelter from the violent storm, instantly transforming the busy road into a deserted cobbled waterway.

Eliza had lived by the sea all her life and was used to anything that the temperamental Atlantic could bestow upon the land, yet the power and violence of this storm worried her. She was sheltering in the dilapidated shack perched precariously at the top of her strawberry strip and she was sure she could feel it slip. It offered very little real shelter as great gushes of water poured through the gaps in the roof and onto her cloak.

Another violent crack of tempestuous electric Armageddon flashed across the valley and prompted Eliza to abandon the flimsily constructed shack of beer crates and driftwood just in time. The disintegrated heap of splintered wood was carried away by a newly awakened spring that pushed it down to the bottom of the strip like a crumpled sledge. She was convinced that she was listening to the sound of God's wrath, and that the power he was unleashing was enough to awaken the dead.

Eliza had hoped to make a start in clearing the strip of brambles before planting up her strawberry runners. Nature had reclaimed what was rightfully hers, and the once highly organised field of perfectly cultivated linear rows of high yielding, money-making fruit had now returned to an abundant wilderness of twisted thorns and pernicious bindweed that was strangling the life and light out of the land. She couldn't live off the charity of her family forever and desperately needed an independent income. Her elder brothers had made it perfectly clear that they resented the return of the Unwanted One and that her presence within the family was unwelcomed.

Eliza understood that she couldn't rely on the protection of her father. The passing of time had not been kind to Thomas Barton since the unexpected demise of his wife. Eliza had barely recognised him on the day he came to the workhouse to reclaim his troubled daughter. He was no longer the proud owner of a successful farmstead with a loving wife and big family, but a man withered and defeated by the cruelty and harshness of his life. Berry Hill farm was half the prize it used to be – much had been sold off over the years to keep farm and family together. They had lost too many children. Every little life lost caused an irreparable tear in the fabric of the family and then the ultimate loss of Lizzie herself was more than it could bear.

Then there was the guilt. They had both learned to live with the burden of having betrayed their daughter at a time of scarcity and had given away the most precious thing in her life to someone undeserving. They also had to live with the knowledge that they had encouraged Eliza to take up service at the Hamilton's - knowing that Esther had suffered at the hands of their nephew some years before. The bitter regret of separating mother and child twisted and knotted deep inside them both. They knew that they could never repair the damage caused or regain the love and trust that had been lost. They all missed the Little Maid and were angered and hurt that Esther no longer had time for the Bartons and rarely visited.

Eliza realised there was no point in waiting for the storm to pass. The ground was thoroughly sodden and there was little chance of clearing any more of the strip that day. She re-traced her steps down to the beach. The stream was speeding violently down from the village - deep, dangerous and the colour of stewed milky tea. The sea was calm, but grey and the two waters met with differing forces, turning the liquids into a foaming, unhealthy sepia spume. She perched herself on the old tree trunk and despite the raging tempest, instantly willed herself back to that fateful day when she had sat on the beach after a hard day picking fruit, sitting in the sun, and listening to the sound of her younger brothers playing with the Little Maid. For a moment or two she could feel the blush of the sun radiate across her tingling face and convinced herself that she could hear children splashing about in the calm waters as they played. That instant captured the peak of her happiness, a gift from time that reminded her that she could find joy in the simplest of things.

The sound of something rushing past her and the crashing of wood splintering on the rocks brought her back to reality. She opened her eyes. She saw, to her horror, a wooden coffin had been transported by the river and was wedged between a couple of boulders. Great torrents of orange coloured water and detritus smashed against the casket. She thought she could see something between the cracks in the splintered, polished pine. She gently wiped away the mud from the brass plate: -

"In Loving Memory of William Evans 1871 – 1891."

The hairs on her arms stood up on end and she visibly shuddered as she realised this was not the first time that bloody Billy Evans had interrupted her favourite moment. She'd heard that he had met with a violent end - his neck fatally slashed with a broken bottle. He'd been left for dead in a pool of his own congealing hatred after a night of boozing in the Pack and bad-mouthing the locals. Tom and Will had come under suspicion when it was reported that the Evans boy had been making accusations about their whoring sister. They were both capable of permanently silencing him, but they would never have bloodied their hands to defend the Unwanted One. Besides, they both had alibis from their doe-eyed female admirers who would never let the Barton boys go to the gallows for defending the likes of Eliza. No one was ever going to come forward to bear witness to the assault. Most people in the village thought that the gobby little bastard had it coming and were surprised he had managed to get to twenty before someone finally shut him up.

Eliza deduced that Billy had been buried along the riverbank in the churchyard and that the wall had been breached by the violence of the storm. More debris came gushing down and she decided to hurry back to the church to make sure her mother's grave had not been desecrated in the same way.

It was hard work running upstream against the flow and force of the storm water. The cobbles of the High Street were treacherous, and she slipped several times before reaching the churchyard. To her relief, other locals had been alerted to the macabre exodus of the graveyard and many were in the river trying to prop up the old crumbling wall. She scanned the yard for her mother's resting place. Her father was waist-deep in the water, desperately trying to keep his wife's casket from being claimed by the torrent. Eliza jumped in. The shock of the cold and the force of the water stole her breath away. She waded towards her father.

The rain had washed most of the soil away from the grave, exposing the coffin and pushing it down the shallow embankment, close to the greedy river. There was no point in shouting - the sound of the storm, the water and the mayhem drowned out everything else. Her father gestured for Eliza to take his position against the wall. She could feel the mud squeeze through her fingers as the wall crumbled under the sheer weight of the shifting embankment. Thomas Barton hauled himself out of the water and started to dig away the mud at the top of the grave with his bare hands. The earth suddenly sank deeper, forming a slipway for the macabre cargo. A rush of men jumped into the torrent to help Eliza catch the descending casket. The force pushed them all back to the opposite embankment, but the coffin was secured. Elizabeth Barton was hauled back to safety on higher ground - the integrity of her casket ensured.

A further breach of the wall upstream pushed several paupers' graves into the grasp of Hades - carrying them off into the watery underworld. Eliza could see a small bundle bobbing up and down coming towards her in the water. She managed to grab it before it rushed past. She knew it was the remains of a baby wrapped tightly in bandages made from ripped sheets. She could feel its tiny frame crumble gently within her arms. Eliza made her way to the bank and was helped from the water by her father. He offered to take the pathetic bundle from her, but she couldn't let it go. She stood dazed. All the trauma in her life was symbolised by this tiny disintegrating bundle of human remains. For that moment it was hers, and she needed some time alone to cradle and rock the husk that was once a child.

"Get that away from her! Don't let her touch it ... she's cursed!" screamed a woman hysterically from the bridge. Her histrionics signalled a surge of further superstitious vitriol from other village women who were watching the morbid spectacle.

Eliza seemed oblivious to the pathetic cries of the gaggle. Another vicious creature waddled up to her and hissed a long hate-filled diatribe of nonsensical mutterings leaving Eliza bemused and speechless. Thomas Barton rallied to his daughter's defence, but still the women continued to spew out spiteful speeches of speculative and spurious imaginings.

"Only a she-devil could waken the dead like this... this is HER doing! Thomas Barton you should be ashamed of bringing this baby-killer back to our village. Take this unnatural whore back to the hellhole where she belongs and leave us good people in peace!" screeched one particularly maniacally malicious mother.

This woman was so zealous in her rantings that she completely ignored the safety of her own children. They were only just saved from falling to a certain death in the treacherous torrent by an heroic passer-by.

Eliza could feel the rage and injustice of the last few years swell within her. She couldn't bear the village women turning against her beloved father and was on the verge on screaming in response, when an almighty crack of jagged silvered light struck the church tower with ear-bursting power. The ranting women dispersed in fear of their lives.

"Come maid, let's return this little one where it belongs and get off back home. Take no notice of these stupid women. They don't know what they're talking about. Last year it was Billy Evans, this year it is you. This will soon settle when they will have someone else to pick on, never you mind!" said Barton soothingly.

He gently led his daughter away from the mayhem. Still stunned to silence, Eliza lovingly placed the crumbling package alongside other retrieved bundles of human misery.

"I was found not guilty!" she cried.

A jury of strangers had found her innocent, and yet her family and the villagers were quick to assume her guilt. They seemed to take pleasure in publicly demonising her. Why were the people she knew and loved happy to torment and hate her? How could they fail to understand that she tortured herself daily? She continued to re-live the traumatic events in minute detail, always wondering if there was anything else she could have done in the circumstances.

They watched as the undertaker removed the excavated coffins onto the back of his cart to be returned to the morgue until the bank and wall had been stabilised.

On the first occasion Eliza had been denied the right to say farewell, so she welcomed the prospect of a re-internment. It would be some small consolation for the bizarre events of the afternoon. Thomas Barton placed his arm lovingly round Eliza's shoulders. He was the only man alive that Eliza would allow to be this close to her, yet she still had to fight against an instinct to recoil from his touch.

After a few moments of silent reflection, father and daughter started to make their way home. As they left the graveyard Eliza was struck by a sharp pain between her shoulder blades. She looked round to see a couple of brazen fishwives throwing rocks. She picked up a stone to retaliate, but Barton firmly gripped his daughter's arm.

"Leave it be girl, leave it be!"

Another missile narrowly missed her, but she ignored it and they retreated to the safety of the farmstead and the familiar hostility of her brothers.

28

Three Doors Close

Clement's eyesight was getting worse. She was squinting furiously to see who was outside the front door. Some waif and stray begging for hand-outs, no doubt. No matter how hard she tried clarity was beyond her, and she had to request the help of the new maid.

"I know who that is, I'll sort this out!" said the servant.

Within a blink of an eye, she was at the door giving the vagrant a piece of her mind. Clements could hear raised voices and knew she had to intervene before the Mrs. started banging her broomstick handle on the overly abused and cracking ceiling.

"What's all this about?" asked Clements. "Oh, my word if it isn't the Twig! Come in maid, but don't let 'er upstairs hear!"

Bundled with haste into the redundant dining room, Eliza was instructed to wait while the cook finished her task. After a couple of minutes, the maid brought in some tea.

"I know exactly who you are! You deserved to be hung!" she hissed.

"Maybe you're right. I should have been hung. It would have been a blessed release from this cursed existence."

At this point she recognised this judgemental zealot to be Amanda Lively's young disciple who had helped to pull her from back from the brink of oblivion. Shocked by Tilly's lack of empathy, Eliza felt that she needed to be enlightened: -

"Have you ever been caught by a lecherous glance or felt the unwanted touch of a hand across the back of your skirt? Have you ever lain awake in dread, listening for the footsteps of your master outside your bedroom door? Have you ever been told that to refuse the advances of your betters would be to neglect your duties? Have you ever been made you feel that you are unworthy to breathe the same air as them? If you haven't, then you are a very lucky girl, and I shall trouble you no further. If you can say yes to any of this, then perhaps you shouldn't be so quick to judge..."

"But what about your poor innocent babes? They played no part in what happened to you. Why did you make them suffer? Why make them pay for such wickedness?" asked Tilly.

This was the first time anyone had directly asked Eliza about the reasoning behind the fate of those children. The truth be told, she had never really considered them as hers. They didn't belong to her. They were the unwanted consequence of unfortunate events beyond her control... thrusted upon her without invitation. She only had one child - she was her life, and she would willingly die for her.

Eliza paused and carefully contemplated her answer. Her tongue nervously played with her chipped tooth, a lasting souvenir from that fateful encounter with Lincoln. She took a deep breath: -

"They didn't suffer. They weren't destined for this world and they're better off where they are. They're not in pain, nor hungry, nor cold. They're not begging on the streets or fighting for survival in a poorhouse. They escaped the clutches of misery, and I am glad!"

The room was shrouded with an awkward silence. Eliza had answered as truthfully as she could without contradiction or incrimination. Tilly glared at Eliza, spat forcefully in her tea, and slammed it hard on the table.

Eliza felt the calming presence of her father's ethereal hand upon her shoulder and resisted the temptation to throw the contents of her cup back at her juror. Instead, she calmly reached for the teaspoon and fished the lumpy mass of phlegm out of her cup and into the saucer.

"Delicious!" she remarked as she sipped her tea.

The disgruntled Tilly made her retreat, was promptly reprimanded by Clements and threatened with dismissal should she involve the mistress. The ageing cook took her place at the table, eager to hear Eliza's side of the whole sorry affair.

"Now then maid, why in God's name have you come back?"

Eliza hesitated. She found being back at Usbourne's unsettling. Long buried emotions were starting to bubble up, but before they got the better of her, she needed to get the old girl on her side.

"I need to speak to the master."

"Whatever for? You've had your fingers burnt once; I'd keep well away if I were you!

"I need his help. I need a reference from him so I can work... I wouldn't normally lower myself, but I'm desperate!"

Eliza recounted her attempts to get a position in Barnstaple, where she'd been told she would not be considered without references or an agency.

"My family turned me away as soon as my father passed. I am not well-liked in the village. I went to the vicarage, but I found that Mrs. Lively died two years ago and there was no point in asking the reverend, because he never took to me."

Eliza was finding recent events too painful to articulate out loud, but she couldn't cry. She knew if she cried, she would never stop. She wouldn't want to stop; she would just keep crying until she could re-write her past. This impossibility rendered crying futile - a waste of the precious energy she needed just to get through the day.

The cook was stunned. She could see how much Eliza was struggling, but there was little she could do.

"He doesn't live here anymore. Not since the inquest. He comes back once or twice a year to see the child, but that's all. He's gone back to the smoke, back to Verity no doubt. I was never privy to his address, and he's left no calling cards."

Eliza's leaden heart started to sink deep into the abyss, along with any expectations of her much-needed lifeline.

"I don't know what else to do."

The cook sat in silence for a moment or two.

"Let me see what I can find out. You can stay in the barn tonight... let's see what the morning brings."

Clements knew her attempts would probably fail to comfort the poor waif. Eliza started to make her way to the barn. But there was one burning question the old cook had to ask: -

"Oh Eliza, just one last thing."
"What?"
"Did you?"
"Did I what?"
"Did you... you know, help them on their way?"
Eliza answered in the only way she knew how:-
"What do you think?"
And she left the room.

***

Eliza passed a reasonably comfortable night in amongst the straw. She dreamt of the nights she used to snuggle up to the Little Maid with Becky's arm protectively curved around her. So intense was her dream that she could almost smell the waft of milky breath and the heaviness of her sister's limb upon her body. She felt warm, happy, and loved. She was desperate to keep the morning at bay and luxuriate in the moment. It was not to be.

She was brusquely awoken by some playful kittens pouncing on her feet, sinking their pin-sharp claws into her toes. She heard a delightful chuckle behind her and realised that Clemency had crept in behind her and it was the arm of the child she could feel draped across her body.

"Oh, my word! How long have you been there for?" Eliza asked, sitting up.

"Just a few minutes. I brought you something to eat."

The child had grown almost beyond recognition. She had an abundance of wild, brown wavy hair, that needed some care and patience. Her face had great potential - not the same as her mother, but a softer, kinder shade of beauty with a playful smile and deep soulful eyes.

"Do you remember me?" Eliza asked cautiously. She didn't know if the child's mind had been poisoned against her.

"Of course I do silly! How could I forget you? You were always my favourite playmate! Why did you leave... didn't you like me anymore... was I too naughty?"

"I'm so sorry. I had to go. My mother was very poorly, and when she died, I had to look after my father and my younger brothers."

Eliza felt ashamed in telling this lie, although it was unlikely that anyone had bothered to give the poor child any other reason for her sudden departure.

"Did you like your mother?"

"Of course I did. I loved her very much and I still miss her every day. I wish I could have taken you with me. You would have loved her too!"

"Why didn't you?"

"Because you were not mine to take... your parents would have missed you!" Eliza instantly realised her mistake.

"Really? Mrs. Usbourne doesn't speak to me, and Papa works in London all the time, so he wouldn't even notice!"

"Mrs. Clements would miss you and what about Tilly?" Eliza was desperately trying to find someone in Clemency's life who would despair at her loss.

"Tilly hates me! She says I'm a wicked child and that when I die, I shall go to hell, because I don't go to church."

Eliza found it hard to believe that anyone could be so desperately cruel to a child, even Tilly.

"Clements likes me, but she's always busy and she says she

can't work here much longer 'cos her teeth are getting too long, or something," continued the child, noticing the concern on Eliza's face. "Never mind. I won't be here too much longer. Tilly says that when Clements leaves, Mrs. Usbourne will pack me off to some fancy school in London, and I shall spend the holidays with my wicked father."

Eliza started to unpack her food parcel and noticed a small calling card with the master's address on had been tucked into the top.

"Did you put this in?"

"Of course I did, silly! I found it in one of Papa's old coats."

"You are clever! It means I can visit you when you go to your new school. Would you like that?"

Eliza watched the child's face beam with excitement. They were interrupted by Tilly's stern voice calling Clemency to come in for breakfast.

"You'd better go. Hurry, I don't want you getting into trouble."

Clemency gave her old friend a big, deep hug and hurriedly kissed her cheek.

"I'll see you in London."

"I promise!"

29

Donna and Eliza. Eliza, London, September 1899

The air was thick with a yellowy, grey acrid smoke that made Eliza's chest tighten as if someone was tugging the strings of her stays. She could see twisted little black smuts dancing in the air. They irritated her nose and made her sneeze, filling her handkerchief with a tar-like substance, blobbed with blood. It was a daily warning, usually ignored, that all was not well. She desperately needed some fresh, clean Devonshire air – not this horrible lungful of London contamination.

Eliza looked back at number eleven Gas House Lane and reflected how far she had fallen. These tumble-down terraced houses were tightly packed and over-crowded. She knew her mother would have described them as shameful slums. This is where the poor gathered; just one step up from living on the streets. Even this misery was now beyond Eliza's grasp. Her landlady's patience had finally snapped and now Eliza was left on the doorstep with nowhere to go.

Eliza was unaware that this was to be her last abode. All the warning signs were there. No money, no job, no hope. Her body had been plagued by some bronchial savagery that had left her mentally fragile and her body permanently weakened. She had hoped that by the time her next rent was due her fortunes might have changed. She had written to the Captain several times in the hope that he would feel guilty enough to provide a simple reference to release her from the slavery of low paid jobs that didn't even pay her rent. She wasted weeks waiting for replies that never came and now she was desperate.

Destitution and homelessness finally provided the courage she needed to confront her former employer, to demand that he should compensate her for her misery. Armed with the precious piece of card that Clemency had given her, she set out to walk to Clapham to confront the only person that could possibly save her from the poor house.

***

DONNA – AUGUST 2012: -

"You've got it upside down! This was definitely Gas House Lane, look!" Algie carefully rotated the map.

Donna looked up at the newly built 'Chandler's Heights' - a block of luxury apartments for 'Manhattan-style living' for the upwardly mobile. The starting price of £1.5 million truly belied the history of misery of this site and gave the impression that the area had always been blessed by affluence.

"It's hard to believe that this is where poor Eliza ended up. According to Becky's letters this is her last known address. There's no reference to the site's history whatsoever. I'm just not feeling it," said Donna.

"What do you mean you're just not feeling it?"

"Oh, I don't know. All this nascent gentrification is just candyfloss, its fluff! It's a betrayal of all the dirt, grime and poverty that was here before. There's no reference or acknowledgement that people lived here under the shadow of the power station, in crowded squalor, living dirty, dangerous lives just to survive. It doesn't seem right. She didn't die here...that's just a hunch!"

Donna was reluctant to share with Algie the fact that she had experienced visions of opulent surroundings and red stains on a marble floor. She was convinced that Eliza had met with a violent end. She couldn't explain it, but she knew she was right.

"Forgive me for pointing this out, but we've been guided by your hunches and intuition for the last three days, and yet we're still no closer to finding out what happened to her!" Algie's normally boundless patience was beginning to discover its limits.

"OK. We'll drive over to my old house in Clapham and look there," instructed Donna.

"Why?"

"Because it was owned by the Captain and there's the outside chance that Eliza worked for him after she left Gas House Lane."

"But there would be nothing left. No association with Eliza or Usbourne."

"Well, my parents sold the house to the Society of War

Artists before we emigrated. They wanted to open a small museum celebrating the life and work of various war artists. That included my great-grandfather, Charles Ruskin. There's a slim chance there might be some clue, some hint of what might have happened."

"OK, but only on the condition that this is the last port of call. If we don't find anything there, we're going back home."

"Deal!" Donna had the irrational conviction that something would turn up.

A flustered Algie unceremoniously dumped Donna outside her old house and sped off in search of a parking space. He didn't hold out too much hope. The road was crammed full of 4x4 vanity projects with the occasional flash sporty types to break the monotony. In the distance he could see a traffic warden meticulously inspecting parking tickets. Algie could almost sense the glee when the warden found an expired ticket. Algie opened his glove compartment and counted his collection of unpaid dockets. He couldn't afford to get another one.

Donna's childhood home seemed smaller, more modest than she remembered and brought back a whole myriad of conflicting emotions. But she needed to focus on the task in hand. No time for any further diversions.

Outside the white Georgian townhouse was a sign identifying the abode as property of the War Art Appreciation Society. Donna paid her entrance fee and scanned the rooms for clues. Donna knew she had to be quick. Parking had been a nightmare throughout their three days in the capital and Algie was building up an impressive collection of parking tickets. She didn't want to push his good nature or their friendship too far, but she didn't want to waste time either.

The first room bore little fruit, but a stunning portrait of her great-grandmother was hanging on the landing wall. She remembered how surprised Joanie had been when they discovered it in the attic just before the move. Donna had been disappointed that she didn't want it shipped out to Canada. Her mother was determined to have a fresh start, with no reminders of the past - especially of her super-dysfunctional family. The painting had been renovated. Layers of darkened varnish had been stripped back and the brightness of the original colours and the delicacy of stroke had been restored. It was hard to believe that the same hand that sketched brutal studies of war and destruction could be the same one that created this delicate study of spirited beauty. Charles Ruskin was often considered ahead of his time, but the contrast between the two styles was startling. Donna made a mental note to correct some of the society's assumptions on its provenance.

She was about to purchase a catalogue when she noticed a sign advertising the exhibits upstairs. It was the notice for 'The Captain's Study' that caught her eye.

"Excuse me. Was the Captain a war artist?" she asked the lady behind the counter.

"Strictly speaking no. The Captain was Ruskin's father-in-law and lived in the house before the artist moved in with his new wife. It became Ruskin's study...its where he sketched."

Donna thought that the bespectacled woman bore a striking resemblance to Xanthe from the Records Office.

Donna went up the stairs. Early childhood memories of climbing the stairs two at a time and sliding down the banisters were a far cry from her current abilities. As she approached the room, she realised that it was in fact her mother's old private study. This magical place had been strictly a child-free environment, but Donna had been known occasionally to break into this temple of mother when she was left alone in the house. The walnut veneered bureaux would prove too enticing to resist and the budding journalist would sit and write about her day in her diary until one of her parents returned from work and would catch the little sneak. On one occasion Donna had been so absorbed by the emotions of the 'worst day in her life ever' that the entry of "fuck, fuck, fuck!" had over run the edge of her cheap Woolies diary and were etched into the finish of the wood.

The room was pretty much as she had remembered. Painted white with a large circular window that would flood the room with a warm, golden aura in the late afternoon. A glorious bureau remained the centrepiece of the room, with swirls of walnut outlined with a darker brown, forming patterns that were almost floral.

The walls of the room were clad with beautiful ancient leather-bound volumes in red and brown. Some were tattered at the edges, but still commanded respect. This temple still smelt of barely disguised damp with overtones of lavender and rose.

The desk was covered with old sketches and pencils. Donna delicately shifted one of the drawings and saw that the patina of the veneer was indeed indented with the word "fuck!" It was hard to remember why she been having the worst day ever or why she had felt compelled to write 'fuck" all over her diary, but she experienced a strangely misplaced feeling of pride. Her teenage rampage was proof that she had left her mark in the world after all!

As Donna glanced over the contents on the desk she noticed a small silver, topless case containing age-yellowed calling cards. She looked furtively over her shoulder to see if anyone was watching. The coast was clear, and she thumbed through the various cards. They were mostly connected with Ruskin, but right at the bottom was a card for The Millen Club - a well-known gentlemen's club.

Donna made her way downstairs and went back to the Xanthe clone to purchase the artist's catalogue.

"Sorry to trouble you again but are you familiar with The Millen Club?" she asked.

Lacking the relevant knowledge, the cashier shouted out for assistance from Mr. Bryce, who made his way over to the desk. This elderly gentleman looked vaguely familiar to Donna, but she could not place him.

"The Millen Club was considered a place of sanctuary for a certain type of gentlemen. It was in the West End, and in its heyday was one of the best in London," Bryce quoted, as if from the brochure.

"Does it still exist?" asked Donna.

"Good grief no! It closed just after the turn of the twentieth century. It closed, despite its popularity, after the Prince of Wales withdrew his patronage. There was some scandal involving the suicide of a young servant girl, and the young Prince didn't want his reputation tarnished by his association with the club. There was never any suggestion that he was involved in the scandal, but he left, and many of the most prestigious members left with him."

"Do you know what happened?" Donna asked. She had a strong sense that she might finally be on to something concrete.

"I'm afraid not," replied Bryce with a sense of deflation.

Donna thanked him and paid for the brochure. She hurried outside to find Algie double-parked with his engine still running. She got into the car.

"Let's get out of here before Rita the meter maid clocks us!" said Algie, impatiently.

"I think Eliza might somehow be connected with the Prince of Wales!" exclaimed Donna – a look of utter disbelief on her face.

30

The Captain and Eliza, September 1899

It was late afternoon and Captain Usbourne was still feeling bloated after a late lunch. He swirled his cognac anti-clockwise and pondered how far he had come. Since his rapid retreat from Devon his fortunes had greatly improved. His wife of independent means was no longer such an emotional burden and she seemed to be running the estate smoothly and without any cause for concern. All hint of the wretched affair with the servant girl had settled down and had been safely locked away deep in the heart of Devonshire. His only true connection with the past was his daughter - an affectionate child, with a wild and impetuous nature. She was unlikely to fit into the sophistication of city life with her country ways without a great deal of expensive coaching. Still, one would broach that difficulty if needed.

Life was good. He was sat in the reading room of the Millen, surrounded by good company with outstanding connections and deep pockets. His reputation as a successful and entertaining gamester had earned him the introduction to one of the most exclusive establishments in London. He was fine dining on partridge and grouse, supping the best cognacs and oak-aged single malts and had access to some of the richest and most gullible gamblers of the city. Long gone were the days when he was easily parted with his money down at the Quay. He had served his apprenticeship the hard way. He had learned to read faces for confidence, bluff, and disappointment. He had turned it into a craft. No detail was ignored; every little nervous tick, bead of sweat and hint of whimsy was crucial. He had learned to cheat with such sophistication, daring and charm that he was never suspected. He had earned the respect and company of the great and not so good and he was revelling in the moment. Even the Prince of Wales had just been marshalled through. He knew it would be unlikely, but he longed for the chance to part the Prince from some of his fortune and truly become the talk of London.

Usbourne was approached by a footman bearing a silver salver with a small note. He recognised his housekeeper's hand and was alarmed to hear that his only daughter was in grave health and that a servant urgently needed to speak with him. He hurried to one of the private reception rooms where he had been instructed to wait. Three minutes had passed before a hidden door in the panelling opened, and a petrified Eliza shuffled her way nervously into the room. Recognition was immediate and mortifying. He knew he had been duped.

"Why the hell are you here?"

"You know why! You never replied! All I need is for you to give me a reference so I can earn a crust and I shall trouble you no more."

"I owe you nothing but the back of my hand! Leave, or I shall call to have you removed!"

The Captain could taste her fear. He approached her and grabbed her arms tightly and squeezed hard until he could feel the blood pounding in her veins. He relished the moment... it took him back to when her fear was an invitation. He pulled her close and kissed her violently, biting her lip until it ripped. She stamped hard on his foot with all her might, and slipping from his grip, ran to the door and escaped into the passageway.

"Bastard!" she yelled.

She felt her tattered lip. There was only a small tear this time, but a little blood goes a long way. Her instinct to bolt was measured by her curiosity. There was a slim crack in the panelled doorway. She approached it with caution. Eliza had to duck down quickly, as she saw his eye scanning furtively through the opposite side of the crack. He was hoping to see her melting like a sorry chip of ice in the sun but could see nothing but the darkness of the hallway. The eye retreated. Usbourne turned his back and straightened his attire. He was unruffled, and unmoved by her pathetic state.

Eliza meandered through the corridor safe in the knowledge that Usbourne would never lower himself to follow her into this secret realm of servitude. She grabbed a buttered roll from an abandoned serving trolley and found herself in a linen cupboard. She realised that her strategy was all wrong. She should never had confronted him alone. She needed to get under his skin in public. She needed witnesses.

"I'll make 'im pay!" she thought, wiping the blood from her mouth. Eliza's need to make him suffer was starting to outweigh her need for a reference.

Usbourne returned to the reading room. Luckily his chair was still empty, and his half-filled glass had not been removed. His unfortunate encounter with the servant girl already was consigned to history - easily forgotten and firmly in the past. The room had started to fill with more patrons and their cigar smoke filled the air with a colonial entitlement and a wispy curtain of grey. As he started to read his newspaper, he observed the Prince of Wales seated in a secluded corner of the room, engaged in lively conversation with one of his entourage. Something was amusing his majesty. Usbourne sat contemplating how he could gain an introduction to the Prince's gaming table that night. Seated and lost in deep thought he was approached by the edge of a silver salver. He instinctively grabbed for the glass as the contents were thrown into his lap.

"For heaven's sake!"

All the eyes in the room were suddenly upon him, silently searching for an immediate explanation. Eliza stared silently in triumph. She had been longing to do that for years and it felt good. A simple yet rewarding act. Unsure of her strategy she bent down to his ear and whispered: -

"Now will you give me a bloody reference?" She paused and looked around at her audience.

"Not so cocky now are you!" she taunted. All the ears in the room were listening too.

At last, she had his attention, but he still seemed unmoved by her demand. Was he still denying her? Could she detect the faint shaking of his head? What would it take to bend him her way? It was at this point that Eliza lost all hope of obtaining what she needed. It would be an admittance of failure on his part and that was never going to happen. The aromatic smoke was beginning to irritate her fragile lungs as she took a deep breath,

"Excuse me gentlemen!" she shouted. There was a pause until she had their full attention, and she suppressed the need to cough.

"I would like to introduce you to the REAL Captain Usbourne. He is not the gentleman you think. What kind of a man spends his wife's fortune playing cards and then abandons her and their child in Devon? I'll tell you…this man! This is the man who took me against my will and let our children die! He left me to rot before the law, but I was found INNOCENT! It was this man who demanded satisfaction from the poor doctor who had told the judge that Usbourne was the father of those innocent babes and was horsewhipped within an inch of his life by this scoundrel!"

She relished the moment. The sheer pleasure of watching him fall in front of royalty was priceless.

"This man is a nasty piece of work! He is a fraud, a cheat, and a MURDERER!"

"You lying bitch!" shouted the Captain.

He would have happily throttled her, but he could see that the Prince of Wales was beckoning to a steward, who then approached the Captain: -

"Sir, will you kindly observe the club rules. Will you please leave?"

Usbourne's and Eliza's eyes were locked in each other's mutual discomfort. The polite request went unheeded.

"Sir, you need to deal with your personal problems outside. Otherwise, your membership will be revoked," the steward insisted.

The smoky grey filled room seemed to turn to a deep shade of fury. Usbourne could no longer contain his loathing and lashed out at the poor steward, who fell to the floor with a bloodied nose. The Prince was instantly surrounded by his men and escorted into the foyer in what seemed to be a well-rehearsed manoeuvre. He could not afford to get dragged into another damning scandal... no matter how tentative the connection.

The Captain had lost all reason and was violently hitting out at anyone who dared approach him. He was incensed. The very notion that he had been asked by that bastard steward to leave in front of that bloody servant girl was demeaning and belittling. She was nothing but a liar and a whore. She would get what she deserved. He would make sure of it! He could feel the scorn by those in the room who were happy to judge him. How dare they! Who were they anyway? They were all pathetic, entitled arses that couldn't hold their own at a gaming table or wipe their own noses. He had nothing but contempt for these upper-class bastards. Fuck them! Fuck their connections. Fuck their opinions! He didn't need their approval anyway!

Amidst the hubbub and confusion, Eliza was able to disappear quietly into the safety of the hidden corridor. Not knowing from where she could have found such energy, she sped up three flights of cold stone stairs. She avoided various attempts by the staff to apprehend her and found her way onto the balcony above the foyer. She saw Usbourne being forcibly manhandled away from the reading room. She saw a crowd gathered around the Prince in the foyer below. Her bittersweet victory would be short-lived. She knew that she had lost everything…there was no going back.

She felt her chest being squeezed like a concertina. The restriction was unbearable. She gasped for air like a stranded mackerel.

She looked down at her audience. The height was dizzying. Exhaustion and confusion were a heady mix, making sensible decisions almost impossible. She climbed up onto the top of the balcony rail, her legs dangling over the precipice.

Eliza commanded everybody's attention. She wanted to say so much more. She could barely breathe and was starting to panic. Her desperation was palpable. She felt something strange in her pocket. It was her father's lucky rabbit foot. She stroked the silky fur and felt comforted. Far down below she could see her father. He was smiling and beckoning to her. She longed to feel the warmth of his fatherly embrace.

"For God's sake let go maid, let go!" she heard him say. She was lost in the moment.

"This is for you!" she yelled. And pushed herself away from the balcony edge, arms outstretched.

Witnesses' opinions differed. Had she deliberately thrown herself from the balcony or had she merely lost her balance? The result was the same. Eliza fell from a great height. There was a grace to her descent; her scream visceral and silent. Some said they thought she was smiling as she flew towards the floor. She could never have imagined that her last few moments of life would bring such notoriety. She plunged face down, smashing her skull, and spilling her teeth like bloodied pearls over the icy marble floor.

There was stunned silence.

The Prince and Usbourne were securely led away from the carnage. The Prince returned to his haven of luxury; his reputation untarnished.

Usbourne portrayed a solitary figure. His reputation publicly and irretrievably shredded. The Captain was certain he had now fallen so low there would be no way of picking his way out. His humiliation was complete. He was totally ruined.

He felt something sharp rubbing his ankle. He bent down to rummage through the top of his shoe. To his horror he withdrew a bloodied tooth, neatly broken. He remembered her fondly. The gap in her tooth, her broad smile, her generous nature. Then he remembered her name.

"I'm not like Lincoln. Lincoln's a bastard! I am not like Lincoln at all!" he muttered in shock.

31

Donna's Research Notes

THE MILLEN CLUB (LONDON)

The Millen Club was a London card-playing club. It was considered one of the oldest card clubs in the capital. Founded some time before 1815. It boasted an impressive clientele including the nobility. Little is known about the club, as the Millen prided itself on its two main values of secrecy and discretion.

SCANDAL The Millen Club was rocked by the apparent suicide of a servant girl in 1899. The horrific event was witnessed by many that were in the foyer of the club. The victim was reportedly an employee of one of the club's members, who publicly accused him of fathering her children and being responsible for their deaths. One anonymous witness came forward who thought her name was Eliza, but not knowing of her surname was buried under the name of

Millen. The club reportedly paid for the poor unfortunate's funeral.

CLOSURE The club's reputation was forever associated with the tragedy and closed shortly after due to many of its most prestigious clients withdrawing their patronages.

CURRENT STATUS The club has been repurposed and changed ownership and names several times since its closure. It is now a private residency currently owned by the Sidorov family who own many hotels and prestigious buildings in London.

32

The Wake, November 2012

The funeral had been a dignified and mercifully dry affair. It had been one of the wettest, windiest autumns on record, but there had been a lucky break in the weather. Donna was relieved that everything had gone smoothly and that everyone seemed genuinely moved and touched by Eliza's story. This was Eliza's day and had been a long time coming. She would have been comforted by the amount of interest that her long-dead bones were generating and delighted that some of her family had made the effort. Her two granddaughters Elin and Prue were the head mourners, and they were surrounded by their children and grandchildren. Eliza was back where she belonged, in a grave next to her beloved Ma and Pa, buried with the remains of little Eliza and Becky.

Donna had every reason to be proud of herself in tracking down Eliza's remains and repatriating her back where she belonged in the bosom of her long-lost family. But she felt uneasy. Her back was aching after sitting upright on one of the uncomfortable pews for ages and her head was mildly pounding to the time of the church organ. During the internment she was aware that someone's eyes had been boring deep into the back of her head and had caught a glimpse of someone shifting in order to get a better glimpse of her mountainous proportions.

The woman in question was very well turned out. Her cascading red hair softly embraced her neck and shoulders. Shrouded in brown and neutral tones her whole image smacked of success and sophistication. This woman knew how to impress. The only comfort Donna could gain was she noticed that the woman's camel coloured coat had massive globules of splashed mud and shite on the back a la Jackson Pollock.

The throng hurriedly made for the car park and back to the Dog and Lamppost for the wake. Donna felt instantly displaced. The wall of family gathered around Elin and Prue and ancient family photographs were distributed and commented upon. Tea and booze were brought round, and the buffet unwrapped. A local journalist made requests for enlightenment and the woman and her camel coat grabbed Algie's arm and escorted the two outside to be interviewed.

"Don't worry about her, she always needs to be in charge. She can't help herself" exclaimed Sophie as she passed around some mushroom vol-au-vents.

Donna felt someone gently squeeze her shoulders.

"Thank you so much for this! You have no idea how much this means to us",

Donna turned around to find a watery eyed Elin smiling at her unnervingly.

"It's the least I could do given the circumstances."

"I know that the outcome was so desperately sad, but at least she's back with us, where she belongs. We shall always be grateful for that." Elin noticed that Donna seemed distracted by the events outside.

"Thank you!" she replied absent-mindedly. She was mesmerised by the over-familiar body-language of the woman that Algie had been hijacked by and how he seemed immune to her outrageous flirting and exaggerated laughter.

Donna was brought back abruptly to reality from her fluffy mind-cloud by the dulcet tones escaping from her phone.

"Sorry Elin, I need to take this." she said as she rummaged through her over-laden shoulder bag. She studied her text message and left the phone on a nearby table.

The exes returned to the steamy warmth of the pub.

"What are you smiling about?" asked Algie as he stooped over Donna's shoulder.

"Good news. My solicitors have managed to settle out-of-court with the land agents, and they are going to pay compensation for swindling my Mum and Gran out of a lifetime's rent for the estate."

Algie gave her a congratulatory hug and a peck on the cheek.

"Dad, we need a new barrel!" interrupted Sophie from the bar.

"On my way!" he replied as he managed to squeeze through his nearest and dearest.

The camel coat made her way over to Donna.

"I hope you don't mind. The reporter is a sort of friend of mine and was curious about Eliza's story. I hope I didn't steal your thunder! I'm Natasha by the way, Algie's ex." She held out her elegant, manicured hand. She still wore her wedding ring.

Donna started to offer her rough and chubby hand in response, but Natasha had already turned away to kiss the cheek of her daughter Chloe and immersed herself in another conversation.

Donna thought she had managed to escape the awkwardness of speaking to the ex, when Natasha returned to speak to her,

"Sorry, where were we?" she half-heartedly enquired,

"Oh yes...YOU are?" she continued with an air of superiority.

A ruffled Donna made the effort to be polite,

"Donna... Algie's friend. I helped in locating Eliza in London." Natasha's eyes were already registering boredom and had started to scan elsewhere. Donna noticed that her bump was being evaluated.

"Due soon?"

"In a couple of weeks actually..." replied Donna who was lulled into the security of false interest.

"Left it a bit late haven't you!" quipped Natasha.

"Excuse me?" Donna responded, as she altered her tone.

"I mean to have a baby at your time of life. its unusual, isn't it? I do hope you're not relying on Algie on bringing this little one up. He's already been through it once...it wouldn't be fair!" she twisted.

"Excuse me, I don't know who the fuck you think you are, but you are making an awful lot of assumptions about my relationship with Algie and my ability to look after myself!"

Not wanting to sour Eliza's big day, she picked up her bag

and made her way to the front entrance. A concerned Algie made his way over.

"What's been said?" he asked.

"Nothing of any importance. Bad head. Got to go! Please send my regards to everybody!"

"Are you sure everything's alright? ... Are we still good?

"We're great! I'm just really tired and I've a thumping head and not really in the mood to make small talk. Please enjoy the rest of the day with your family. I promise I'm fine!" she said as she left.

Algie wandered over to Natasha.

"Your new friend's a bit touchy, isn't she?" gloated Natasha.

"Oh, Nat... you've got shite on the back of your coat!" he said with great satisfaction.

33

Charlie, November 2012

Donna had been tossing and turning all night. Her head was still pounding. She was convinced that someone was pressing their knee into the small of her back, grinding the base of her spine.

God was moving her piano again and every so often the room would illuminate and shudder under the strain. The courtyard was alive with the music of heavy raindrops smashing into the ground, and torrents of water slushed down the drainpipes, displacing all other sound.

Donna heaved her lumpy mass out of bed to fetch another blanket. The light strobed dramatically. A blood-stained sheet writhed menacingly as she opened the blanket box.

A strong smell of vomit filled the air and Donna could taste blood. She made a bolt for the bathroom and stuck her head down the toilet. Her body convulsed as she retched, her intercostal muscles heaving with every spasm. It left her stretched and pained. She splashed some cold water across her face, and a swish of minty mouthwash helped to banish the bitter acid taste.

The kaleidoscopic effect of the damaged mirror caught her attention. Her slightly puffy face flushed with chloasma stared back.

And so did those haunting, deep brown eyes.

They didn't belong to her. It was someone else.

Ignoring the interloper, she fixed upon the various images of herself trapped in the fractured fabric of the mirror. A strike of bright blue light intruded. The image of haunting eyes flashed deep into her own, captured like a negative.

A shock of adrenaline electrified her body.

The lights cut out. Intermittent flashes of piercing blue punctured the darkness. Donna stepped back and slipped on the bathmat, cracking the back of her head on the protruding radiator. Bruised and tender, she got up and rubbed the egg-shaped wound. Her attention was diverted by the grinding sound of an opening latch. She held her breath as she concentrated on the persistent metallic grating.

She made it back to her bedroom and picked up the telephone. The line was dead. She frantically searched through her bag, spilling the contents on the floor in a desperate bid to find her mobile.

'Fuck!' She had left it in the pub. Her vulnerability was eased slightly by the return of some light, and she cautiously waddled downstairs to investigate the sound.

"Bugger off Jack, I told you I'm not well, come back when I've sorted myself out," blasted a spectral voice.

Relieved, Donna sat on the stairs and listened to the familiar drama that had been playing out over the last few months. A gap in transmission had given Donna the false hope that the melodrama might have ceased.

As she focussed her attention on the small hallway, the image of Eliza slowly faded into view. The poor weeping child shuffled her way to the door, stopping periodically to lean on the wall for support. Another wave of pain hit her hard and she started to pant rapidly.

"For goodness' sake Eliza, open up!" the voice yelled. He thumped on the door.

"Shut up, you'll wake the master!"

"You look like death! What have you been doing?"

"I told you I'm not well..." Eliza shuddered as chills vibrated through her body.

"I'm so cold Jack, will you light the fire?" she said weakly.

There was a snap of kindling and an odour of sulphur, as the lad struck a match. A faint glow of orange and yellow offered little cheer.

"What's that blood on the floor?"

The sounds of the past faded in and out. Donna needed to concentrate and re-tune. She strained to catch the sound...

"Keep away from it... don't kill ..." The voices just out of reach again.

"Please Jack, I beg of you. I've done nothin' wrong...I promise!"

Jack thumped upstairs, pushing a great rush of negative energy through Donna's body. She shuddered violently.

The desire to check on Eliza encouraged Donna to investigate the kitchen. A feeble cry echoed hauntingly.

Eliza sat with the tiny, shrouded bundle, gently swaying in

a futile bid to comfort it. She carefully pulled back the cloth from the infant's face. The baby's bulging, blood-shot eyes fixed on its mother. Bloody crystals around its mouth and nose made it difficult to draw breath. A dark bruise was prominent on the windpipe.

It was deeply shocking.

Donna was tuning out. She couldn't keep her focus on the mother and child. She looked again, but they had gone. As she climbed the stairs back to her bedroom the signals became stronger again.

The lid of the blanket box remained opened; she approached it with caution. She could still detect weak movement from a blooded sheet. A man rushed in and scooped up the bundle to reveal a tiny scrap of a child barely clinging to life. He commanded the servant to pass the baby to its semi-conscious mother on the bed.

"Fetch the other child."

The woman hurried away.

Eliza lay inert on the bed, incapable of nurture. The Captain reclaimed the still moving bundle. He looked directly into the child's face and saw nothing but his own disgrace. He held the object of his embarrassment for a few moments and then placed it back into the unresponsive arms of its mother.

The servant returned with the baby girl. "Eliza what have you done to the child?" she asked.

The doctor came in and muttered something about a warm bath and sugared water. The agitated baby coughed and spluttered.

Donna's silent tears flooded down her face as the baby girl drew her last breath.

Thunder cracked through the house like gunshots as the storm passed directly overhead. The pain in the small of Donna's back intensified and her temples felt as if they were being crushed in a vice.

In a futile bid to make her way to Jude's house, she put her dressing-gown on and started to descend the stairs. The disembodied sounds of Eliza's self-delivery filled the passageway.

The visual jarred. Instead of witnessing the spectre of Eliza's frail body pushed up against the wall, she saw herself. Transfixed and immobilised she could only view the spectacle with disbelief.

Donna felt the warmth of her broken waters run down her weakened legs. She panicked. Giving birth at home without her birthing partner was not part of her plan. Every time her doppelganger convulsed with pain Donna's body echoed in sympathy. Their shared ordeal was intense.

Acceptance that the pain would crescendo and dissipate was the only way to cope. Surge after surge crashed over her. She needed a new coping strategy. The well-rehearsed chants of 'breathe and release' didn't seem to cut-it somehow. Donna tried to focus on her breathing, but the pain kept interrupting.

The doppelganger wasn't coping well either. She needed someone to tell her that everything would be alright, to hold her hand and mop her brow.

Donna became disassociated. Her body felt lifted and free. Liberated, she joined her counterpart's struggle on the floor.

The storm eased. A thin grey light marked the weak division between night and day. Time was meaningless.

The need to push was over-whelming. Donna could feel someone hold her hand. She squeezed with no mercy as the internal tourniquet tightened across her abdomen. All mutterings of comfort were gratefully accepted.

The breaks between pain brought a welcome relief, but they were short-lived.

The urge to push harder was impossible to resist. This time there was no progress. The mutual struggle was obvious - the baby was stuck.

The urgency to complete the mission over-rode the agony.

'Pant!' demanded her internal coach.

The baby started to emerge. Donna leaned forward to touch the slippery, waxy head. The next heave made no progress, nor the next.

A desperate Donna grabbed the child just under the head and pulled. Gently at first and then with more force. The effort out measured her remaining energy.

Tormented by morbid, twisting thoughts, Donna lost confidence in her ability to cope alone. She thought she was losing the battle. She feared her body was shutting down. Through a blurred curtain, she could just make out the silhouette of a comforting female presence. Calm was restoring,

"Hold on. Don't give up! Hold on!"

Eliza's softly spoken words were beyond Donna's comprehension. Her ethereal birthing-partner coaxed and reassured.

Momentarily, she felt disassociated from herself again. She was merely a bit player in her own drama. She witnessed the two of them from above, working in perfect partnership.

They were approaching the endgame. With one last push, the baby was born.

Something was wrong. The baby was silent and blue.

Donna returned with a violent jolt. The thick, veiny cord

Thunder cracked through the house like gunshots as the storm passed directly overhead. The pain in the small of Donna's back intensified and her temples felt as if they were being crushed in a vice.

In a futile bid to make her way to Jude's house, she put her dressing-gown on and started to descend the stairs. The disembodied sounds of Eliza's self-delivery filled the passageway.

The visual jarred. Instead of witnessing the spectre of Eliza's frail body pushed up against the wall, she saw herself. Transfixed and immobilised she could only view the spectacle with disbelief.

Donna felt the warmth of her broken waters run down her weakened legs. She panicked. Giving birth at home without her birthing partner was not part of her plan. Every time her doppelganger convulsed with pain Donna's body echoed in sympathy. Their shared ordeal was intense.

Acceptance that the pain would crescendo and dissipate was the only way to cope. Surge after surge crashed over her. She needed a new coping strategy. The well-rehearsed chants of 'breathe and release' didn't seem to cut-it somehow. Donna tried to focus on her breathing, but the pain kept interrupting.

The doppelganger wasn't coping well either. She needed someone to tell her that everything would be alright, to hold her hand and mop her brow.

Donna became disassociated. Her body felt lifted and free. Liberated, she joined her counterpart's struggle on the floor.

The storm eased. A thin grey light marked the weak division between night and day. Time was meaningless.

The need to push was over-whelming. Donna could feel someone hold her hand. She squeezed with no mercy as the internal tourniquet tightened across her abdomen. All mutterings of comfort were gratefully accepted.

The breaks between pain brought a welcome relief, but they were short-lived.

The urge to push harder was impossible to resist. This time there was no progress. The mutual struggle was obvious - the baby was stuck.

The urgency to complete the mission over-rode the agony.

'Pant!' demanded her internal coach.

The baby started to emerge. Donna leaned forward to touch the slippery, waxy head. The next heave made no progress, nor the next.

A desperate Donna grabbed the child just under the head and pulled. Gently at first and then with more force. The effort out measured her remaining energy.

Tormented by morbid, twisting thoughts, Donna lost confidence in her ability to cope alone. She thought she was losing the battle. She feared her body was shutting down. Through a blurred curtain, she could just make out the silhouette of a comforting female presence. Calm was restoring,

"Hold on. Don't give up! Hold on!"

Eliza's softly spoken words were beyond Donna's comprehension. Her ethereal birthing-partner coaxed and reassured.

Momentarily, she felt disassociated from herself again. She was merely a bit player in her own drama. She witnessed the two of them from above, working in perfect partnership.

They were approaching the endgame. With one last push, the baby was born.

Something was wrong. The baby was silent and blue.

Donna returned with a violent jolt. The thick, veiny cord

was wrapped tightly around the baby's throat. Her partner instinctively placed two fingers under the noose and slipped it over the head. The baby instantly flushed with colour.

The rose-pink child cried with vigour and was immediately welcomed by the embrace of its mother. Donna noticed a blue bruise the size of a thumbprint on the baby's throat. She shuddered.

Donna placed the baby on her chest, feeling its skin next to hers. She inhaled deeply. The bond was instant and forever, and her love for this child was utterly overwhelming.

There was a tentative knock at the door. Algie popped his head round and realised what had happened. He had been trying to phone for hours.

He thought she might like her mobile back.

"Bloody hell!" he exclaimed. "Are you alright?"

Donna nodded weakly. She looked around the passageway. But Eliza had gone...

About the Author

Annie Roche is proud to be a Blow-In! Born in London to a London-Irish family, brought up in Surrey, Kent and Suffolk and eventually settling with her husband and three children in North Devon! Her career has been as varied from dancer to historian, music administrator, shop and café proprietor, teacher and now author.

Annie always wanted to write, even as a child and spent much of her childhood writing incomprehensible stories that nobody really understood. She has been writing stories in her head for her entire life and after an enforced career change has finally found the courage to put pen to paper.

The Blow-Ins is her debut novel and has been inspired by original research into infanticide cases in North Devon for her History Master's Degree. Her research proved that infanticide was prolific nationwide during a time of poor or no contraception and little welfare provision. The majority of these mothers were young servants, many of which had been abused or sexually assaulted by their masters or left high and dry by their lovers. Being stranded with an unwanted baby with no money, family support and little hope of gainful employment drove many desperate women and young girls to commit the ultimate taboo of new-born child murder or face starvation and societal scorn. Many of these historical cases were screaming out to be explored and the voices of these women needed to be heard.

Annie loves living in the stunning Devonshire countryside, close to the dramatic North Devon coastline and has found this wild landscape the inspiration for her novel. Apart from writing she enjoys growing fruit and vegetables, reading and after a few unexplained experiences an interest in the supernatural. Usbournes is loosely based on a remote eighteenth century farmhouse and surrounding hamlet that she and her family used to live in and some of the unusual experiences have been included.

She is currently writing a sequel to the Blow-ins based on another case that was included in her dissertation and hopes to publish in 2025.

Keep in touch with Annie at annierocheauthor@gmail.com

www.ingramcontent.com/pod-product-compliance
Lightning Source LLC
Chambersburg PA
CBHW072147070526
44585CB00015B/1036